ROGER BACON
COMPENDIUM OF
THE STUDY OF THEOLOGY

STUDIEN UND TEXTE ZUR GEISTESGESCHICHTE DES MITTELALTERS

HERAUSGEGEBEN VON

Dr. ALBERT ZIMMERMANN

PROFESSOR AN DER UNIVERSITÄT KÖLN

BAND XX

ROGER BACON

COMPENDIUM OF
THE STUDY OF THEOLOGY

ROGER BACON

COMPENDIUM OF
THE STUDY OF THEOLOGY

EDITION AND TRANSLATION
WITH INTRODUCTION AND NOTES

BY

THOMAS S. MALONEY

E.J. BRILL
LEIDEN • NEW YORK • KØBENHAVN • KÖLN
1988

Library of Congress Cataloging-in-Publication Data

Bacon, Roger, 1214?-1294.
    Compendium of the study of theology

    (Studien und Texte zur Geistesgeschichte des
Mittelalters, ISSN 0169-8125; Bd. 20)
        Translation of: Compendium studii theologiae.
        Bibliography: p.
        Includes index.
        1. Signification (Logic)—Early works to 1800.
2. Theology—Early works to 1800. I. Maloney, Thomas S.
II. Title. III. Series.
B765.B23C6613 1988   160   88-2824
ISBN 90-04-08510-6 (pbk.)

ISSN 0169-8125
ISBN 90 04 08510 6

PRINTED IN THE NETHERLANDS BY E. J. BRILL

Et opus animae rationalis praecipuum est verbum,
et in quo maxime delectatur.

The principal creation of the rational soul is
the word, in which it takes its greatest
delight.

Roger Bacon, *Opus tertium*

CONTENTS

ACKNOWLEDGMENTS

While accepting the flaws of this work as my own, I would publicly express a huge debt of gratitude to the late Jan Pinborg and Paul Spade for their encouragement and untold hours in helping to bring this work to completion. I am also grateful to Paul Matthews and William Schuyler for their comments on the translation.

INTRODUCTION

If Roger Bacon is known for anything today it is for his association with the medieval beginnings of what we now call experimental science, especially optics. Along with a few others of his time he placed great emphasis on empirical verification as a method of validating the claims of deductive science. But his significance extends considerably beyond this. He was a man of extraordinary vision and the vision stopped short of nothing less than a call for a complete revision of the educational system of the second half of the thirteenth century, a call for correction of the procedural errors in the intellectual life of his times. Over and over he decried the failure of the theologians and masters of arts to accord the sciences their proper role: all knowledge, experiential, inferential, and divinely revealed, must make its contribution to a morally ordered society. Prompted by the persuasion that treasures of great worth were still locked up in the writings of Greeks and Arabs, and that Latin theologians were barely aware of the way their own language could serve, if properly understood, to eradicate some of what he considered egregious blunders in current semantic theories, the call did not fail to incorporate a summons to greater emphasis on the study and analysis of language.

Bacon describes his plan in a work written in 1267, later referred to by him as his *Opus maius*.[1] He sent this work, along with others, to Pope Clement IV with the hope that the latter would use his influence in getting the plan adopted. What the Pope thought of it, or whether he ever even received the works, is not known. Nevertheless, Bacon continued to call for a reorganization of Christian learning and in the last year of his life, 1292, returned to two of its central issues and wrote the treatise *Compendium studii theologiae* (*Cst*) here presented in a new edition and translation. He wrote it, he tells us, at the insistence of others to write something useful for theologians, i.e., to put at their disposal an expertise not other-

---

[1] *'Opus maius' of Roger Bacon*, 3 vols., ed. John Henry Bridges (1897-1900); reprinted Frankfort on the Main: Minerva, 1964). Vol. 3 is a supplement containing a revised text of Parts 1-3 of vol. 1 with corrections, emendations, and additional notes for vols. 1-2. (Henceforward this work will be cited as *Opus maius*, ed. Bridges, followed by volume, page, and line.) For Bacon's "Introduction" to this work see F.A. Gasquet, ed., "An Unpublished Fragment of a Work by Roger Bacon," *English Historical Review* 11 (1897) 494-517; for a more recent and complete edition of Part Seven of the *Opus maius* (on moral theology) see *Rogeri Baconis Moralis Philosophia*, ed. Eugenio Massa (Zurich: Thesaurus Mundi, [1953]). Translations of Latin texts will be my own unless otherwise noted, though page references to Burke's translation of the *Opus maius* will also be given for those who wish to pursue the context of the translated remarks. (See Robert Belle Burke, *The Opus Maius of Roger Bacon*, 2 vols. [Philadelphia: University of Pennsylvania Press, 1928].)

wise available, and to guage the significance of this remark one needs to appreciate some of the forces that helped shape his life.[2]

Bacon was born in England around 1214[3] and seems to have come from a family of above average means, possibly even of noble stock.[4] He himself mentions having a brother, and there may have been other children in the family.[5] Assuming normal progression towards a Master of Arts degree which he is known to have acquired, he must have begun his undergraduate studies at Oxford around 1227 during which time he would have studied grammar, rhetoric, and logic (the Trivium) and then moved on to arithmetic, geometry, astronomy, and music (the Quadrivium).[6] More importantly, however, he would also have studied the so-called natural books and *Metaphysics* of Aristotle, works denied students at Paris during this time.[7] In consequence when Bacon completed his course-work and teaching requirements and had become a

---

[2] Several biographies or studies including biographical data exist but I shall rely principally on Stewart C. Easton's *Roger Bacon and His Search for a Universal Science: A Reconsideration of the Life and Work of Roger Bacon in the Light of His Own Stated Purposes* (New York: Russell and Russell, 1952; reprinted 1971), henceforth cited as Easton, *Roger Bacon*, and to a lesser extent on Theodore Crowley's "Roger Bacon's Life and Works" in his *Roger Bacon: The Problem of the Soul in His Philosophical Commentaries* (Louvain: l'Institut Supérieur de Philosophie; Dublin: James Duffy, 1950, pp. 17-78), henceforth cited as Crowley, *Roger Bacon*. Easton is Bacon's most thorough biographer and, along with Crowley, takes into account not only the earlier biographies but also Robert Steele's editions of Bacon's Parisian works which were unavailable to most of the earlier biographers. For a list of other biographies and Easton's evaluation of each see his *Roger Bacon*, pp. 237-240.

[3] The date is inferred by A.G. Little (*Roger Bacon Essays Contributed by Various Writers on the Occasion of the Commemoration of the Seventh Century of His Birth*, collected and edited by A.G. Little [Oxford: Clarendon Press, 1914; reprinted New York: Russell and Russell, 1972], p. 1) on the basis of the usual age when boys entered Oxford in Bacon's time (twelve or thirteen) and the latter's remark in his *Opus tertium* of 1267 that except for two years he had been "*in studio*" for the past forty years. (*Fr. Rogeri Bacon Opera quedam hactenus inedita*, ed. J.S. Brewer [London: Longmans, 1859; reprinted Nendeln: Kraus Reprint, 1965], p. 65.6-9, henceforward cited as *Opus tertium*, ed. Brewer.) For further discussion of the date see Easton, *Roger Bacon*, pp. 9-11, and for Crowley's option of not before 1219-1220 see his *Roger Bacon*, pp. 17-18 and 195.

[4] Easton, *Roger Bacon*, p. 10.

[5] Ibid., p. 9.

[6] The date has relevance for remarks in this work on a Master Edmund of Canterbury and a Master Hugo (see below, #14, meaning Translation, paragraph 14.) but is an inference based on the same data used to infer Bacon's date of birth. Crowley, given his later date for Bacon's birth, suggests the year 1234. (For the dates see Easton, *Roger Bacon*, pp. 10-12, and Crowley, *Roger Bacon*, pp. 20-21 and 195.) Easton's calculations have Bacon becoming a Master of Arts in 1235 at the age of about twenty-one and Crowley's in 1240-1241 at roughly the same age. (See Easton, *Roger Bacon*, p. 18 and Crowley, *Roger Bacon*, p. 195.)

[7] For a general description of his studies at Oxford and their relevance for his later works, including the reference to the ban of 1210 at Paris, see Easton, *Roger Bacon*, pp. 12-18. See also Crowley, *Roger Bacon*, pp. 19-22.

Master of Arts his credentials would have been the envy of any of his Parisian peers.

Sometime in or shortly before 1245 Bacon accepted an invitation to teach in the faculty of arts at the University of Paris,[8] and judging by the works we know of that he wrote at that time and others to which he alludes he must have taken his profession quite seriously. During his first Parisian period it seems certain that he wrote at least eight sets of *questions* on Aristotle's natural treatises and *Metaphysics* and one commentary.[9] Within the *questions* he makes reference to five other "books" which Robert Steele thinks of as other *questions* and Stewart Easton suggests may well have been commentaries.[10] In addition to these, and still early in his career, he wrote three works which in one way or another touch on the study of language, his *Summa grammatica, Sumule dialectices*, and *Summa de sophismatibus et distinctionibus.*[11] The second of these is of special interest because of its relation to the present work. There, in the section on appellation, Bacon proposes what is, as far as is known, a claim uniquely his own, i.e., that of themselves names are names only of presently existing entities.[12] The question is whether a term like 'Caesar' said of a living and dead person equivocates, and in discussing the matter he makes his position quite clear on two issues: the application of his theory to inferences involving infinite, privative, and negative terms,[13] and the

---

[8] Easton argues this date cannot be later and Crowley suggests 1240-1241, the latter drawing on Bacon's remark in his *Opus minus* that he had seen Alexander of Hales in Paris with his own eyes. Alexander died in 1245. (See Easton, *Roger Bacon*, pp. 26-27; Crowley, *Roger Bacon*, pp. 23-25 and 195; and *Fr. Rogeri Bacon Opera quaedam hactenus inedita*, ed. J.S. Brewer [London: Longmans, 1859; reprinted Nendeln: Kraus Reprint, 1965], pp. 325.26-27 and 326.9-11, henceforth cited as *Opus minus*, ed. Brewer.) For a study of the academic life at Paris at this time see James A. Weisheipl, "The Parisian Faculty of Arts in Mid-thirteenth Century: 1240-1270," *American Benedictine Review* 25 (1974) 200-217.

[9] These works have been edited by Robert Steele (two by Ferdinand Delorme and one by A.G. Little and E. Withington) in *Opera hactenus inedita Rogeri Baconi*, 16 vols. (Oxford: Clarendon Press, 1905[?]-1941), henceforward cited as *Opera*, with editor and volume indicated. The one commentary is *Liber de sensu et sensato* (ibid., 14, ed. Steele) and Easton defends its ascription to Bacon in an appendix. (See his *Roger Bacon*, pp. 232-235.) For the notion of a "*question*" see below, #1, n. 4.

[10] Easton, *Roger Bacon*, pp. 59-61.

[11] For the first two see *Opera*, 15, ed. Steele; for the third ibid., 14. The text of the *Summa de sophismatibus et distinctionibus* is in need of emendation and is currently being re-edited by H.A.G. Braakhuis. Steele says that it possibly dates from Bacon's Parisian career but cautions that it "might well have been part of an Oxford course." (See *Opera*, 14, p. viii.) Easton is inclined toward a Parisian setting. (See his *Roger Bacon*, p. 61.) Henceforward the *Sumule dialectices* will be cited in the notes as *Sd*.

[12] See *Sd*, pp. 277.17-282.37, especially p. 280.16-32. However it should be noted that while no others are known to hold this theory Bacon himself introduces it under the form "Some say", at the same time granting that it is not a common opinion. (See *Sd*, p. 277.31-36.)

[13] See *Sd*, pp. 284.1-287.10.

uselessness of appeals to such notions as habitual being (*esse habituale*)[14] and confused as opposed to determinate being (*esse confusum et determinatum*) to describe the existential condition of the significates of names.[15] All of these issues are discussed explicitly in the present work with no change in position, and the fact that he expressly states here that he aired these difficulties some forty years previously dates the *Sumule dialectices* to about 1250.[16] Whether the work was written at Paris or immediately upon Bacon's return to Oxford is now a matter of debate.[17]

Whatever the case with the *Sumule dialectices* the use of Aristotle's natural treatises, the *Metaphysics*, and the works of Avicenna and Averroes during his Parisian career permits one to speak of Bacon as a pioneer in Aristotelian studies. And one should note that his early works give absolutely no hint of his later *special* interest in semantics, theology, and science in general. Had he continued to labor in this vein history would have recorded his contribution to the development of Aristotelian studies but would have found little else upon which to remark. But something happened to set him on a radically different course, for he was soon seized by the desire, already mentioned, to reorganize the whole of Chris-

---

[14] Ibid., p. 287.11-18.

[15] Ibid., p. 287.19-32.

[16] For the theory in general see below, #85-111. For the application to privative, infinite, and negative terms see below, #106; for rejections of the notions of habitual and confused being (the latter here called common being [*esse commune*]) see below, respectively, #101 and #99.

[17] Robert Steele, its editor, and Easton place it at the end of Bacon's first tenure at Paris. (See *Sd*, p. xx and *Roger Bacon*, p. 61, respectively.) Support for this claim can be petitioned on the internal grounds that Bacon, attempting to elucidate the kind of supposition involved in the expressions "The Seine flows" and "England is a good land," chooses the former for extended analysis and on the external grounds that it would have been quite natural for an arts professor at Paris to have written such a work, given Bacon's teaching responsibilities and his other works known to have been written there. (See *Sd*, pp. 272.20-273.6; cf., e.g., his *Questiones supra libros octo Physicorum Aristotelis* where he says, "... as if my palm would touch the Seine ..." [*Opera*, 13, ed. Delorme, p. 226.5-6].) More recently, however, Alain de Libera has pointed to an English commentary on the sophism "*Omnis homo de necessitate est animal*" attributed to Robert Kilwardby which, he says, "very probably" provides evidence that the author was directly aware of the *Sumule dialectices*, thereby supporting an Oxfordian setting. (See below, "Introduction," p. 19.) If one looks to the present work for help in deciding the issue one finds data difficult to interpret. (See below, #85-86 and cf. #111.) Assuming that the errors and madness mentioned refer to the theory that names univocally signify entities and nonentities, Bacon offers the confusing claim that they were invented by Richard of Cornwall both at Paris (after leaving Oxford) and at Oxford (before going to Paris). To resolve the paradox in favor of an Oxfordian setting one would have to assume that the errors and madness are not the same. This would then have Bacon claiming that the madness was begun by Richard at Oxford and that he was later reproved at Paris for (other) errors he invented there. This distinction, however, seems to be unsupported by the context. Given, then, the conflicting data from all available sources, the question of where the *Sumule dialectices* was written remains unresolved.

tian learning, giving particular emphasis to its practical applications. His later works indicate that he had become greatly interested in the relation of the sciences to theology and we know from his own words that he had access to the Pseudo-Aristotelian *Secretum Secretorum* while at Paris.[18] Easton suggests that it was this work more than anything else that prompted his new vision.[19] Hence upon his return to Oxford sometime around 1250[20] he began delving into things scientific and wrote several treatises, drafts of some of which were later incorporated into the *Opus maius*,[21] all the while spending the enormous sum of £2,000 on secret books, instruments, and tables.[22] Shortly after his return he followed the example of many of the scholars of his time and became a Franciscan.[23] Up till about 1254 his work proceeded smoothly, but by 1257 presumably the enthusiasm with which he pressed his case for the new vision landed him in considerable disfavor with his superiors, for in that year he was removed to Paris where he spent the next ten years,[24] years, however, that show no slacking of his endeavors to demonstrate the usefulness of the sciences for the study of theology. Easton attributes several works to this period among which are his *De multiplicatione specierum* (1262) and

---

[18] *Secretum secretorum cum glossis et notulis Fratris Rogeri*, ed. Steele, *Opera*, 5, p. 39.31-35. For additional information on this work see below, #13, n. 53.

[19] See Easton, *Roger Bacon*, pp. 80-86, and Crowley, *Roger Bacon*, pp. 52-54.

[20] The date of his return to England is uncertain. Easton says not later than 1250; Crowley suggests around 1247. (See Easton, *Roger Bacon*, p. 87, and Crowley, *Roger Bacon*, pp. 28-29.) Much depends on the place and dating of his *Sumule dialectices*, and possibly his *Summa de sophismatibus et distinctionibus*, though even should these be shown to have been written in England after 1250 enough time at Paris must be postulated to account for his known Parisian works.

[21] For a tentative reflection on some of the major discrepancies that appear in Bacon's own statements about his scientific writings, including those that preceded the *Opus maius*, and on a possible chronology of the works themselves see Easton, *Roger Bacon*, pp. 100-117.

[22] See *Opus tertium*, ed. Brewer, p. 59.4-12.

[23] The date of his entry into the Franciscan Order is not recorded. Easton suggests about 1252 (*Roger Bacon*, p. 139); Crowley about 1257 (*Roger Bacon*, p. 32). For a discussion of Bacon's motives see Easton, *Roger Bacon*, pp. 118-126.

[24] Easton suggests that he was sent away from Oxford because of his Joachite leanings rather than for any of his investigations into magic and astrology, etc. (For Easton's general assessment see his *Roger Bacon*, pp. 126-143.) Crowley on the other hand reflects on Bacon's relation to Bonaventure and points to the opposition raised by theologians who lectured and preached against the pursuit of mathematics and the sciences on which Bacon was so vocal. (See his *Roger Bacon*, pp. 50-60.) Finally, James A. Weisheipl seems to imply that recuperation from physical illness was associated with the return to Paris. (See his "Bacon, Roger," *New Catholic Encyclopedia*, Catholic University of America, ed. [New York; St. Louis; San Francisco; Toronto; London; Sydney: McGraw-Hill, 1967], pp. 552-553.)

Part One (and possibly a section of Part Two) of his *Communia naturalium* (1260-1267), all of which treat of issues relevant to the present work.[25]

Equally significant for events to follow was the fact that in 1260 the new Minister General of the Franciscans, the renowned Bonaventure, had ordered that no member of the Order was to go to the Pope on any matter without permission from the Minister General or to circulate any of his own works without permission from the General or the member's Provincial.[26] Determined to pursue his grand design, desperate for the recognition he thought he deserved, and anxious to extricate himself from disfavor, he twice sought by means of an intermediary the support of Guy le Gos de Foulques, once when the latter was a Papal legate and again, within a year, when he had become Pope Clement IV.[27] Guy responded with interest both times but enjoined secrecy.[28] Bacon, strapped for funds and unable to proceed openly, delayed for two years, but finally in the spring of 1267 assembled much of his writings since the early 1250s, revised them and added new material, and composed his most celebrated work, the *Opus maius*. Within about a year he also composed his *Opus minus* and *Opus tertium*.[29] Parts One and Three of the *Opus maius* are especially relevant for the *Cst*. The first is on the general causes of error and the third on the study of languages. It is readily apparent that Part One of the *Cst* is a condensed version of the material in Part One of the *Opus maius* and that Part Two is a shortened adaptation and partial

---

[25] For the *De multiplicatione specierum* see David C. Lindberg, *Roger Bacon's Philosophy of Nature: A Critical Edition, with English Translation, Introduction, and Notes of De multiplicatione specierum and De speculis comburentibus* (Oxford: Clarendon Press, 1983). The *Communia naturalium* (*Liber primus communium naturalium Fratris Rogeri*, ed. Robert Steele, *Opera*, 2-3 [Oxford: Clarendon Press, n.d. and 1911]; *Liber secundus communium naturalium Fratris Rogeri de coelestibus*, ed. Robert Steele, *Opera*, 4 [Oxford: Clarendon Press, 1913]) seems to have been written in various stages though published in its present form shortly after 1267. Presumably since Book One, Part One, also treats of the theory of species found in the *De multiplicatione specierum* Easton dates it 1260-1267. (*Roger Bacon*, pp. 50, 111, and 188; see also Steele, *Opera*, 3, p. iii.) For the suggestion that at least one section of Book One, Part Two, was also written during this time see below, p. 10, n. 47.

[26] For the relevant parts of this decree see Easton, *Roger Bacon*, pp. 142-143.

[27] The intermediary was Raymond of Laon, a clerk in the service of Guy le Gos de Foulques. Guy became Pope in February, 1265, and died in November, 1268.

[28] Secrecy was enjoined because permission had not been sought under the rules of Bonaventure's injunction of 1260.

[29] For a chronology of the events that led to the writing of these works see Easton, *Roger Bacon*, pp. 146-166 and Crowley, *Roger Bacon*, pp. 34-50. For the *Opus minus* see ed. Brewer, pp. 313-389 and for the *Opus tertium* see ibid, pp. 3-310; *Un fragment inédit de l'Opus tertium de Roger Bacon précédé d'une etude sur se fragment*, ed. Pierre Duhem (Quaracchi: College of St. Bonaventure, 1909), pp. 75-193; and *Part of the Opus tertium of Roger Bacon Including a Fragment Now Printed for the First Time*, ed. A.G. Little (Aberdeen: University Press, 1912; reprinted Farnborough: Gregg Press, 1966), pp. 1-89. Easton argues that the *Opus tertium* was neither completed nor sent to the Pope (*Roger Bacon*, p. 166); Crowley thinks it was "probably" sent (*Roger Bacon*, p. 47).

reorganization of the central themes in a recently discovered section of Part Three of the *Opus maius*.[30] Hence if one is to look for the period in Bacon's life when the theories elaborated in the *Cst* were worked out, one would be safe in focusing on the years 1250-1267.

Bacon presumably returned to Oxford shortly after writing the works of 1267 and probably continued to revise his scientific writings, giving the *Communia naturalium* its final form.[31] The times however were rather hectic. There was increasing rivalry between the Franciscans and Dominicans, and the long seething friction between the seculars and Orders erupted in a series of polemics over the true notion of evangelical poverty. At Paris Siger of Brabant was challenging the teaching of the more orthodox theologians, a challenge that resulted in Bishop Tempier's condemnation of various propositions at Paris in 1277.[32] Given these

---

[30] To compare Part One of each work see ed. Bridges, 3, pp. 1-35, transl. Burke, 1, pp. 3-35, and below, #2-14. Part Two of the *Cst* is on signification and its modes, and the editors of Bacon's *De signis* correctly argue that this treatise should be added after the material now presented in Part Three of the *Opus maius*. (For their argument and the text of the *De signis* see K.M. Fredborg, Lauge Nielsen, and Jan Pinborg, eds., "An Unedited Part of Roger Bacon's '*Opus maius: De signis*'" in *Traditio* 34 (1978) 76-79 and 81-136, respectively. Henceforth this treatise will be cited as *Ds* followed by section numbers.) The editors speak of the *De signis* as a *second* chapter of that Part (ibid., pp. 75 and 76) and this requires that the present material in Part Three as found in Bridges' first volume be thought of as Chapter One—there are no divisions by chapter in that edition—and that the fourteen chapter divisions in the revision in Volume Three be ignored. The latter is no great loss when one recognizes that they are sometimes arbitrary (the first three reasons for studying languages are grouped in the first chapter while the rest are in separate ones; cf. ed. Bridges, 3, pp. 80-83 and, e.g., 84) and in one place ignore the type of rubric in MS. J. that is the basis given for the other divisions (see ibid., p. 101, n. 1). For a description of the major differences between the relevant parts of the *Opus maius* and the *Cst* see below, pp. 9-11.

[31] See Easton, *Roger Bacon*, pp. 186-188 and above, p. 6, n. 25.

[32] For a thorough discussion of the condemnations by Bishop Stephen Tempier at Paris in 1277 see John F. Wippel, "The Condemnations of 1270 and 1277 at Paris," *Journal of Medieval And Renaissance Studies* 7 (1977) 169-201. Wippel gives no indication he believes Bacon was condemned at this time and Easton rejects an earlier thesis that some of Bacon's astrological theories were included in the condemnations, a thesis more recently maintained by Fernand Van Steenberghen. (See Easton, *Roger Bacon*, pp. 196-197, and Fernand Van Steenberghen, *La philosophie au XIIIe siècle*, Philosophes Médiévaux 9 [Louvain; Publications Universitaires; Paris: Béatrice-Nauwelaerts, 1966], p. 422.) Eleven days after Tempier's condemnations Bishop Robert Kilwardby issued another series of condemnations at Oxford. Again, Easton is not disposed to see any connection between these condemnations and Bacon, but more recently Alain de Libera suggests a possible link, depending on whether Kilwardby is the author of an anonymous treatment of the sophism "*Omnis homo de necessitate est animal*" found in MS. Erfurt 4°, 328, f. 7vb-10rb. (See Easton, *Roger Bacon*, p. 197 and de Libera, "Roger Bacon et le problem de l'*appellatio univoca*" in *English Logic and Semantics: From the End of the Twelfth Century to the Time of Ockham And Burleigh*, Acts of the 4th European Symposium on Mediaeval Logic And Semantics, Leiden-Nijmegen, 23-27 April 1979, ed. H.A.G. Braakhuis, C.H. Kneepkens, and L.M. de Rijk, *Artistarium Supplementa* 1 [Nijmegen: Ingenium, 1981], pp. 219-220 and below, p. 19.)

unsettling events, Bacon's bitter disappointment over the failure of his *Opera* to achieve their end, and a lingering resentment of his past and continuing treatment at the hands of his own Order, we should not be surprised to find that in 1272 another of his works fairly teems with invective. This was his *Compendium studii philosophiae*, probably written as an introduction to what for years he had intended to be his *scriptum principale*, a work never completed but to which he made frequent reference. As Easton remarks, it was "nothing but a scurrilous attack upon his contemporaries in every rank of society."[33] Although it is not certain that this work was ever published, surely the sentiments expressed in it were often on Bacon's lips at this time and they clearly could not have endeared him to his superiors and many of his peers. Shortly thereafter he wrote grammars of Greek and Hebrew, without, however, the same degree of animus.[34] Nevertheless, he was once again headed for exile.

It is recorded in the *Chronicle of the Twenty-four Generals* of 1370 that Bacon was imprisoned by order of Jerome (of Ascoli) for "suspected novelties."[35] Clearly something happened to Bacon during this period for we know of no writings by him during the 1280s. However, there are good reasons to doubt that imprisonment was the cause. Easton discusses the issue at length, refers to various theories, and concludes that at most Bacon was again sent to France and placed under a kind of house arrest. He also suggests that it was more the person of Bacon that may have been condemned than any of his particular theories.[36] There is no record of his release, though, if one accepts Easton's hypothesis about Bacon's involvement in the Joachite controversy and takes this (as Easton does) as at least partial explanation for his "imprisonment," then he would probably have been released in 1290 when other such dissidents were freed by the new Minister General of the Order, Raymond de Gaufredi.[37] At that point he probably returned again to Oxford.

With mention of this third return to Oxford, one has all the significant events in Bacon's life to approach the *Compendium studii theologiae*. Bacon

---

[33] For the work see *Fr. Rogeri Bacon Opera quaedam hactenus inedita*, ed. J.S. Brewer (London: Longmans, 1859; reprinted Nendeln: Kraus Reprint, 1965), pp. 393-519; for Easton's comment on it see *Roger Bacon*, pp. 69-70.

[34] For these works see E. Bolan and S.A. Hirsch, *The Greek Grammar of Roger Bacon And a Fragment of His Hebrew Grammar* (Cambridge: University Press, 1902). For a study of Bacon as philologist see S.A. Hirsch, "Roger Bacon And Philology" in A.G. Little, ed., *Roger Bacon Essays* (Oxford: Clarendon Press, 1914; reprinted New York: Russell and Russell, 1972), pp. 101-151.

[35] *Analecta Franciscana*, 3 (1897), p. 360.

[36] See Easton, *Roger Bacon*, pp. 192-202; Crowley agrees (*Roger Bacon*, pp. 67-70).

[37] See Easton, *Roger Bacon*, pp. 201-202. Crowley argues that Bacon's release "probably came earlier" since "we have no reason to believe that he had any sympathy for them [the Spirituals] or they for him." (*Roger Bacon*, pp. 71-72.)

himself gives its date of composition as 1292 and tradition records the same year as that of his death and burial at Oxford.[38] The *Cst*, as we have it, is divided into two unequal Parts and there are several references to one or more chapters and to a third Part which are still missing.[39] Bacon provides a clue to what he wrote in the third Part when he recalls in the *Opus tertium* the subject matter of a parallel (and also missing) final section of the *De signis*:

> For the rest I have considered how a vocal sound in Sacred Scripture signifies a spiritual sense with the literal and in which modes of a sign; how the literal sense signifies the spiritual; and how the Old Testament is a sign of the new; and how sacraments are signs. And I have inserted many difficult things, e.g., about the first language of Adam and how he gave names to things and whether boys nurtured in a desert would have used some language on their own (*per se*) and, should they meet each other, how they would indicate mutual feelings, and many other things which I cannot now explain.[40]

As mentioned previously, the *Cst* is thoroughly dependent on material found in Parts One and Three of the *Opus maius*. One will also recognize the subject matter of Part Two, Chapter Four, of the *Cst* as a return to issues treated in the *Sumule dialectices* of about 1250 and also found in the *De signis*.[41]

But even given this dependence, the effort of 1292 is not to be considered a mindless re-presentation. It is clear that Bacon selects his material with a keen eye on current affairs, passing over some items, ex-

---

[38] See below, #14 and #86 and A.G. Little, "Introduction: On Roger Bacon's Life and Works" in A.G. Little, ed., *Roger Bacon Essays* (Oxford: Clarendon Press, 1914; reprinted New York: Russell and Russell, 1972), p. 28.

[39] A third Part is explicitly mentioned in the *Cst* on two occasions, once in a context of discussing the relation of natural human acts to original sin (see below, #40) and the other when mentioning the signification of the spiritual sense of the Scriptures and sacraments (see below, #83). On six other occasions Bacon promises a further treatment—three of these speak of subsequent chapters—of such issues as propositions (see below, #103 and #111), the signification of terms like '*ens*' and '*unum*' (see below, #133-134 and #142), and the existence of pure forms (see below, #135), which may or may not be references to the third Part. (Cf. *Ds* 52, 88, 120 and 142 which also refer to discussions that do not appear in the known sections of that work, which also breaks off before the conclusion of *Ds* 173.) Having spoken of the missing "theological" section of the *Cst* as a Part (*pars*), I should note that on the two occasions mentioned above when Bacon makes reference to it he speaks of it as a Treatise (*tractatus*) and this in contradistinction to the way he speaks of the unit comprising the first Prologue and first two chapters of this work: these are called "the first Part." (See below, #1, n. 1). Since the first two units are with justification called "Parts" and since I am not sure whether the consistency with which Bacon uniquely refers to the missing "theological" section as a treatise is significant, I shall continue to speak of it as a third Part.

[40] Ed. Brewer, p. 101.21-30.

[41] The issue is whether words univocally signify (appel) entities and nonentities. (See *Ds* 134-161 and *Sd*, pp. 277.28-287.32.)

panding and adding others, and rearranging topics. Additional historical
data is presented and opponents' theories not previously mentioned are
often supplied. Issues treated with equanimity in the early works are
sometimes here infused with anger, an occasional reminder that the
author of the *Compendium studii philosophiae* is still writing. More specifically, a major change in Part One is the omission of the fourth cause of
human errors mentioned in the *Opus maius*, namely, the hiding of one's
own ignorance by a display of apparent wisdom,[42] and in Part Two the
following are worthy of note. First, the opening sections of the earlier
work offer some observations on the triadic notion of signification—sign,
thing signified, and interpreter—and present a definition of a sign.[43]
These are omitted in the *Cst*, the absence of the latter being especially
significant in view of Bacon's theory that concepts of things outside the
mind are signs.[44] This position requires that the scope of things capable
of becoming signs should not be limited to things susceptible of sensory
perception as in the more traditional Augustinian definition.[45] Second, in
the *De signis* natural signs are divided into three classes on the basis of
whether they convey awareness of something by inference or configuration or whether the sign be an effect (or cause).[46] This tripartite division
is also found in his *Communia naturalium*, but only the first two classes are
found in the *Cst*.[47] Interestingly, the more restricted division is mentioned in the *Opus tertium* where Bacon is giving a summary of the relevant
part of the *Opus maius* (*De signis*).[48] Since the *Opus tertium* was written

---

[42] See below, #7, n. 21.

[43] See *Ds* 1-2.

[44] *Ds* 2.

[45] For Augustine's definition see below, #24, n. 91.

[46] See *Ds* 3-6.

[47] See ed. Steele, *Opera*, 2, pp. 119.29-120.20 and below, #26 and #29. A propos of the
Communia naturalium it should be noted that Book One of the work is divided into four
Parts and that both Steele and Easton contend that what we now have represents a revision of earlier material that took place shortly after the *Opera*. (See respectively *Opera*, 3,
ed. Steele, p. iii and *Roger Bacon*, pp. 50, 111, and 188.) In Book One, Part Two, of the
Communia naturalium Bacon divides signs into those given by a soul and those that are
natural, and then offers the triple subdivision of natural signs. (*Opera*, 2, ed, Steele, p.
119.18-120.20.) If this section had been written after the *De signis* one would expect
natural signs to be mentioned and discussed prior to those given by a soul since this is the
usual order and the one followed in the *De signis* (3-8), *Opus tertium* (ed. Brewer, pp.
100.19-29), and the present work (see below, #26-31). Also, when speaking in the same
passage of the usefulness of a classification of signs one would expect some specific
reference to its relevance for a proper understanding of the Scriptures, assuming that he
had already gone to great lengths in this regard in the (missing) final section of the *De
signis*, yet no such reference is given. I am inclined, therefore, to think of this section of the
Communia naturalium as having been written before the *Opus maius*, sometime during
1260-1267, and included unaltered in the revision that resulted in publication of the work
shortly after the *Opera* of 1267.

[48] See ed. Brewer, p. 100.20-24.

within a year of the latter either Bacon's memory failed or he had second thoughts about the appropriateness of a division based on the fact of something being a cause or effect. And indeed the *De signis* itself suggests that even at the time of its writing Bacon was uncomfortable with the triple subdivision: the first two, he says, are more appropriately classes.[49] Perhaps while reflecting when writing the *Opus tertium* it occurred to him that the knowledge derived from an understanding of causal relations is science in the strict (Aristotelian) sense rather than that knowledge acquired merely from (natural) signs, and that where two things or events are not known to be causally related, though in fact they are so, an adequate account of any significative relation can be given by appeal to concomittance or consequence.[50] Whatever his reason, he makes it clear in both the *De signis* and the *Cst* that he recognizes that causal and sign relations are different, and in the former he points to the relevant cause of distinction: sign relations require an interpreter in order for them to obtain; causal ones do not.[51] Third, Bacon digresses momentarily in the *Cst* to apply the notion of involuntary human acts to the issue of original sin; no such digression appears in the *De signis*.[52] Fourth, in the earlier work connotation is treated after equivocation, but appears before it in the *Cst*.[53] Fifth, no parallel treatment of ampliation and restriction (forms of equivocation) is given in the *Cst*, though the notions are mentioned and a discussion is promised.[54] Sixth, there is likewise no parallel in the *Cst* for the incomplete section in the *De signis* on nugatory predications involving genus and species.[55] Seventh, modes of equivocation are given as five in the earlier work and as six here.[56] Finally, the *De signis* promises a section on supposition but breaks off without it while the *Cst* makes no such promise.[57] As already noted neither treatise as it now stands contains a third Part on theology and Scripture. Other differences of lesser significance will be mentioned in the footnotes.

---

[49] See *Ds* 5.

[50] See also below, #30, n. 101.

[51] See *Ds* 6 and below, #30.

[52] See below, #38-40.

[53] See respectively *Ds* 102-133 and below, #66-83 and #130-142.

[54] Cf. *Ds* 89-99 and below, #85.

[55] See *Ds* 170-173. The discussion, however, is incomplete.

[56] Cf. *Ds* 38-43 and below, #131-139. The sequential enumeration of these modes in the *De signis* is not consistent. (See below, #129, n. 255.) The *Communia naturalium* also speaks only of five modes and there Bacon mentions that he has written more fully on these five modes in his *Metaphysics*. (See *Opera*, 2, p. 51.4-15.) The earlier treatment, however, is not preserved in the fragment published by Steele (*Opera*, 1) entitled *Metaphysica Fratris Rogeri Ordinis Fratrum Minorum de viciis contractis in studio theologie*.

[57] See *Ds* 50, 52, and 88. In *Ds* 52 Bacon makes it clear that he does not want to treat the issue in question in terms of supposition theory but signification.

Bacon was some seventy years old when he wrote this *Compendium*. He was probably burdened with failing health, and certainly disappointed at the papal reception given to his *Opera*. As "the only seer in the country of the blind" he was still resentful of his treatment by his peers and fellow Franciscans and frustrated by the failure to receive the appropriate recognition for one who was offering a complete revision of Christian learning.[58] He had long given up hope of ever completing his *scriptum principale*.[59] Given this state of affairs two questions arise: why did he decide to begin yet another work and why did he select the subject matter represented in the three Parts of the *Compendium studii theologiae?*

As has already been mentioned, he himself gives us a clue to the answer to the first question: he had long been requested to write "some things useful for theology."[60] The remark should probably not be taken completely at face value but should be seen rather as partial justification of his own desire to make one last effort to produce something that would merit recognition. His life's ambition had been to show how all the sciences were useful for theology but he was now, let us speculate, convinced that theologians were not prepared to undergo the training his proposal required and that his universal science was too much for them to grasp. Whatever he wrote would have to be brief—if nothing else, his health and age demanded this—and it would have to treat issues with which his readers were already familiar. Too vast a display of knowledge would only invite the same response as before. Perhaps at this point, reflecting on the unique ways in which the various sciences had been described as useful for theology in the *Opus maius*, he recognized that there was one science which theologians could not escape, with which they were already familiar, and of which they were in desperate need, and it was the science of language. Biblical exegesis requires a proper understanding of the many modes in which words can signify and so does the proper conduct of a disputation on *questions*. In this area theologians were still holding linguistic theories which he considered erroneous. He was especially piqued by the popularity at Oxford of certain theories against which he had (unsuccessfully) fought some forty years previous and of which he was now ready to declare Richard of Cornwall the inventor.[61] If theologians were ill-prepared to see the relevance of all sciences

---

[58] The epithet is Crowley's (*Roger Bacon*, p. 196).

[59] Bacon originally intended to send to Pope Clement a well organized treatise which would be itself an example of his grand plan for the reorganization of Christian learning. Pressed by time, he instead wrote the *Opus maius*, a work which he speaks of as a *persuasio*. For further comment on his *scriptum principale* see Easton, *Roger Bacon*, pp. 149, 152-153, 160, 188, and 191.

[60] See below, #4.

[61] See below, #86 and #128. When Bacon treated these issues in the *Sumule dialectices* and *De signis* Richard was not mentioned by name.

to theology, perhaps they could be brought by one last effort to see the value of the study of language, a proposal far more modest than the grand scheme of the *Opus maius* but one standing in relation to it as the part to the whole. He had written on the subject before and all that was required was to re-work the material, a practice at which he was now adept. He could begin with the general causes of error (at least the first three) and, aware that what he would be advocating would not be popular, would urge his readers to be more skeptical of majority positions. Then would come a treatise on signification, and finally a discussion of its applications to Scripture and theology. This even the handicap of old age permitted, and the result was the *Compendium studii theologiae*.

Bacon's place in the development of logic and semantics has only recently begun to be studied and, even given the body of research on the man that is building up, one can only speak with caution of Bacon's sources, opponents, and followers. Clearly his emphasis on the freedom of the will in naming[62] and his insistence that things rather than their concepts are the principal significates of words[63] are themes central to the thought of later terminists at Oxford like Ockham, yet no direct link with them has been established. The central issues with which he grapples have a long history, and thus the question of his sources and opponents becomes a broad one. Finally, it is distressingly difficult to identify works written at Oxford during the last half of the thirteenth century with which to compare his. Nevertheless work has begun, with most effort directed toward identifying his adversaries.[64]

First mention should perhaps go to Franz Pelster who in 1929 identified Balliol College Oxford Codex 62 containing a commentary on the *Sentences* of Peter Lombard as written by Richard of Cornwall.[65] Pelster edited a section from *Sentences* 3, Distinction 21, pertaining to the question whether Christ could be called a man during the three days in the tomb, and it is there that Richard makes appeal to the notion of habitual being (*esse habituale*) to argue a case for univocal signification, a position

---

[62] The cause of naming is "the free will of the one imposing the name in accord with the good pleasure of his own will." (See below, #81.)

[63] "I say, therefore, that a vocal sound imposed to signify a thing outside a mind signifies only that thing by reason of the imposition ..." (See below, #59). It is a natural sign of the concept of the thing. (See below, #60.)

[64] The following survey of research on Bacon as semanticist (logician) focuses only on published works of a more or less extended nature where Bacon's theories are of principal concern. For a general introduction to Bacon's place in the development of medieval logic see Jan Pinborg, *Logik und Semantik im Mittelalter: Ein Überblick* (Stuttgart-Bad Canstatt: Frommann-Holzboog, 1972), pp. 13, 78, 90, and 93-96.

[65] "Roger Bacon's '*Compendium studii theologiae*' und der Sentenzenkommentar des Richardus Rufus," *Scholastik* 4 (1929) 410-416.

repeatedly attacked (as Pelster notes) by Bacon in Part Two, Chapter Four, of the *Cst*. Twenty years later Pelster returned to the issue with a more lengthy article and supplies what appears to be the complete text of Distinction 22 on the same topic.[66]

In 1970 Sten Ebbesen and Jan Pinborg wrote *Studies in the Logical Writings Attributed to Boethius de Dacia* in which Part Two researches the question whether man can be said to be animal when no man exists.[67] In Chapter 10, "Roger Bacon and the Fools of His Times,"[68] Ebbesen warns against taking Pelster's lead in thinking of Richard alone as Bacon's adversary in Part Two, Chapters Four and Five of the *Cst* (p. 43). He expresses some reservations about Pelster's attribution of Balliol 62 to Richard ("not wholly convincing") and points to works by authors like Siger of Brabant, William of Arnaud, John and Boethius of Dacia, Henry of Ghent, and an anonymous commentary on the *Posterior Analytics* as additional sources for the various theories condemned by Bacon (pp. 43-44). He also notes that Boethius of Dacia agrees with Bacon that 'man' said of an existing and dead man is equivocal (p. 42).

This was followed in 1977 by a very penetrating analysis of Bacon's semantics by H.A.G. Braakhuis who compares theories presented in William of Sherwood'a *Introductiones in logicam* and *Syncategoremata* with those in Bacon's *Sumule dialectices* and the *Cst*.[69] There he shows that both agree that appellation is only of things existing, that the range of things supposited and appellated is the same (pp. 114-117), and that both reject the notion of confused being (*esse confusum*) in favor of determinate being (*esse determinatum*) (p. 123). While it is true, Braakhuis notes (p. 125), that William has a notion of habitual being and habitual supposition, it is also true that the latter contends in his *Syncategoremata* that 'is' is an equivocal term, with the result that "Man is animal" when no man exists is to be judged true or false on the basis of whether actual or habitual being is intended; for Bacon this proposition is false, even *falsissimum*.[70] William grants that when 'is' functions only as a single predicate, as in "Man is," existence is entailed (pp. 124-125). Thus Braakhuis concludes that

---

[66] "Der Oxforder Theologe Richardus Rufus O.F.M. über die Frage: '*Utrum Christus in triduo mortis fuerit homo*'," *Recherces de Theologie Ancienne Médiévale* 16 (1949) 259-280. On the same question see also Arthur M. Landgraf, "Das Problem *Utrum Christus fuerit homo in triduo mortis* in der Frühscholastick" in *Mélanges Auguste Pelzer* (Louvain, 1947), pp. 109-158, where, however, neither Richard of Cornwall nor Bacon are mentioned.

[67] *Studies in the Logical Writings Attributed to Boethius de Dacia, Cahiers de l'Institut du Moyen-Age grec et latin* 3 (Copenhagen: University of Copenhagen, 1970), pp. 13-53 (63-103).

[68] Ibid, pp. 40-44 (90-94).

[69] "The Views of William of Sherwood on Some Semantical Topics and Their Relation to Those of Roger Bacon," *Vivarium* 15 (1977) 111-142.

[70] See below, #128.

William's views in this regard at the most come under only partial condemnation by Bacon. Finally Braakhuis sees both as agreeing that terms
in negative propositions stand only for existing things (p. 128) and that
supposition occurs only within the context of an expression, complete or
incomplete (p. 140).

In 1978 the *De signis* was published and in the following year Ebbesen
again turned to the subject matter relevant to Part Two, Chapters Four
and Five of the *Cst*, discusses the sophism "This is a dead man; therefore
this is a man" and relates it to the Aristotelian fallacy of "Something said
in a certain sense or absolutely (*secundum quid vel simpliciter*) (p. 43).[71]
After offering a few words on the notion of imposition and signification
and underscoring the perceived opposition between signification and
supposition as semantic theories he points out that, while Parisian
masters up to 1250 approached semantics from the point of view of supposition, by the second half of the thirteenth century it was signification
theory that prevailed (p. 47). Problems posed by expressions like 'dead
man' were resolved by appeal to the notion that 'man' was originally imposed to mean both living man and corpse, and that 'man' is thus by
original imposition an analogous term. Words, then, do not lose their
signification (pp. 47-48). Duns Scotus, writing in the 1290s, and Ralph
Brito, at the turn of the century, reject this analysis, the latter however
acknowledging that it was then the common opinion but arguing that
'man' in 'dead man' is simply a case of improper or "similitudinary"
signification (pp. 49-51). This, he felt, saved the theory of signification,
but, as Ebbesen points out,

> he had paid a high price for getting rid of the corpse in the significate of
> 'man' by introducing a signification which does not depend on the power
> allotted to the word on its imposition, for such is his 'similitudinary
> signification' (p. 51).

Given this solution it is not surprising, continues Ebbesen, that one finds
within a few decades a return to supposition theory at Paris in the works
of John Buridan, probably imported from England with Ockham as its
chief inspiration (p. 52). Turning to the question of the prevailing semantic theory at Oxford during the last quarter of the thirteenth century as
reflected in treatments of the 'dead man' sophism, Ebbesen notes the
problem of the rarity of clearly identifiable sources but points to three sets
of *questions* treating *On Sophisticatical Refutations* as the only ones "that
merit consideration at all": those of John of Felmingham, anonymous G
and C-668, and, most importantly, anonymous G and C-611/341
(p. 53). The first two were written around 1300 and, while Ebbesen

---

[71] Sten Ebbesen, "The Dead Man Is Alive," *Synthese* 40 (1979) 43-70.

claims to have formed "no clear impression" of the position taken in either, he speaks of the former as "a 'soft' variant of the Parisian semantics" and usage, a position, he says, that is "roughly like Brito's" (pp. 53-54). However, it is the third work that most captures Ebbesen's interest as a means of discovering Bacon's impact in England. The MS. starts with some *questions* treating *On Interpretation* which, he says, differ little from the approach found in Parisian works of 1270-1290, leading to the acknowledgment that they may even be Parisian (pp. 54-55). However, the rest of the sixty-four *questions* are judged to be English, by the same author, and are dated to around 1280, with the 1270s and 1295 as extreme parameters. The position taken there represents a shift toward supposition theory: while an equivocal term must signify more than one thing, when another term is joined to it as in 'dead man', the whole phrase supposits only one thing. Thus even if 'man' signifies something living it need not stand for it. Ebbeson then concludes his article with selections, edited there for the first time, from G and C-611/341 and from Brito's *Quaestiones super Sophisticos Elenchos* (pp. 56-65).

As can be seen, most attention up to this point has been focused on the question of whether terms univocally signify both things present and things past or future, issues treated in the *Cst* in Part Two, Chapters Four and Five, and, it is Bacon's *Sumule dialectices* and *Compendium studii theologiae* to which reference is made. However, in 1981 Jan Pinborg focused attention on Bacon's notion of natural signification, an issue especially relevant to Part Two, Chapters One to Three, and which Pinborg describes as "one of the more original and one of the unifying concepts of Bacon's schemes."[72] While his remarks are directed principally to the *De signis* their relevance to the *Cst* is obvious, except of course for mention of the tripartite division of natural signs (pp. 406-407). Pinborg gives an excellent description of Bacon's central claims and points to varying degrees of originality in regard to certain features. Bacon, he says, is unique in combining into one work so many elements ordinarily found in separate treatises on grammar and logic (p. 405). His analysis of implied meanings (connotation) is "a first systematical attempt to bring order to this problem before the more comprehensive treatment in Ockham's *Summa totius logicae*" (p. 409).[73] Bacon pays close attention to specifying various grades of equivocation in both the *De signis* and the *Cst* (Part Two, Chapter Six) and Pinborg emphasizes the originality of a systematization which is based not on Aristotle's *Categories* but rather on

---

[72] "Roger Bacon on Signs: A Newly Recovered Part of the *Opus maius*," *Miscellanea Medievalia* 13 (Berlin; New York: Walter de Gruyter, 1981), pp. 403-412. For the quotation see ibid., p. 406.

[73] Connotation is treated in this work in part Two, Chapter Three.

scattered remarks in the latter's *Physics* and *Metaphysics* and on Arab writings (p. 410). Further, Bacon's understanding of universal names as giving more confused (not truer) knowledge than individual names and his requirement that a new imposition be made to designate individuals, Pinborg says, "makes possible a more critical analysis of universal terms" and thereby "opens the way to Scotus and Ockham and continues the development of terminist logic toward its culmination in the early 14th century" (pp. 411-412). Reflecting on Bacon's contribution Pinborg concludes: "When words and concepts are considered as signs which operate according to rules, it becomes possible to use philosophical language critically, but without despair" (p. 412).

In 1981 two excellent papers by Karin Margarita Fredborg and Alain de Libera appeared in the Acts of the 4th European Symposium on Mediaeval Logic and Semantics. The former's "Roger Bacon on '*Impositio Vocis ad Significandum*'" is especially helpful in pointing to Bacon's originality and to those additional sources in reaction to which Bacon may have developed his theories.[74] Fredborg takes his claim that words principally signify extramental objects and his distinction between vocal and tacit imposition as "no doubt his most original contribution[s] to grammar and semantics" (p. 168) and claims that the necessity of renewing impositions was stressed by Bacon "to a degree unusual among his contemporaries" (p. 170). Regarding the question of Bacon's opponents, she suggests—in addition to Richard of Cornwall—William of Sherwood, Magister Abstractionum, and an anonymous English commentator on the *Logica Vetus* as representatives of the view of habitual being condemned by Bacon (p. 170). While Bacon was aware of Pseudo-Grosseteste's theory to explain how words acquire meaning, namely, by means of a "common nature" or bridge formed by the combination in the listener of the speaker's inner word (*species vocis*) and concept (*species rei*), he rejected it, she notes, appealing instead to a combination of conventional and natural significations with no mention of a "common nature" or listener's role (pp. 174-175). And since Lambert of Auxerre tried to explain the same issue by contending that object, concept, and word were all causally linked, Fredborg thinks it "quite possible" that Bacon's own explanation was an implicit attack on him (p. 175). On the question of whether imposition occurs before, during, or after use, she states that John of Dacia allows all three possibilities, Pseudo-Albert chooses the first of them, and Bacon and Pseudo-Kilwardby the second

---

[74] *English Logic And Semantics: From the End of the Twelfth Century to the Time of Ockham And Burleigh*, Acts of the 4th European Symposium on Mediaeval Logic and Semantics, Leiden-Nijmegen, 23-27 April 1979, H.A. G. Braakhuis, C.H. Kneepkens, and L.M. de Rijk, eds., *Artistarium Supplementa* 1 (Nijmegen: Ingenium, 1981), pp. 167-191.

(pp. 176-177).[75] Despite this agreement, however, she argues that in four other respects Bacon disagrees with Pseudo-Kilwardby: since Bacon's inner word is "bereft of any significant function of ensuring the meaning of a word," she says, he rejected Pseudo-Kilwardby's claims that (a) "imposition takes place mediated through the imposition of the 'inner word'"; (b) "the outer sensible word is a natural sign only of the import of the word (*intentio vocis*)"; and (c) "words may retain their meaning, even after the objects signified have perished" (p. 177). In addition, (d) the two differ considerably in the attention they give to an explanation of how a listener grasps the correct meaning of a word: Pseudo-Kilwardby offers suggestions, but Bacon hardly mentions the issue (pp. 177-178). Fredborg concludes by pointing to a certain "somebody" mentioned by Pseudo-Kilwardby who held that "'the outer word acquired its meaning through the inner word, which is signifying naturally'" (p. 178). She thinks that the theory is "too primitive" to be Bacon's but adds, "... it is highly probable that it is exactly from such a view that Bacon in his *De signis* and later in the *Compendium studii theologiae* took his point of departure" (p. 178).

The second paper referred to above, Alain de Libera's "Roger Bacon et le problem de l'*appellatio univoca*," attempts to relate Bacon's theory that terms signify entities and nonentities only equivocally as expressed in his *De signis* and the *Cst* to his theory of "equivocal appellation" as (at least) implied in his *Sumule dialectices* and to situate the latter in the context of Parisian and continental appeals of the early and mid-thirteenth century to restriction and the Oxford use of ampliation.[76] Though Bacon's later works make recourse to signification and a second imposition to explain cases of equivocation de Libera contends that Bacon was in possession of the fundamental themes of his later doctrine as early as 1250, as is clear in the *Sumule dialectices* (p. 196). He searches for the "common doctrine" of appellation in the Oxford tradition—terms appellate something common to both entities and nonentities—to identify Bacon's opponents, noting the problems of finding consistency in that tradition. His search takes him to those formulations in the *De signis* which correspond to issues in the *Sumule dialectices* and he calls attention to the opposition by Siger of Brabant in the second half of the thirteenth century (pp. 196-203). Returning to possible opponents for the formulations found in the *Sumule dialectices* (pp. 203-205) he rejects William of Arnaud (he never taught at Paris or Oxford), Robert the Englishman (for the same reason),

---

[75] Bacon's position in this controversy seems to have changed between the *De signis* and the present work. See below, #126, n. 247.

[76] *English Logic And Semantics*, pp. 193-234.

Bonaventure (he could not have been attacked with such boldness), and Albert the Great (this would give a Parisian context to the polemic, which runs counter to the Oxford tenor of the *Sumule dialectices* and to Bacon's own claims in the *Cst*).[77] He concludes that one must look to or near Richard of Cornwall for "the principal candidate" (pp. 205-207). To this end de Libera singles out two English works for analysis, quoting amply from each, and he compares the texts with various Baconian themes. The first is Pseudo-Kilwardby's *Super Priscianum maiorem* in which views held by Bacon are attacked either directly or indirectly and which de Libera recommends as a good summary of semantic controversies at Oxford (pp. 207-216). The second is a commentary on the sophism "*Omnis homo de necessitate est animal*," also attributed to Robert Kilwardby. There, de Libera claims, one finds in two places texts which "very probably" lend support to the argument that the author, whoever he was, was recalling theories directly from Bacon's *Sumule dialectices* ("An entity is understood in every name") and *De signis*" ("To be is the proper passion of an entity just as … to give light of that which gives light" (pp. 216-220).[78] De Libera concludes with the suggestion that Richard of Cornwall's opinion on the quesion of the three days aroused Bacon's ire more because of the way it opened the way for the "new" semantic theories than for the theological errors Bacon claimed to see in it (pp. 220-221).

In 1983 I published an article "The Semiotics of Roger Bacon" in which I call attention to the originality of Bacon's attempt in the *De signis* to explicate his semantics in the light of a broader semiotics, thereby breaking in part with the tradition of the *summulae* rooted via Boethius in *On Interpretation* 2.[79] For its own purposes the older tradition remained content to distinguish words from all other signs, and Bacon adopted this approach in his *Sumule dialectices*. But, I suggest, by the time he was ready to address the issue again in 1267 (*De signis*) his understanding had developed into an awareness that words signify both naturally (in two different ways) and at pleasure and that in some circumstances they may signify at least five different things in these three ways. What was needed was a new point of departure, one that distinguished not just between agents acting nonrationally and rationally but also between those doing so inanimately and animately. This he found, as he himself notes, in Aristotle's *On the Soul* 2 and it became the foundation (and justification) for a new division of signs and a new approach to semantics: signs originate either from nature or from a soul.[80] Unfortunately, however,

---

[77] See below, #85.

[78] See *Sd*, p. 279.34-35 and *Ds* 117, respectively.

[79] See *Mediaeval Studies* 45 (1983) 120-154.

[80] Bacon refers to *On the Soul* 2 (explicitly in the *De signis* [12-13]) but omits the explicit reference in the present work. (See below, #32 and n. 108.)

when he came to consider the class of signs given animately but instinctively (such as human groans and animal talk), he reverted to the tradition of the *summulae* and spoke of them—unnecessarily, I argue—as signifying naturally, thereby introducing into his semiotics an equivocation of the term 'natural'. The article is organized to show how words function as signs in all of his modes of signification except one.

In 1983 two papers by me appeared in the proceedings of the colloqium "Archéologie du signe," both, however, laboring under the deficiency of having been written before the appearance of the edition of *De signis* and of most of the studies discussed above. The first, "Roger Bacon on the *Significatum* of Words,"[81] focuses on Part Two, Chapters One to Three, of the *Cst*, correlates it with the *Sumule dialectices*, and presents Bacon's theory of signification in regard to terms prior to imposition (pp. 190-193) and after (pp. 194-199), the latter section distinguishing (with Bacon) the significate of words after imposition on themselves (pp. 194-198) and on things outside the mind (pp. 198-199). The last part of the paper indicates the way in which Bacon's theory excludes such things as concepts and connotations as principal significates (pp. 199-209).

The second paper, "The *Sumule dialectices* of Roger Bacon and the Summulist Form,"[82] builds on another given at the same colloquium by Alain de Libera, "Textualite logique et forme summuliste,"[83] and urges that while Bacon and William of Sherwood (like all writers of textbooks on Logic of the thirteenth century) were confronted with the same problem of organizing Aristotle's logical corpus in new and more pedagogically useful ways, Bacon was less "innovative" than William but thereby remained more faithful to the "Boethian" call for a "*terminorum integra cognitio eorumque in propositionem non latens copulatio*" (pp. 235-242).[84] As a result, the treatment of fallacies is, I suggest, better integrated into the subject of Logic in Bacon's textbook than William's. The paper concludes with some very sketchy comparisons between the two authors' views of the properties of terms (pp. 242-248).

Finally, in 1984 I wrote "Roger Bacon on Equivocation" which draws heavily on Part Two, Chapters Four and Six, of the *Cst*.[85] In the first part

---

[81] *Archéologie du signe*, Lucie Brind'Amour and Eugène Vance, eds. Cahier d'études médiévales/Papers in Mediaeval Studies 3 (Toronto: Institut Pontifical d'Etudes Médiévales/Pontifical Institute of Mediaeval Studies, 1983), pp. 187-211.

[82] *Archéologie*, pp. 235-249.

[83] *Archéologie*, pp. 213-234.

[84] See *Sd*, p. 196.25-26; cf. Ps.-Boethius *De disciplina scholarium*, 5. 4, ed. Olga Weijers (Leiden; Cologne: E.J. Brill, 1976), p. 121.5-9.

[85] Thomas S. Maloney, "Roger Bacon on Equivocation," *Vivarium* 22 (1984) 85-112. Two other articles appeared in 1984 which, while not so directly related to the material in the *Cst* to warrant extended comment in this Introduction, are quite valuable in ex-

I contend that while Peter of Spain, William of Sherwood, and Bacon (*Sumule dialectices*) saw the need to speak in more detail about equivocation than Aristotle, they refused to break away from his three types. Peter and William permit themselves the liberty of recasting the three types into two modes, but do not agree on the foundation for their distinctions. But in the *De signis* of 1267 Bacon returned to the issue of equivocation and displays considerable originality. While he preserves Aristotle's definition of equivocation, he distinguishes five modes (expanded to six in the *Cst*), none of which corresponds precisely with Aristotle's three. Where Aristotle and the summulists took 'dog' as an example of equivocation in its purest form, the later Bacon focuses on the case where one term signifies an entity and a nonentity, like 'man' signifying a living and a dead man. In the second part, then, I explicate Bacon's remarks on each of the six modes, and in a final part suggest that the principal explanation for this further example of Bacon's originality was nothing other than his uncommon interest in the philosophy of language itself, especially when it bore upon theological questions of his time.

From these indications it is clear that Bacon's role in the development of semantics is finally being given serious attention. To date I have counted some eighteen sources listed as possible candidates for the role of Bacon's adversary on various issues, principally on the question of whether words univocally signify both entities and nonentities. And since Bacon admits holding a minority view the list could easily be broadened. De Libera's research suggests that Bacon's works were not as completely ignored by his peers as one might fear, given the outspoken references to his colleagues in the *Opus maius* and *Compendium studii philosophiae* and the general disfavor with which he was regarded within his Order. But as Ebbesen says, "... it would also be strange if a brilliant and aggressive teacher with a career of that length did not influence his surroundings in any way,"[86] and one cannot help but think that future rescarch on

---

plicating other themes in Bacon's grammar and logic. See C.H. Kneepkens, "Roger Bacon's Theory of the Double *Intellectus*: A Note on the Development of the Theory of *Congruitas* and *Perfectio* in the First Half of the Thirteenth Century," and Georgette Sinkler, "Roger Bacon on the Compounded and Divided Senses," both in *The Rise of British Logic*, P. Osmund Lewry, ed., Acts of the Sixth European Symposium on Medieval Logic And Semantics, Balliol College, Oxford, 19-24 June 1983 (Toronto: Pontifical Institute of Mediaeval Studies [1985]), pp. 115-143 and 145-171, respectively. For Bacon's position in the controversy over universalsseeTheodore Crowley, "Roger Bacon: The Problem of Universals in His Philosophical Commentaries," *Bulletin of the John Rylands Library* 34 (1951-1952) 264-275, and Thomas S. Maloney, "The Extreme Realism of Roger Bacon," *Review of Metaphysics* 38 (1985) 807-837.

[86] "The Dead Man Is Alive," *Synthese* 40 (1979) 53. Also in 1983 Ebbesen published a sketch of the major developments in semantics that highlights the contributions of the Stoics, Porphyry, supposition theory, and modism and their relation to Bacon, Ockham,

semantic theories at Oxford in the second half of the thirteenth century will clarify the relation of his insistence that words signify at pleasure only existing things to the even greater emphasis placed on this view by Ockhamists in the terminist logic of the early fourteenth century.

As far as I can tell, modern interpretation of Bacon's semiotics and semantics has yet to produce any major controversies. However, Bacon's claim in the *Cst* that he discovered his initial division of signs—from nature and given by a soul—before coming across it in Augustine's *On Christian Doctrine* is viewed more guardedly by Pinborg and Fredborg than by myself.[87] Pinborg speaks of Bacon "... taking as his over-all frame of reference the semiotics outlined in Augustine's *De doctrina christiana*" but acknowledges:

> Generally, the Augustinian inspiration did not effect medieval discussions on logic; Bacon is here an interesting exception, a fact which is further underscored by his drawing also on the *De dialectica* and the *De magistro* which is a quite exceptional thing to do for a medieval logician.[88]

Fredborg is somewhat more explicit. Granting the fact that "the late *Compendium*, in comparison with the *De signis*, shows a fuller reading and a more ready acknowledgment of Augustinian sources," she remarks in reference to Bacon's claim to originality, "This statement should hardly be interpreted too literally."[89] Both writers speak cautiously and are aware of inconsistencies in the data, and the contexts of their remarks suggest that they are rather stating the issue than attempting to resolve it. In support of their hesitation one can also point to references in the *Opus maius* to Book Two of *On Christian Doctrine*[90] and to Bacon's statement in the *Opus tertium* summarizing material in the *Opus maius* (*De signis*): "I

---

and Buridan. See Sten Ebbesen, "The Odyssey of Semantics from the Stoa to Buridan" in Achim Eschbach, ed., *Foundations of Semiotics*, vol. 7, Achim Eschbach and Jurgen Trabant, eds., *History of Semiotics* (Amsterdam; Philadelphia: John Benjamins, 1983), pp. 67-85, esp. pp. 75-77.

[87] Bacon's remarks entail (at least) two claims: (1) his fundamental division is the product of his own efforts and (2) the division is the same as Augustine's. For the text and the translation of Bacon's remark see below, #25. For Augustine's division of signs and what follows see *De doctrina christiana* 2. 1. 2-2. 2. 3, ed. Joseph Martin, *Corpus Christianorum, Series Latina* 32, pp. 32.12-33.18, transl. D. Robertson, Jr., *St. Augustine: On Christian Doctrine* (New York: The Liberal Arts Press, 1958), pp. 34-35.

[88] "Roger Bacon on Signs: A Newly Recovered Part of the *Opus maius*," *Miscellanea Medievalia* 13 (Berlin: New York, Walter de Gruyter, 1981), p. 405.

[89] *English Logic And Semantics*, p. 173. In the *De signis* Bacon makes explicit mention of the *De dialectica* twice (*Ds* 88 and 135) and the Ps.-Augustinian *Categoriae* once (*Ds* 46). In the *Cst* the *De doctrina christiana* is referred to in #25 and #36; the *De dialectica* in #55 and #120; the *De magistro* in #63 and the *Categoriae* in #95.

[90] Ed. Bridges, 3, p. 30.3 and ed. Bridges, 1, pp. 178.7-12 and 180.3-6; transl. Burke, 1, pp. 30, 198, and 199.

have attempted to point out those modes [of signification], just as Augustine teaches in the second and third book of *On Christian Doctrine* that some signs are natural and some are given by a soul.''[91] Thus it must be granted that Bacon had at least some kind of knowledge of the material in Book Two of that work, either from the work itself or by hear-say, before he wrote the *De signis* and that he was in some sense aware of Augustine's way of dividing signs at least immediately after writing that work.

Without attempting here the lengthy task of fully documenting an argument in support of accepting Bacon's claim at its face value, I would point to the following considerations. First, as far as I am aware no references in the *Opus maius* to *On Christian Doctrine* pertain directly to the division of signs. It is not at all inconceivable that when writing the *Opus maius* Bacon was unfamiliar with the very brief section containing the division itself. Pinborg has noted how unique it was for a logician of Bacon's time to use this work at all. Semiotic considerations in the *summulae* tradition rested squarely on Aristotle's *On Interpretation* 2 as transmitted by Boethius. Second, Bacon gives every sign in the *Opus ter-tium* and the *Cst* of being quite happy to acknowledge openly the confir-mation provided by Augustine's work. Why then, if he had known of the latter's division when writing the *De signis*, would he have been reluctant to draw benefit from it immediately? Instead he appeals to *On the Soul* 2. At the time he himself was most probably not yet even aware of the need for an *Opus tertium* in which Augustine's blessing could be claimed. Third, and most significantly, Bacon's division is not Augustine's, even though he claims it to be so. Augustine's division is, for all practical pur-poses, that found in the *summulae* tradition and in Bacon's own *Sumule dialectices* with, however, one difference: Augustine cannot make up his mind just how to classify human groans and animal talk. Bacon is quite clear on this issue in the *Sumule dialectices*, the *De signis*, and the *Cst*. Augustine's fundamental division is based on the presence or absence of *human* intent; the *De signis* makes a classification on the basis of the presence or absence of a more general kind of intent, one which includes sensitive (instinctive) as well as rational intent. If there is a measure of duplicity in Bacon's remarks it pertains not so much to the issue of originality as to a second claim, the pretense (witting or unwitting) to be speaking with Augustine's authority. The terminology with which the divisions are expressed are the same, but the equivocation in 'nature' and 'soul' masks an important difference. Finally, though of lesser significance for the present issue, Bacon's definition of a sign is not the

---

[91] Ed. Brewer, p. 100.16-20.

same as Augustine's since it admits as signs things which are imperceptible to the senses. Bacon, recall, needs a definition that allows concepts to be the natural signs of things of which they are admittedly likenesses. Once again it is what he, granted erroneously, takes to be Aristotle's requirements of signification that guide him, not Augustine's. Theologians may have been familiar with the latter's definition in order to discuss sacramental theology, but that was not Bacon's immediate concern. He was moving away from the *summulae* tradition on the basis of *On the Soul* 2 and both of these were of Aristotelian parentage.

For these reasons, then, I think it quite reasonable to accept Bacon's (first) claim in the *Cst* at its face value and add his division of signs to the other original views already described. In saying this I recognize that at some time in his early career he may have heard that Augustine divides signs into natural signs and signs given by a soul, or that he may even have observed the distinction in *On Christian Doctrine*. Nevertheless, given the similarity in terminology between it and the *summulae* tradition and the overriding importance of the latter for logicians, it is quite believable to me that, if Bacon ever knew of the Augustinian source, he soon forgot it and that it played no part in the development of his semiotics in the *De signis*. Later when he had become aware (or was reminded) of the Augustinian division, but was under the extreme pressure of getting his *Opera* off to the Pope as quickly as possible—he was already under a second, and this time Papal, mandate—he failed to see beyond the similarity in terminology, took Augustine's division to be the same as his own, and attempted to reap the benefit in his *Opus tertium*, never again bothering to compare his own classification to that given in *On Christian Doctrine*. Immediately his interests turned elsewhere and when he returned to the issue in 1292 his recollection was that of the *Opus tertium*. From this point of view, then, the issue concerns not so much his claim to originality but who or what brought his attention to the Augustinian division between the writing of the *Opus maius* and *Opus tertium*. Unfortunately no clues are given in the *Opus minus* or the later works as far as I can tell.

Having given in the foregoing some biographical data and a description of the status of current research on Bacon's semantics, it only remains to say a few words about the Latin text here presented and the conventions employed in the translation. At present there are two known MSS. of the *Compendium studii theologiae*. The older and principal one, Royal MS. 7 f. vii (ff. 78r-83r), is from the late thirteenth century, double columned, averaging sixty lines a page, highly contracted, and held in the British Museum. On p. 13 of the volume in which our text (R.) is found (along with parts of other treatises by Bacon and others) one finds the following (erased) inscription: "*Iste liber est de ordine fratrum minorum concessu W. Herbert qui eum ad ordinem procuravit.*" At one time the volume was in the Lumley Library but in the seventeenth century it was acquired by Prince Henry's chaplain, John Prideaux, Bishop of Worcester (1641-1650), who made a copy, omitting some of the more troublesome readings and on occasion contenting himself with the gist of the text. This apograph (O.) is now in the Bodleian Library, Oxford, and is identified as University College No. 47 (ff. 45r-64r). The volume containing MS. R. was presumably acquired by John Theyer from Prideaux since it bears his name and the date 1651.

In 1911 Hastings Rashdall edited a text under the title *Fratris Rogeri Bacon Compendium studii theologiae* using the thirteenth century MS. as his principal source.[92] Without gainsaying Rashdall's contribution in producing the first printed edition, deficiencies occur on practically every page. A few are substantial, many are failures to indicate corrections, and some reflect undue reliance on MS. O. The editors of the *De signis* have graciously provided me with a list of emendations which they developed while preparing that work, and in preparing the Latin text for this edition I have doubled the list, consulting MS. R. itself for readings unclear on the microfilm.[93] The sole source for the present edition is, of course, Royal MS. 7 f. vii (R.). Paragraphing follows modern norms and the orthography has been normalized to bring the Latin text into harmony with that of the *De signis*. Alternate spellings such as in '*quotiens*' ('*quoties*'), '*alico*' ('aliquo'), '*mangna*' ('*magna*'), '*Aristotilis*' ('*Aristoteles*'), '*quatinus*' ('*quatenus*'), and obvious misspellings like '*parlogizantur*' ('*paralogizantur*') are not indicated in the critical apparatus.

In regard to the translation itself medieval scholarship, like its present day counterpart, developed its own concepts and terminology, and the endurance of these over the centuries is checkered at best. A name today is not what it used to be and current theories of meaning and reference are too precise to square nicely with the medieval notion of signification.[94] All things considered, I have aligned myself with those who argue that the first translation of a technical treatise such as this should be as literal as good grammar and the canons of intelligibility permit. Literalness is not nearly the obstacle to scholarship that an approach

---

[92] (Aberdeen, 1911; reprinted Farnborough: Gregg Press, 1966), pp. 25-69.

[93] The list of their emendations appears at the end of Karin Margarita Fredborg's "Roger Bacon on '*Impositio Vocis ad Significandum*'," *English Logic And Semantics*, pp. 187-191.

[94] See for example Alan Perreiah's "Approaches to Supposition-Theory," *New Scholasticism* 45 (1971) 381-408.

bordering on paraphrase is. My hope is that those already well versed in the field and in the Latin language will find this translation of use in identifying theories for further investigation in the Latin text. For those less equipped a literal translation with explanatory notes recommends itself as the best hope of getting into the concepts of the period. Those accustomed to less than literal translations will already have noticed certain variations, principally four, in this "Introduction." Since they will be continued in the text itself, a few words of explanation are in order.

Medieval writers in general, Bacon in particular, use the expression "*Nomen imponitur rei*" to indicate how names come to be attached to things. Most often one sees this translated as "A name is imposed *on* a thing," and for all practical purposes the intent of the Latin is preserved. However, in the opening section of the *De signis* Bacon is at pains to emphasize that the object of imposition is to be stated grammatically in the dative case. Unfortunately not everything he has to say on the point is immediately clear, but it is clear that he wants to stress the relational nature of a sign. While the previous (and customary) translation of '*impositio*' and its cognates can be understood, it would seem that the relational aspect of a sign and the force of the dative case can better be served by "A name is imposed *for* a thing."[95]

A second issue arises when medieval writers discuss the semantic consequences of words that no longer signify the things for which they were imposed: "*Nomen cadit a sua significatione.*" Ordinarily one would find this rendered by "A name has lost its signification," which, again, gets the point across well enough, but in so doing loses the metaphor couched in the Latin. Literally it reads, "A name falls away from its signification." While I am unaware of the origin of the metaphor, I can see no particular advantage in failing to preserve it. It is certainly more justified by the text than the more customary notion of *losing* signification, itself a metaphor.

Finally there is the more troublesome phrase '*ad placitum*'. Boethius introduced it to translate Aristotle's '*kata synthêken*' and to distinguish the way in which a certain class of signs including language comes into being from the way in which all others do. Referring to language it connotes the role played by human freedom and rationality in establishing the link between a word or expression and that for which it was imposed. A question arises as to whether it is best rendered by 'conventionally' or (literal-

---

[95] Cf. below, #68, where Bacon speaks of a name being placed in an expression "for its significate." So far as I am aware Bacon employs the phrase 'on a thing' in regard to imposition only twice and both times in the *De signis* (130 and 131): imposition and the natural signification of connotative terms are said (by way of metaphor) to fall upon (*cadunt super*) different significates. However, it should also be noted that in the same context he also speaks of imposition *for* a thing (*imponitur rei*).

ly) 'at pleasure'. The former enjoys almost universal acceptance but to the modern ear can easily connote a kind of pact between speaker and listener. Indeed some support for it can be sought in the medieval definitions of signification all of which make reference to the role of an interpreter. Bacon is even more explicit than most: "... unless someone could conceive through a sign, it would be empty and worthless (*cassum esset et vanum*); indeed, it will not be a sign ..."[96]

But the issue is not quite this simple. While medieval definitions invite a discussion of the role of interpreter in receiving signs, once their authors begin to talk about signs that arise by rational intent, that role fades into the background. Granted Fredborg mentions an attempt by Pseudo-Kilwardby to explain how a listener may grasp the intended meaning of a word used by another, the discussion breaks off with, "But if somebody could give better reasons, I shall not be distressed."[97] Bacon has several opportunities in the *Cst* (and the *De signis*) to develop any collective dimension to imposition which he sees when treating of various cases of linguistic use. For example he could have done it when discussing tacit imposition (*apud intellectum*), a change in signification without expressed warning, but contents himself with simply saying that those hearing the expression understand it in the same sense as the speaker.[98] While we might be somewhat disappointed at such unsuccessful analyses, they serve, I think, to underscore something to which J. Engels called attention a few years ago:

> A curious fact: whereas the definition of a sign formulated by Augustine passed down through the Middle Ages, the collective aspect of the linguistic sign, although pointed out by him, has been almost eclipsed by the Boethian 'ad placitum'.[99]

Engels contends that Boethius had a much more individualistic notion of imposition than Augustine: one imposes as one pleases, with little acknowledgment of any kind of collective rapport between speaker and listener, much less between the speaker and the community at large. While I am not prepared to speak for other medieval writers—though I suspect the case is much the same—it is clear to me that in the *De signis* and the *Cst* Bacon's principal concern is with the giving of signs, the efficient cause of speech, and not their reception. This is not too surprising

---

[96] *Ds* 1.

[97] "Roger Bacon on '*Impositio Vocis ad Significandum*'," *English Logic And Semantics*, p. 178.

[98] See below, #125.

[99] "La doctrine du signe chez Saint Augustin" in *Studia Patristica* 6, ed. F.L. Cross (Berlin: Akademie-Verlag, 1962), p. 373. See also his "Origine, sens et survie du terme boécien '*secundum placitum*'," *Vivarium* 1 (1963) 87-114.

when one recognizes that any notion of naming, i.e., signifying *ad placitum*, would have had to have been able at that time to be reconciled with the case of Adam's naming all the creatures around him before Eve was created.[100] Somewhat similar to this is the appeal frequently found in medieval treatises to the naming of infants at baptism and the naming of pets. Bacon himself speaks of this as vocally expressed imposition (as in "I call this dog 'Rover'") and designates it as "the first, principal, and customary" form in contradistinction to tacit imposition, but again with little hint of a collective dimension.[101] Bacon distinguishes himself by recognizing that not all linguistic differences originated at the Tower of Babel; knowledgeable persons (*sapientes*) or experts (*periti*) can construct them by art, as happened, he says, in the case of the old Angles and Saxons.[102] But the method he prescribes for this institution is far more suited to the establishment of a code than of a language rooted in a collective effort. The highly individualistic tone to which Engels refers is also well illustrated in this work when Bacon says that names can be (equivocally) imposed "at the pleasure of the impositor (*ad placitum imponentis*)" and that the cause of naming is "the free will of the one imposing the name in accord with the good pleasure of his own will."[103]

Nevertheless, none of these remarks should be taken to imply that in cases other than Adam's no collective rapport would be defended by medieval writers in general and by Bacon in particular. As was pointed out, all signification requires an interpreter. But they do, I think, support Engel's recourse to the notion of an eclipse of a collective aspect and suggest that a translation of '*ad placitum*' by 'conventionally' says too much to the modern ear, at least in regard to Bacon. What is needed is an expression that is open to the collective dimension but allows it to lie dormant while bringing to the fore the impositor's role in this kind of signification. To this end the literal version 'at pleasure' seems more suited, and in consequence names are said to signify *at pleasure* in this translation. It is tempting, of course, to make the phrase a little more pleasing to the ear by adding a reference to the speaker, as in "signs at one's own pleasure," and we have just noted two instances where something like that occurs in the text. But on all other occasions the phrase appears starkly as '*ad placitum*', and the reason for this is, I think,

---

[100] Bacon mentions this case explicitly in the *Opus tertium*. See above, p. 9.

[101] See *Ds* 154-161, esp. 158, and below, #97.

[102] See *Ds* 156. Elsewhere the role of impositor of language is explicitly assigned to the metaphysician. See His *Questiones supra libros prime philosophie Aristotelis* (ed. Steele, *Opera*, 10), p. 96.25 and *The Greek Grammar of Roger Bacon*, ed. Edmond Nolan and S.A. Hirsch (Cambridge: University Press, 1902) pp. 57-58.

[103] See below, #73 and #81 respectively. For similar kinds of statements see also below, #53, and #58, and #81-82, and *Ds* 97, 154, and 157.

simple enough: by Bacon's time the phrase had long since become a technical term. The translation then seeks to preserve this historical note by rendering '*ad placitum*' simply by 'at pleasure' and asks the reader to hear in it a technical term with a venerable history.

The remaining issues center on such terms as '*vox*', '*oratio*', '*nomen*', '*verbum*', and '*dictio*'. As far as I am aware there is no one English equivalent that will do the work of '*vox*' in all contexts. In its most basic sense, Bacon says, it refers to the sound made by the rush of air from the lungs and intentionally (instinctively or rationally) modulated by oral factors such as tongue, palate, teeth, and lips, and in this sense it is distinguished from all other sounds (*sonus*).[104] Thus it can be translated by 'articulate sound', 'voice', or 'vocal sound'. The temptation is to render it by 'word' since a *vox* that signifies at pleasure is a word and '*vox*' will have this sense almost exclusively in most of Part Two of this work. However, Bacon will also be seen to speak of the instinctive *voces* of brutes and people and these are not linguistic entities in the strict sense. He also needs to refer to what we would now call nonsense utterances but which he speaks of simply as *voces* and to distinguish on occasion the two components of a name, i.e., its *vox* and the attribute it acquires in virtue of imposition, signification at pleasure: a name is a *vox* that signifies at pleasure. With these problems in mind and desiring to reflect Bacon's almost exclusive preference for '*vox*' to the other options at his disposal, even when he is speaking of linguistic units in and outside discourse, I have consistently rendered the term by 'vocal sound' in the translation while allowing myself greater latitude in explicating his remarks here and in the notes.

When vocal signs at pleasure are strung together in such a way that they all signify at pleasure something independently of that which each signifies in virtue of its own imposition one has an *oratio*.[105] But Bacon speaks of *oratio imperfecta* and *perfecta* depending on whether the implementation of the two prerequisities entailed in the notion of *oratio* results in an incomplete or complete thought, expressed grammatically on the one hand as a phrase or clause and on the other as a sentence. In view of these considerations, I have chosen the term 'expression' to translate '*oratio*', allowing the context to indicate whether an incomplete or complete expression is intended.

While medieval grammarians divide speech into its eight parts, medieval logicians speak of only two, *nomen* and *verbum*, which signify in expressions respectively the subject of predication and what is

---

[104] See *Sd*, p. 233.6-20.
[105] For this and the distinctions that follow immediately see *Sd*, pp. 240.14-241.11.

predicated.[106] (The reference, of course, is to complete expressions.) Because Bacon speaks (primarily) as a logician in the *Cst* '*nomen*' will be translated by 'name' and '*verbum*' by 'verb'. The latter is unfortunate because of its grammatical overtones but I know of no appropriate substitute.

'*Dictio*' is a term (ordinarily) used to designate a part of an expression about which one wants to speak. Since such can be either an individual word, phrase, or clause, the translation allows the context to determine whether 'word', 'phrase', or 'clause' is appropriate.

Finally a word on style. Those familiar with medieval Latin manuscripts will know that paragraphing follows anything but modern norms. I have taken the usual liberty of breaking up lengthy sections and convoluted sentences whenever this could be done without detriment to the author's intended sense. Then, too, Bacon sometimes writes highly complex conditional sentences with several objections in the antecedent and a (sometimes single) response in the consequent. It has seemed advantageous in these instances to translate them in the indicative mood and set the objections in separate sentences, lest the import of the individual objections be lost. Such changes are duly noted and affect in no way the issues under discussion. In general I have adhered relatively strictly to the syntax but have felt free to substitute the obverse "No x exists" for "There is not an x," the latter Bacon's preferred manner of expression. Also, where the context is clear, '*est*' is rendered by 'exists'. Finally, brackets are used to enclose notions not expressly in the Latin text but which are in harmony with it and serve to make the translation more coherent. In a very few cases where the Latin supplies a pronoun whose reference is ambiguous, I have substituted a bracketed noun to remove the ambiguity. Care has been taken, however, not to do this when to remove the ambiguity would force an arbitrary or less than obviously warranted interpretation.

---

[106] See ibid., p. 240.16-17, and for an exception below, #73, n. 166.

TEXT AND TRANSLATION

COMPENDIUM STUDII THEOLOGIAE

[1] *Incipit compendium studii theologiae et per consequens philosophiae, et potest et debet servire theologicae facultati, et habet duas partes principales. Prima ⟨circa⟩ liberalem communicationem sapientiae investigat omnes causas errorum et modos er-*
5 *randi in hoc studio, ut verae causae et veri modi appareant evidenter. Secunda pars descendit ad veritates ipsas stabiliendas, et ad errores cum diligentia excludendos.*

⟨PARS PRIMA⟩

⟨PROLOGUS⟩

[2] Quoniam autem in omnibus causis auctoritas digna potest et debet
10 valere plurimum, ut ait Tullius primo libro *De quaestionibus tusculanis*, atque Plinius in prologo *Naturalis philosophiae* dicit, ''Benignum arbitror et ingenui pudoris fateri per quos profeceris,'' propter quod primum librum sui voluminis constituit de nominibus auctorum quorum sententiis utitur in omnibus aliis libris xxxvi, ideo saltem huius operis primordia et in-
15 super, ubicumque iustum fuerit, volo dignis auctoritatibus confirmare. Et quoniam principalis occupatio theologorum istius temporis est circa quaestiones, et maior pars omnium quaestionum est in terminis philosophiae cum tota disputatione, et reliqua pars, quae est in terminis theologiae, adhuc ventilatur per auctoritates et argumenta et solutiones
20 philosophiae, ut notum est omnibus sufficienter literatis, ideo, ut conformem me aliis, auctoritatibus et rationibus philosophicis uti cupio abundanter. Et varia introducam quia ''nihil est iocundum nisi quod reficit varietas,'' ut ait Seneca libro *De copia verborum*, quia identitas generat fastidium, et mater satietatis ab omnibus comprobatur. Etiam
25 causa specialis me movet, ut excitem lectorem ad quaerendum libros auctorum dignos, in quibus magna pulcritudo et dignitas sapientiae reperitur, qui nunc temporis, sicut a multitudine studentium, sic a doctoribus eius, quasi penitus ignorantur.

---

19 adhuc] adhunc   23 reficit] reficitur   24 mater] mart

COMPENDIUM OF THE STUDY OF THEOLOGY

[1] [*Here*] *begins a compendium of the study of theology and in consequence of philosophy. It can and ought to be of service to the discipline of theology and it has two principal Parts. The first,* [*on*] *the liberal sharing of wisdom, investigates all the causes of error and the ways of erring in this discipline so that causes that lead to truth and valid methods* [*of seeking wisdom*] *may appear in clear light; the second Part moves on to establish these truths and to exclude errors with diligence.*[1]

[PART ONE]

[PROLOGUE]

[2] Since, however, among all the causes [of truth] worthy authority, as Tully says in the first book of [his] *Tusculan Questions*, "can and ought to count for much,"[2] and [since] Pliny says in the Prologue of his *Natural Philosophy*, "I consider it pleasing and of honest decency to acknowledge [those] through whom you have progressed" (because of which he made the first book of his volume to consist of the names of the authors whose opinions he uses in all the other thirty six books),[3] thus I wish to confirm at least the beginnings of this work with worthy authorities, and thenceforth wherever it will have been appropriate. And since the principal focus of theologians at this time is on *questions*, and the major part of all *questions* is [presented] in the language of philosophy [along] with all the types of disputation, and [since] the remaining part, which is in the language of theology, is still aired through authorities, arguments, and solutions of philosophy (as is known to all sufficiently literate), thus to conform myself to others I desire to use authorities and philosophical reasons abundantly.[4] And I shall introduce various things, since "nothing is enjoyable except that which variety refreshes," as Seneca says in his book *On the Abundance of Words*, because sameness generates aversion and the mother of bounty is approved by all.[5] A special cause also moves me, [namely,] to stir up the reader to seek out worthwhile books of authors in which are found the great beauty and dignity of wisdom, which [books] are more or less at the present time entirely unknown by the multitude of students and its teachers alike.

CAPITULUM PRIMUM

[3] Haec autem pars prima sive libellus primus habet capitula...
Primum est de communicatione sapientiae liberali.

[4] Saepe igitur et multum requisitus et diu exspectatus ut scriberem
5 aliqua utilia theologiae, impeditus tamen multipliciter, ut notum est
multis, insuper conscius superfluae difficultatis quae non potest excludi
audiendo et legendo, sed requiritur multitudo experientiae et longi temporis examinatio diligens, tandem favens amicis, quantum efficatius
potui, festinavi, considerans illud sapientis Solomonis, "Spes quae dif-
10 fertur affligit animam," sicut secundum Terentium, "Nil gravius tor-
quet quam spes destituta," et Ovidius ait, "Spes anxia mentem/
Distrahit, et longo consumit gaudia voto." Seneca etiam septimo libro *De
beneficiis* ait, "Gratius venit quod de facili, quam quod de plena, manu
sumitur," et in eodem dicit, "Ingratum est beneficium quod diu inter
15 manus dantis haesit." Et adhuc dicit, "Cum roganti suffundatur rubor,
qui hoc remittit, multiplicat munus suum," quia ut in eodem ait, "Nulla
res gravius constat quam quae precibus empta est." Et Salustius, secundum Ieronimum auctor certissimus, dicit in *Iugurtino*, "Animo cupienti
nihil satis festinatur," quam sententiam Seneca libro *De copia verborum*
20 continuat dicens, 'Ipsa etiam celeritas desiderio mora est."
[5] Sed, licet secundum has sententias et consimiles ad omnia
beneficia debemus esse prompti secundum possibilitatem nostram,
tamen promptissimi debemus esse ad beneficia sapientiae talia com-
municanda si possumus, quia excedit omnia alia. Et facillime possumus
25 hoc adimplere et secundum quod ait Ieronimus in epistola *De correctione
psalterii*, "In hoc beneficio, quanto plus solvimus, plus debemus."
Propter quod in libro *Sapientiae* dicit auctor, "Quam ⟨f.78rb⟩ sine fic-
tione didici, et sine invidia communico, et honestatem illius non abscon-
do." Alexander quidem, magnus Aristotelis discipulus, requirens
30 Dimidum regem Bragmanarum de communicatione sapientiae ait,
"Libera res est communitas sapientiae, et nesciens pati dispendium cum
in alterum participata transfunditur, sicut ex una luce si lumina plura
succenderis, nullum damnum principali materiae generabis, quae
quidem accipit facultatem plus lucendi, quoties causas invenit plus
35 praestandi." Insuper tantae dignitatis est sapientia, ut non communicata
pereat, et in avaro deficit possessore. Et Seneca libro *Primarum epistolarum*

---

2 capitula....] *spatium c. 5 lit. seq.*   7 experientiae] experientia   10 affligit] affrigit
18 cupienti] cuepienti   20 celeritas] sceleritas   26 quanto] quantam

[CHAPTER ONE]

[3] *This first Part or first little book, moreover, has chapters. ... The first is on the liberal sharing of wisdom.*

[4] Often, therefore, much requested and long expected to write some things useful for theology, but blocked in many ways (as is known to many), and further conscious of the extraordinary difficulty which cannot be removed by hearing [lectures] and reading, but [for which] there is required much experience and prolonged, diligent study; finally, favoring my friends, I hastened [to respond] the more efficiently I could, reflecting on that of wise Solomon, "Hope which is deferred afflicts the soul," just as according to Terence, "nothing tortures more severely than empty hope."[6] And Ovid says, "Anxious hope distracts the mind and consumes joy by [its] long promise."[7] Seneca also says in the seventh book of *On Benefits*, "That is received more graciously which comes from a willing than that from a full hand,"[8] and in the same [work], "Ill-received is the benefit which has remained long in the hands of the donor."[9] And in this regard he says, "Since a seeker blushes, who relieves this multiplies his gift,"[10] because, as he says in the same [work], "nothing is more burdensome than that which is bought with entreaties."[11] And Sallust—a very reliable author according to Jerome—says in [his] *Jugurthian War*, "Nothing hastens quickly enough for the soul that desires,"[12] which judgment Seneca continues in [his] book *On the Abundance of Words* when he says, "Even swiftness itself is delay to desire."[13]

[5] But, granted according to these sayings and those similar we ought to be ready to [bestow] all benefits, yet we ought to be most ready to share the benefits of wisdom if we can, because [wisdom] exceeds all others. And we can fulfill this [responsibility] quite easily and in accord with that which Jerome says in his letter *On the Correction of the Psalter*: "The more we pay, the more we owe."[14] Because of this the author says in *The Book of Wisdom*, "What I learned without guile I share without grudge, and her integrity I do not hide."[15] Alexander, the great disciple of Aristotle, questioning Dimidus, King of the Bragmanae, about the sharing of wisdom, says: "The sharing of wisdom is a free thing, not knowing loss when, shared, it is transferred to another, just as if you kindle many lamps from one flame you cause no loss to the principal matter which acquires the ability to kindle more as often as one finds reasons for it to manifest [itself] the more."[16] Further, of such dignity is wisdom that, unshared, it perishes and in a greedy owner dwindles. And Seneca

sexta dicit epistola, "Gaudeo addiscere ut doceam, nec me ulla res delectabit, licet sit eximia et salutaris, quam mihi uni sciturus sum. Si enim quod cum hac exceptione detur mihi sapientia, ut illam inclusam teneam, nec enuntiem, reiciam. Nullius enim boni sine socio iocunda est
5 possessio." Et Boethius in prologo libri *De hypotheticis syllogismis* ait, "Nullum quidem bonum est quod non pulchrius elucescit, si plurimorum notitia comprobetur." "Sapientia enim abscondita, et thesaurus invisus, quae est utilitas in utrisque," quod dicit Solomon; nulla penitus invenitur.

---

1 Gaudeo addiscere] gaude addicere   2 licet] sed   8 dicit] dicat

says in the sixth letter in his book *First Letters*: "I rejoice to learn more so that I may teach; nor will any thing please me which I am about to know for myself alone, granted it be exceptional and beneficial. For if [it would be the case] that wisdom be given me with the provision that I hold it hidden and that I do not proclaim it, I would refuse it, for an enjoyable possession is of no value without a partner."[17] And Boethius says in the Prologue of [his] book *On Hypothetical Syllogisms*, "No thing is indeed good which does not shine more beautifully if it be confirmed by the awareness of a greater number."[18] "For hidden wisdom and concealed treasure—what is the usefulness of each?" which Solomon says; none at all is found.[19]

CAPITULUM SECUNDUM

[6] *Capitulum secundum de causis generalibus humanorum errorum.*

[7] Sed nisi causae generales et speciales humanae ignorantiae et erroris evacuentur, persuasio vana est. Primo igitur de malitia et infec-
5 tione venenosa causarum generalium loquens, dico quod tria sunt viden-dae veritatis offendicula: fragilis et indignae auctoritatis exempla, con-suetudinis diuturnitas, sensus multitudinis imperitae. Primum inducit in errorem, secundum ligat, tertium confirmat. De quorum trium reproba-tione, etsi omnes sapientes consentiant, Seneca tamen libro *Secundarum*
10 *epistolarum* propre finem colligit haec tria, simul egregia auctoritate con-demnans. Dicit igitur, "Inter causas malorum nostrorum est quod vivimus ad exempla, nec ratione componimur, sed consuetudine ad-ducimur. Quod, si pauci facerent, nollemus imitari; cum plures facere ceperint, quia frequentius, quasi honestius id facimus. Et sic apud nos
15 recti locum tenet error ubi publicus factus est." Consimilem sententiam ponit Marcus Tullius in prologo tertii libri *Tusculanarum quaestionum* dicens, "Simul atque postquam editi in lucem susceptique sumus, in omni continua pravitate et summa opinionis perversitate versamur, ut paene a lacte nutricis errorem suxisse videamur. Cum vero parentibus
20 traditi et magistris redditi sumus, tunc ita variis imbuimur erroribus, ut vanitati veritas et opinione confirmata ipsa natura cedat." Accedent etiam poetae ⟨qui⟩ addiscuntur ⟨et⟩ leguntur et mentibus nostris longa consuetudine inhaerescunt. Cumque accedunt, quasi quidem magister, populus et omnis undique ad vitia consentiens multitudo, tunc plane tan-
25 ta opinionum inficimur pravitate, et a natura discedimus, ut nobis in-vidisse videatur.
[8] Quanta vero discretione examinanda est auctoritas, Aristoteles primo *Ethicae* testatur dicens, "Duobus existentibus amicis, Platone et veritate, magis consentiendum est veritati quam amicitiae Platonis." Et
30 secunda translatio dicit, "Duobus existentibus amicis, sanctum est honorare veritatem." Similiter in *Vita Aristotelis* legitur Plato dixisse, "Amicus est Socrates, sed magis amica veritas." Etiam idem dixit Aristoteles de Platone, sicut scribitur in eadem. Sed pauci volunt ex-aminare dicta suorum magistrorum, quod reprobat Boethius libro *De*
35 *disciplina scholarium* dicens, "Miserrimi ingenii est semper inventis uti, et

---

5 venenosa] venenonosa   8 reprobatione] reprobatio   17 editi] edidi edidi   19 suxisse] sugisse   31 veritatem] *spatium c. 38 lit. seq.*

[CHAPTER TWO]

[6] *The second chapter is on the general causes of human errors.*[20]

[7] But unless the general and specific causes of human ignorance and error be eliminated, persuasion is in vain. Speaking first, therefore, of the wickedness and poisonous infection of general causes I say that there are three things that are obstacles to the necessary vision of truth: examples of weak and unworthy authority, the longevity of custom, [and] the opinion of an unexpert multitude.[21] The first leads to error; the second binds; [and] the third confirms.[22] Even though all who are wise would agree on the condemnation of these three, yet Seneca gathers these three together near the end of his book *Second Letters*, at one and the same time condemning them with distinguished authority. He says, therefore, "Among the causes of all ills is that we live by imitation. We are not gathered together by reason, but led by custom. We would be unwilling to imitate something if [only] a few were doing [it]; should many have begun to do [it], we hold it as if more proper because more frequent. And thus error holds the place of right among us where it is made public."[23] Mark Tully places a similar judgment in the Prologue of [his] third book of the *Tusculan Questions* saying: "As soon as and from the time we are brought forth into the light and received we engage in every ongoing depravity and the highest perversity of opinion, with the result that we seem to have almost suckled error from the milk of our nurse. When we are handed to [our] parents and turned over to teachers we are by then so tainted with various errors that truth succumbs to vanity and to opinion confirmed by nature itself."[24] Poets are also added [who] are learned, read, [and] remain fast in our minds by dint of long custom. And when the populace and the vice-indulging crowd join as a sort of teacher, then clearly we are infected with their depravity and we depart from nature so that they seem to look upon us with scorn.

[8] With just how much discretion authority is to be examined Aristotle bears witness in the first book of [his] *Ethics* when he says, "If two friends exist, Plato and Truth, one should align oneself more with Truth than the friendship of Plato." And a second translation says, "If two friends exist, it is pious to honor Truth.[25] Likewise in the *Life of Aristotle* Plato is read to have said, "Socrates is a friend but Truth more a friend."[26] Aristotle also said the same of Plato, as is written in the same [work]. But few wish to examine the words of their teachers, which Boethius condemns in [his] book *On the Training of Scholars* saying: "A

numquam inveniendis; stultiusque est ma ⟨f. 78va⟩gistratus orationibus
confidere omnino. Sed primo credendum est ⟨donec videatur⟩ quid sen-
tiat; postea fingendum est eundem in dicendo errasse, ut sic reperire
queat quid commisse ⟨objiciat⟩ sedulitati.'' Tullius etiam in *Hortensio*
5 tales reprobat evidenter dicens, ''Multi primum tenentur astricti opi-
nionibus, antequam quid verum sit iudicare potuerunt. Obsecuti amico
cuidam, aut alicuius quem audierunt oratione capti, de rebus incognitis
iudicant; et ad quamcumque disciplinam quasi tempestate delati, tamquam ad saxum inhaerescunt.''
10 [9] Consuetudinem vero causam magnorum errorum et periculosam
ostendit Ieremias propheta dicens, ''Numquid potest Aethiops mutare
pellem suam, aut pardus varietatem suam? Sic non potest homo
benefacere cum didicerit male.'' Et Solomon, ''Adolescens iuxta viam
suam, cum senuerit, non recedet ab ea.'' Et Salustius ait in *Iugurtino*,
15 ''Ubi adolescentiam habuerunt, ibi senectutem agunt.'' Et propter hoc
dicit Aristoteles secundo *Ethicae*, ''Non parum differt sic vel sic assuesci a
iuventute,'' quia decimo *Ethicae* dicit, ''Non enim possibile est vel non
facile quae ex antiquo consuetudinibus comprehensa sermone
transmutare.'' Et alia translatio planius dicit, ''Impossibile enim aut non
20 facile mutare per sermonem eum, qui iam induratus est moribus antiquis
tempore longo''; propter quod adiungit quod iuvenes consueti ad errores
non possunt castigari, nisi per poenas a legibus constitutas. Aristoteles
etiam primo *Metaphysicarum* asserit consuetudinem esse causam errorum
dicens, ''Tu potes videre quanta mala facit consuetudo in civitatibus,
25 nam apologi et fabulae magis recipiuntur quam veritates.'' Et ideo
Tullius primo libro *Quaestionum* dicit, ''Magni animi est cogitationem a
consuetudine reducere.'' Horum autem omnium quae per consuetudinem inducuntur causa est quod consuetudo est altera natura,
secundum Aristotelem libro *De memoria et reminiscentia*, hoc est, alterat
30 naturam. Et primo generat naturam corruptam, quia Hippocrates dicit,
''Sub molli culcitra iacere non consuetis fagitat naturam,'' et postea,
''Placet naturae quando continuata est,'' ut quilibet experitur in se
multis modis.
[10] Sensum vero multitudinis et testimonium multorum Aristoteles
35 ponit primo *Metaphysicarum* causam nostrorum errorum ubi dicit Commentator quia opposita principiorum, cum fuerint famosa, magis reci-

---

4 sedulitati] *spatium c. 16 lit. seq.*   8 ad] quod *add.*   9 saxum] sexum   17 enim possibile]
impossibile   30 Hippocrates] ypocras

low-grade talent always uses the things [already] discovered and never those [yet] to be discovered; and it is [even] more foolish to trust entirely the sayings of academic authority. But one should first believe [until] what it holds [be seen]; afterwards one should imagine that the same has erred in speaking so that one can thus find out what [one might object] one has granted to overzealousness."[27] Also Tully clearly condemns such in his *Hortense* saying: "Many at first are held fast by opinions before they were able to judge what is true. Following a certain friend or captivated by a speech of someone whom they heard, they make judgment on things unknown, and they cling as to a rock to whatever theory they have been carried as though by a storm."[28]

[9] Jeremiah the prophet shows custom [to be] the cause of great errors and dangerous when he says: "Can an Ethiopian change [the color of] his skin or a leopard his spots? So a man cannot do well when he has learned poorly."[29] And Solomon [says], "A youth with inveterate habits, having grown old, will not depart from them."[30] And Sallust says in *The Jugurthian [War]*, "Where they spent their youth, there they pass their old age."[31] Because of this Aristotle says in the second [book] of the *Ethics*, "It makes no little difference [whether we] are accustomed one way or another from our youth,"[32] because, as he says in the tenth [book] of the *Ethics*, "for it is not possible or [at least] not easy to change by thorough argument things which [are part of us] from of old through customs."[33] And another translation says more clearly, "For [it is] impossible or [at least] not easy to change by argument him who has already been imbued for a long time with ancient mores."[34] Because of this he adds that youths accustomed to errors cannot be punished except through penalties established by laws.[35] Aristotle also asserts in the first [book] of the *Metaphysics* that custom is a cause of errors saying, "You can see how many evils custom perpetrates in the cities, for apologists and fables are better received than truths."[36] And thus Tully says in the first book of the *[Tusculan] Questions*, "It takes a great mind to lead thought away from custom."[37] The cause, moreover, of all these things which are induced through custom is that custom, according to Aristotle in [his] book *On Memory And Reminiscence*, is an alternate nature, that is, it alters nature.[38] And first it generates a corrupt nature because, [as] Hippocrates says, "to those unaccustomed it fatigues nature to lie beneath a soft coverlet," and later, "it is pleasing to nature when it is continued," as anyone knows in many ways from experience itself.[39]

[10] In the first [book] of the *Metaphysics* Aristotle posits the opinion of the multitude and the testimony of the many as a cause of our errors where the Commentator says that things opposed to principles, wherever they are trumpeted, are better received than the principles themselves.[40]

piuntur quam ipsa principia. Propter quod sanctus Iohannes Chrysosto-
mus super *Mattheum* dicit, "A veritate se nudos esse professi sunt, qui in
multitudine se armaverunt. Multi vero sunt vocati ad veritatem Dei,
pauci vero electi." Secundum quod Plato dixit in *Timaeo*, "Intellectus
5 paucorum est." Tullius etiam prologo libri *Secundarum quaestionum* egregie
loquitur   dicens,   "Philosophia   paucis   est   contenta   iudicibus,
multitudinem ipsam consulto fugiens, eique ipsi suspecta et invisa." Et
in ipso libro *Secundarum* quemlibet alloquitur dicens, "Te autem, etsi sis
in oculis multitudinis, tamen eius iudicio stare nolim, nec quod ipsa putet
10 idem putare pulcherrimum," et paulo post, "Quoniam etiam lauda-
biliora videntur omnia, quae sine populo teste fiunt." Et Seneca libro *De
vita beata* dicit, "Nulla res nos maioribus malis implicat, quam quod ad
rumorem componimur, optima rati quae magno assensu recepta sunt,"
et post pauca, "Non ita bene cum rebus humanis agitur, ut meliora
15 pluribus praepateant." Et ideo concludit dicens, "Quaeramus ergo quod
optime factum est, et non quod usitatissimum, non quod vulgo interpreti
veritatis pessimo probatum sit." Et ideo dicit sacer textus, "Noli sequi
turbam ad faciendum malum," quasi eius proprium sit, vel ad quod de
facili inclinatur.
20   [11] Cum igitur hae sententiae sanctorum et aliorum sapientium insuper aliae ⟨f.78vb⟩ innumerabiles reprobant has tres causas errorum
humanorum, nequeo satis admirari quod omnes faciunt haec tria
argumenta pessima ad eandem conclusionem, "Hoc exemplificatum
est," "Hoc consuetum est," "Hoc vulgatum est, ergo tenendum est,"
25 cum in pluribus oppositum conclusionis potest stare cum praemissis et
directe sequitur ex eisdem, quod per experientiam quilibet potest probare
in se et in aliis evidenter. Omnes enim scimus a pueritia usque in finem
vitae, quod a parentibus et a magistris et sociis et aliis pro uno exemplo
bono et veraci ac perfecto recipimus quasi infinita exempla imperfecta et
30 falsa et vana, inferentia nobis ineffabilia damna tam in studio quam in
vita. Et iterum novimus omnes quod quae ab ineunte aetate traximus in
consuetudinem facilius ⟨retinemus⟩, et libentius mala et falsa et vana, et
in pluribus bona et vera et utilia negligentes.
     [12] Scimus etiam quod multitudo humani generis semper erravit tam
35 in philosophia quam in sapientia divina. Nam de divina patet, quod

---

6 iudicibus] in *add.*   7 eique] ei quia‖ suspecta] suscepta   9 nolim] noli   11 libro] libre
12 res] nisi ulla res *add.*   17 veritatis...sit] veritatem pessime probant sic   31 ineunte]
ineunta est

Because of this St. John Chrysostom says [in a homily] on *Matthew*, "They have acknowledged themselves to be divested of truth who have armed themselves with the multitude; many indeed are called to the truth of God, but few [are] chosen [to receive it],"[41] [because], according to what Plato said in the *Timaeus*, "understanding belongs to a few."[42] Also Tully speaks admirably in the Prologue of [his] book *Second Questions* when he says, "Philosophy is content with few judges, deliberately avoiding the multitude because [philosophy is] an object of suspicion by [the multitude] and hostile to it."[43] And in the same book *Second* [*Questions*] he speaks to anyone saying, "I, however, would not have you stand by its judgment even though you be [esteemed] in the eyes of the multitude, nor think the same quite beautiful which it might think [to be so],"[44] and a little later, "[Be wary of its judgment] also because all things seem more praiseworthy which come to be without public witness."[45] And Seneca says in [his] book *On the Happy Life*, "Nothing involves us in greater evils than the fact that we are disposed for rumor, convinced that the best things [are those] which have been received with the greatest approval,"[46] and after a bit, "[The case] is not so well off with human affairs that better things are more clear to the many."[47] And thus he concludes saying, "Let us seek, therefore, that which is the best done and not what [is] the most commonly [done], not that which might be approved by the rabble, the worst interpreter of truth."[48] And hence the sacred text says, "Do not follow the crowd in pursuit of evil," as if it were proper to it, or [that] to which it is easily inclined.[49]

[11] Since, therefore, these judgments of the saints and other wise people along with other innumerable ones condemn these three causes of human errors, I cannot sufficiently be amazed that they use these three quite perverse arguments for the same conclusion: "This has been exemplified," "This is customary," "This is widely accepted, therefore it must be held," since in many [cases] the opposite of the conclusion can stand with the premises and follow directly from the same, which anyone can clearly prove directly and in other [ways] through experience. For we all know from [our] youth to the end of life that in place of a good, true, and perfect example we receive from [our] teachers, companions, and others more or less infinite, imperfect, false, and vain examples that bring us unspeakable harm both in [our] academic labors and life [in general]. And again, we have all known that we retain more easily those things from our earliest age [which] we drew from custom, [retaining] bad, false, and vain things the more willingly, neglecting in many [instances] those good, true, and useful.

[12] We also know that the majority of the human race has always erred both in philosophy and with regard to divine wisdom.[50] For it is

pauci homines respectu totius multitudinis mundi receperunt veritatem
Dei, ut patriarchae et prophetae, et alii iusti etiam, ita ut non solum
multitudo totius generis humani rebellis fuerit legi divinae, sed vulgus
Iudaeorum, quibus lex data fuit, repugnabat Deo, sicut sacra scriptura
5 multipliciter contestatur. Et cum per praedicationem apostolica ecclesia
congregata est, pauci remanserunt in fide vera, et adhuc pauci sunt
respectu multitudinis mundi, scilicet, illi qui Romanae ecclesiae sunt
subiecti. Tota reliqua multitudo errat, ut pagani, idolatri, Iudaei,
Sarazeni, Tartari, haeretici, schismatici, respectu quorum cultores veri
10 Christianae fidei sunt valde pauci. Et si isti dividantur in paucitatem et
multitudinem, multitudo, licet fidem habeat, tamen informis est, et sine
rectis operibus mortua secundum sanctum Iacobum comprobatur. Pauci
enim probant fidem suam bene vivendo, quia multitudo Christianorum,
licet confiteantur se nosse Deum, factis tamen negant, ut ait Apostolus,
15 et hoc videmus occulta fide. Et si illos, qui fide et operibus dignis vigent,
dividamus in multos et paucos, ipsa multitudo est nimis imperfecta, et
viam perfectionis paucissimi apprehendunt.

[13] Similiter possumus videre in philosophia, nam, testante Iosepho
in *Antiquitatum* libris et Aristotele in libro *Secretorum*, Deus a principio et
20 lapsu temporis paucis dedit veritatem philosophiae, scilicet, aliquibus
patriarchis et prophetis et quibusdam aliis Haebreis iustis, antequam
Latini et Graeci et aliae nationes habuerunt philosphiae principium. Post
quos, ut ait Aristoteles, secuti sunt viri qui vocati sunt philosophi, qui ab
Haebreis receperunt principia scientiarum et artium, ac maxime Graeci,
25 "quia magis fuimus studiosi," connumerans cum aliis semetipsum. Sed
isti fuerunt paucissimi respectu totius humani generis. Et si istos
dividamus in multitudinem et paucitatem, soli Peripatetici Aristoteli con-
sentientes remanserunt in veritate philosophiae, quia Pythagoricos et
Platonicos et Stoicos invenit errantes et omnes sectas philosophantium.
30 ⟨Et⟩ evacuavit errores, et mille volumina scientiarum conscripsit, ut
legitur in *Vita* sua. Et Aristoteles, ut ait Tullius in *Topicis*, "Admodum,
id est valde, paucis, notus fuit." Nam secundum ipsum Tullium quinto
De quaestionibus tusculanis et quinto *Academicorum* libro, quindecim
successores eius reliquit, et cum illis petiit exilium ut iret in perpetuas
35 peregrinationes, numquam ad propria reversurus, quatenus cum illis
paucis vacaret sapientiae, quia haec vita magis est similis vitae Dei et

---

3 fuerit] fuit   8 errat] erat   11 licet] sed || informis] informi   26 istos] istis   34 reliquit]
reliquid

clear in the case of divine [wisdom] that measured against the whole multitude of the world few people received the truth [given] by God, like the patriarchs, prophets, and also other just ones, so that not only the majority of the whole human race was in rebellion against divine law but [also] the horde of Jews to whom the law was given was opposing God, as sacred scripture confirms in many places. And when the apostolic church was gathered together through preaching, few remained in the true faith, and up to this time they are few when counted against the multitude of the world, namely, those who are subject to the Roman Church. All the remaining multitude is in error, like the pagans, idolators, Jews, Saracens, Tatars, heretics, [and] schismatics, in comparison with whom the supporters of the true Christian faith are very few. And if these be divided into a minority and a majority, the majority, granted it would have the faith, yet [its faith] is without form, and according to St. James without good works [faith] is shown [to be] dead.[51] For few demonstrate their faith by living well, because the multitude of Christians, granted it may confess it knows God, yet, as the apostle says, it denies [this] by [its] deeds, and we see this by a hidden faith.[52] And if we should divide those who live by faith and fitting works into the many and the few, the multitude itself is too imperfect, and very few embrace the way of perfection.

[13] We can see something similar in philosophy, as Josephus bears witness in [his] books *Antiquities* and Aristotle in [his] book *Secret*, from the beginning and throughout time God has given the truth [arrived at] by philosophy [only] to a few, namely, some patriarchs and prophets and to certain other just Hebrews, before the Latins and Greeks and other nations had the tool of philosophy.[53] After these, as Aristotle says, there followed men who were called philosophers, who received the principles of the sciences and the arts from the Hebrews, and especially the Greeks ("because we were more studious"), numbering among others himself.[54] But these were very few when measured against the whole human race. And if we should divide these into a majority and a minority, only the Peripatetics (who are in agreement with Aristotle) have remained in the truth of philosophy, because he found the Pythagoreans, Platonists, and Stoics and all the [other] sects of those who philosophize to be in error.[55] He eliminated [their] errors and, as is read in the *Life* [*of Aristotle*], he wrote a thousand volumes on the sciences.[56] And Aristotle, as Tully says in [his] *Topics*, "was known to a mere, that is, very, few."[57] For according to that same Tully in the fifth [book] of the *Tusculan Disputations* and fourth book of the *Academics* he left with his fifteen followers and went into exile with them, never to return to his own, in order to be free with those few for [the pursuit of] wisdom, because this life is more similar to the life

angelorum. Vitavit igitur multitudinem, et cum paucissimis philosophatus est, sciens multitudinem ineptam ⟨f. 79ra⟩ sapientiae, ut in praesentibus efficaciter est ostensum.

[14] Tarde vero venit aliquid de philosophia Aristotelis in usum
5 latinorum, quia naturalis philosophia eius et *Metaphysica* et commentaria Averrois et aliorum similiter his temporibus nostris translata sunt. Et Parisius excommunicabantur ante annum Domini 1237 propter aeternitatem mundi et temporis, et propter librum *De divinatione somniorum*, qui est tertius *De somno et vigilia*, et propter multa alia erronee translata.
10 Etiam logicalia fuerunt tarde recepta et lecta. Nam Beatus Edmundus, Cantuariae Archiepiscopus, primus legit Oxoniae librum *Elencorum* temporibus meis. Et vidi magistrum Hugonem, qui primo legit librum *Posteriorum*, et librum eius conspexi. Pauci igitur fuerunt qui digni habiti sunt in philosophia praedicta Aristotelis respectu multitudinis Lati-
15 norum, immo paucissimi, et fere nulli usque in hunc annum Domini 1292ᵐ, quod in sequentibus capitulis copiosissime et evidentissime patefiet. Et tardius communicata est *Ethica* Aristotelis et nuper lecta a magistris et raro. Atque tota philosophia reliqua Aristotelis, in mille voluminibus in quibus omnes scientias tractavit, nondum translata est,
20 nec communicata Latinis, et ideo fere nihil dignum de philosophia Aristotelis scitur. Et usque nunc fuerunt tres qui de illis paucis quae translata sunt potuerunt iudicare veraciter, sicut statim multis modis efficacibus probabitur diligenter.

---

1 igitur] Dei *add.*   13 librum eius] verbum eius   22 multis] multis *add.*

of God and the angels.[58] Hence he avoided the multitude and philosophized with very few, knowing the multitude [to be] ill-suited for wisdom, as has been effectively shown [to be the case] in present [times].

[14] Only lately has something of Aristotle's philosophy come into use among the Latins, because his natural philosophy and *Metaphysics* and the commentaries of Averroes and of others like [him] have been translated in these our times.[59] And at Paris they were under the ban of excommunication before the year 1237 because of [positions taken in regard to] the eternity of the world and of time and because of the book *On Prophesying by Dreams*, which is the third [book] of *On Sleep and Sleeplessness*, and because of many other things erroneously translated.[60] Even the logical [treatises] were [only] lately received and lectured on. For Blessed Edmund, Archbishop of Canterbury, [was] the first at Oxford to lecture on the book [*On Sophistical*] *Refutations* [and this he did] in my time.[61] And I saw Master Hugo, who was the first to lecture on the book *Posterior [Analytics]*, and I perused his book.[62] Hence there were few who were held proficient in the previously mentioned philosophy of Aristotle when measured against the multitude of Latins, indeed very few and practically none up to this year of the Lord 1292, which will become abundantly and quite evidently clear in the ensuing chapters. And even more lately has the *Ethics* of Aristotle been communicated, and [only] recently and rarely lectured on by teachers.[63] All the remaining philosophy of Aristotle in the thousand volumes in which he has treated of all the sciences has not yet been translated nor communicated to the Latins, and thus almost nothing representative is known about Aristotle's philosophy.[64] And up to now there were three [people] who could make accurate judgments on the few [things] that are translated, as will immediately be diligently proven in many convincing ways.[65]

⟨PARS SECUNDA⟩

⟨PROLOGUS⟩

[15] *Incipit prologus libri secundi de* Compendio studii theologicae facultatis.

5   [16] Determinata parte prima huius *Compendii de studio theologiae* in qua investigavi omnes causas errorum et modos errandi tam in substantia studii quam in modo, ut stabiliantur causae veraces et modi veri, nunc sequitur pars secunda in qua volo descendere ad ipsas veritates certificandas, et ad errores vacuandos in particulari et in propria disciplina.

10   [17] Quamvis autem principalis occupatio studii theologorum deberet esse circa textum sacrum, sciendum est, ut probatum est multipliciter in priori parte, tamen a quinquaginta annis theologi principaliter occupati sunt circa quaestiones, quod patet omnibus per tractatus et summas et honera equorum a multis composita. Non sic circa sacratissimum textum

15 Dei. Propter quod proniores sunt theologi ad recipiendum tractatum de quaestionibus quam de textu. Et ideo volo deservire eis, primo in his quae magis diligunt, quoniam prima pars prudentiae est, eius cui loqueris aestimare personam.

[18] Sed Palladius libro *De agricultura* asserit eleganter, ''Ceterum

20 maior profunditas sapientiae et magnificentia sine comparatione, et ideo maior difficultas, est exponere textum quam in quaestionibus.'' Et secundum Aristotelem nata est nobis via cognoscendi a facilioribus ad difficiliora, et ab humanis ad divina. ''Humana,'' dico, quia maior pars quaestionum in studio theologorum cum tota disputatione et modis

25 solvenda est in terminis philosophiae, ut notum est omnibus theologis qui exercitati fuerunt ad plenum in philosophicis, antequam veniebant ad theologiam. Et alia pars quaestionum in usu theologorum, quae est in terminis theologiae, ut de Beata Trinitate, et lapsu primorum parentum, et de gloriosa Incarnatione, et de peccatis, et virtutibus, et donis, et

30 sacramentis, et de desideriis, et paena, ventilatur principaliter per auctoritates et rationes et solutiones tractas ex philosophicis considerationibus. Et ideo quasi tota occupatio quaestionum theologorum est iam philosophica tam in substantia quam in modo.

---

3 libri secundi] *alia manu add.*   15 proniores] sermires(?)   19 eleganter] elegatum
25 est in] et in   30 desideriis] desideria

[PART TWO]

[PROLOGUE]

[15] [*Here*] *begins the Prologue to the second book of the* Compendium of the Study of the Discipline of Theology.

[16] Now that the first Part of this *Compendium on the Study of Theology* has been completed (in which I examined all the causes of errors and the ways of erring in the substance of that study as well as [its] method), there now follows a second Part in which I wish to move on to give a correct understanding of the issues themselves and eliminate specific errors in each discipline, so that causes that lead to truth and valid methods may be made secure.

[17] Although it ought to be recognized that the principal focus of the work of theologians ought to be on the sacred text, as was repeatedly proved in the preceding Part, yet theologians have been principally occupied for the past fifty years with *questions*, which is clear to all from the treatises, summas, and horseloads composed by many.[66] [This is] not the case with the most holy text of God. Because of this theologians are more prone to receive a treatise on *questions* than on the text [of the sacred scripture], and hence I wish to serve them first in those things they love the more, since the first part of prudence is to take into account the type of person to whom you are speaking.

[18] But Palladius elegantly asserts in [his] book *On Agriculture*, "There is, moreover, a greater depth of wisdom, a magnificence without comparison, and hence a greater difficulty in exposing a text than in *questions*.[67] And according to Aristotle there is innate in us a way of knowing [that proceeds] from easier things to the more difficult,[68] from the human to the divine. I say "human" because the greater part of *questions* in the theologians' discipline, along with all the types of disputation and its varieties, is to be conducted in the language of philosophy, as is known to all theologians who have labored to the full in philosophical matters before coming to theology.[69] [There is] another part of *questions* used by theologians which [is discussed] in theological language, for example, [*questions*] concerning the blessed Trinity, the fall of our first parents, the glorious Incarnation, sin, virtues, gifts, sacraments, desires, and punishment. [Yet this too] is aired principally through authority, reason, and solutions derived from philosophical considerations. And hence almost the whole focus of the *questions* of theologians is now philosophical in substance as well as method.

[19] Propositum igitur meum est tradere omnia philosophica spe-
culativa quae sunt in usu theologorum, et multa quae necessaria sunt eis,
quorum usum non habent, et certificare omnia per ordinem a primis ad
ultima, et tunc quae pertinent ad unam materiam exponere in suo loco,
5 ut, cum quasi infini⟨f.79rb⟩ties prae multitudine quaestionum una et
eadem res requirat, secundum considerationum diversitatem et con-
tradictionum eius, exquiram omnia quae eius sunt in uno loco, ut quod
infinitis quaestionibus variatur, uno loco istius libri reperiatur.

[20] Verbi gratia, cum in tota disputatione reali requiratur ratio ter-
10 minorum et propositionum et argumentorum, hoc suo loco reperietur
quidquid in tota rerum disputatione exigitur. Similiter, cum ratio
specierum et virtutum, quae fiunt ab agentibus in hoc mundo, requiratur—sive fiat mentio de actione divina sive angelica, sive celestium in
inferiora sive inferiorum ad invicem, sive fiat actio in sensum sive in in-
15 tellectum, et universaliter de tota cognitione cognoscentium et Dei et
angelorum et intellectus humani et sensus—hoc in parte determinata
huius libri invenietur quod in locis dispargitur infinitis. Et intelligendum
est de omnibus in hoc modo; melius enim est simul in uno loco omnia
reperire, quam per innumerabilia diverticula partes minimas et singulas
20 perscrutari. Quoniam vero tota difficultas disputationis circa reales
veritates dependet ex terminis et orationibus et argumentis, et summa
prolixitas et maximi errores hic multiplicantur, et vanitates innumerabiles et indignae theologicis occupationibus, ex quibus per totum
corpus realium quaestionum accidit corruptio infinita, prima distinctio
25 huius tractatus circa quaestiones demonstrabit quid verum, quid falsum,
quid dignum vel indignum, quid vanum, quid utile fuerit iudicandum.

[21] Hic autem requiritur potestas metaphysicae usque ad
undecimum librum de substantiis separatis, et logicae, quia Aristoteles
dicit, "De eisdem est metaphysica et dialectica, sed differunt in regimine
30 vitae." Hoc est ⟨verum⟩ secumdum Avicennam primo *Metaphysicae* in
modo non in re, quantum ad substantiam considerationis utrobique.
Nam qui bene scit *Metaphysicam* videbit quod primus liber docet inven-
tionem scientiarum via sensus, memoriae, et experientiae, quam logica
in fine libri *Posteriorum* docet. Et in principio illius libri *Posteriorum* et in
35 secundo multa tanguntur de origine scientiae, et in aliis libris logicae

---

4 tunc] aut *add.* 6 requirat] requiratur 7 contradictionum] condictionum 18 hoc
modo] hunc modum 25 demonstrabit] demonstrabitur 32 Nam] falsam

[19] My proposal, therefore, is to set forth all the philosophically speculative [principles] which are used by theologians, along with many that are necessary for them but whose use they do not have, and to give a correct understanding of everything in an orderly way from first to last. Then, too, [I propose] to set forth in its own place that which pertains to one topic, so that, although one and the same issue requires almost an infinity of *questions* because of its different considerations and conditions, I shall be probing in one place all its aspects. The result is that what is distributed throughout an unlimited number of *questions* [in other writings] will be found in one place in this book.

[20] For example, since [an understanding of] the notion of terms, propositions, and arguments is required in all types of disputation on real things, whatever is needed in all types of disputation on [these] matters will be found in its proper place.[70] Similarly, since a notion of the likenesses and forces which come from agents in this world is required—whether mention be made of divine or angelic action, whether of heavenly [agents acting] on those below or of those [acting] on one another, whether the action be on a sensory faculty or the intellect, and [whether mention be made] in general of all the knowledge possessed by anything that knows, namely, God, angels, the human intellect, and senses—this will be found in a designated part of this book, which [in other works] lies scattered in an infinite number of places.[71] Everything is to be considered in this fashion, for it is better to find everything in one place at the same time than to search through countless byways for each minute part [of every issue]. And because the whole contention in a disputation on real truths depends on terms, expressions, and arguments, and [because] there are multiplied here the greatest excesses, the most significant errors, and innumerable vanities unworthy of theological attention, from which an unlimited corruption permeates the whole corpus of real *questions*, the first distinction in this treatise on *questions* will demonstrate what had ought to be judged true, what false, what worthy or unworthy, what vain, and what useful.

[21] Here, however, is required the help of metaphysics up to the eleventh book [of the *Metaphysics*] on separated substances and of logic because Aristotle says, "Metaphysics and dialectic treat of the same things while they differ in regard to a rule of life."[72] According to Avicenna in the first [book] of his *Metaphysics* this is [true] of their method but not of their subject matter, as far as the substance of what each considers is concerned.[73] For who knows the *Metaphysics* well will see that the first book teaches that the discovery of the sciences is by way of senses, memory, and experience, which logic treats at the end of the book *Posterior* [*Analytics*].[74] And many things on the origin of knowledge are

haec metaphysicae consortia satis patent. Secundus liber *Metaphysicae*
continet fundamenta magna logicae in diversis locis, de quibus postea fiet
mentio. Tertius liber est totus logicus, sicut liber *Topicorum*, quia in illis
disputat per argumenta dialectica positiones philosophorum. Quartus
5 liber communicat valde cum logica propter divisionem entis et unius, et
propter declarationem huiusmodi principiorum logicae: "De quolibet affirmatio vel negatio et de nullo ambo." Et quintus liber totus est
logicalis, quia ibi distinguuntur vocabula, ut de modis per se, et aliis
quae sunt communia logicae et metaphysicae. Sextus liber est de vero et
10 falso, et de veritate propositionum de futuro, et de ente per accidens,
quae sunt logicalia. Septimus et octavus sunt principaliter de definitione,
de qua docetur sexto *Topicorum* et libro *Posteriorum*. Nonus liber est de
potentia passiva et activa, et de potentia rationali et irrationali, de quibus
docetur fine libri *Perihermenias*. Decimus explicat divisionem entis et
15 unius, et quattuor genera oppositionum, de quibus in *Praedicamentis*
docetur.

[22] Hoc ideo dixi ut advertatur quod metaphysicus in decem libris
eadem tractat secundum Aristotelem et Avicennam in substantia quae
logica, licet in modo differat. Et licet Aristoteles in secundo et septimo et
20 alibi aliqua tangat de principiis et causis rerum et scientiarum, tamen hoc
facit per argumenta dialectica, quia dialectica ad ⟨principia⟩ omnium
methodorum viam habet, ut Aristoteles dicit in *Topicis*. Quoniam vero
brevitati quantum possibile est semper insistendum est, docente Horatio,

    Item quid praecipies esto brevis, ut cito dicta
25   Percipiant animi dociles teneantque fideles;
    Omne supervacuum de pleno pectore manat,

non opportet primo numerare problemata ⟨f. 79va⟩ cum magna ostenta-
tione, nec corpus problematum cuiuslibet per argumenta ad utramque
partem distendere. Sed, ubi plane declaratur veritas, nec indigetur con-
30 tradictio, nec esset multiplicatio cavillationum inutilium. Et ubi propter
difficultatem requiritur obviatio iusta, exposita veritate per suas rationes,
statim signentur obicienda in contrarium et solvantur, quia longe melius
sic iudico procedere, eo quod, exposita veritate sufficienter, multa
sophismata inutilia excluduntur, ut sufficiat recitare ea quae vim habent,
35 et breviter dissolvantur.

---

1 haec...consortia] h^c m^e consor^{ia} 30 nec esset] ne cesset   32 solvantur] solvatur

touched upon at the beginning and in Book Two of the *Posterior* [*Analytics*].[75] These minglings of logic and metaphysics are [also] sufficiently clear in other books. The second book of the *Metaphysics* contains in various places the great foundations of logic, about which mention will be made later.[76] The third book is wholly logic, as [is] the book *Topics*, because in them he disputes the positions of philosophers with dialectical arguments. The fourth book shares much with logic because of the distinction between entity and one and because of this kind of a statement of the principles of logic: "A thing can be either affirmed or denied, but not both."[77] And the whole fifth book bears the stamp of logic, for there words are distinguished, for example, in regard to *per se* modes and others which are common to logic and metaphysics.[78] The sixth book is about that which is true and false, about the truth of propositions regarding the future, and about accidental entity, which are topics in logic.[79] The seventh and eighth are principally on definition, which is taught in the sixth book of the *Topics* and in the book *Posterior* [*Analytics*].[80] The ninth book is on passive and active potency and on rational and irrational potency, which is taught at the end of the book *On Interpretation*.[81] The tenth explains the distinction between entity and one and the four kinds of opposition, which are taught in the *Categories*.[82]

[22] I have made these remarks that one might advert to the fact that according to Aristotle and Avicenna a metaphysician treats in ten books substantially the same things as logic, granted they differ in the way [they do this].[83] Granted, too, that in the second and seventh book and elsewhere Aristotle touches on matters relevant to the principles and causes of things and sciences, nevertheless he does this through dialectical arguments because dialectic gives access to [the principles] of all methods [of inquiry], as Aristotle says in the *Topics*.[84] Since brevity is always to be insisted upon as much as possible—as Horace instructs, "Whatever you will teach, be brief, so that minds ready to learn may quickly hear what is said and hold it faithfully; everything superfluous flows off when the heart is full,"[85]—it is not necessary to single out problems with great display first, nor stretch the corpus of problems in both directions through just any kind of arguments.[86] Where truth is plainly stated contradiction is not needed and no multiplication of useless quibbling would ensue. And where legitimate opposition is required because of some difficulty, once truth has been exposed on its own merits, objections to the contrary may be immediately indicated and met. I judge it to be far better to proceed in this way because, once truth is sufficiently exposed, many useless sophistries are excluded. In consequence it suffices to recite those things that carry weight and [anything to the contrary] quickly fades away.

[23] Quia vero hic modus non servatur in scriptis, detestanda super-
fluitas cumulatur. Et, quoniam hi qui virtutum nominum sunt ignari
saepe paralogizantur, secundum Aristotelem in *Elenchis*; et "parvus error
in principio est magnus in fine," secundum eundem primo *Caeli et mundi*;
5 atque magna pars errorum circa orationes et argumenta oritur ex malo
intellectu terminorum, ut patebit; oportet secundum doctrinam Boethii
libro *De disciplina scholarium* in primis tradi cognitionem integram terminorum, nam qui minima spernit paulatim decidet, secundum *Ec-
clesiasticum* 19° capitulo. Et cum multa sint consideranda circa terminos,
10 primum estimo considerandum de significatione terminorum.

_____

7 tradi] tradidi   10 significatione] significatis

[23] Because, however, this method is not adhered to in writings, there results an excess that ought to be detested. And, since those who are ignorant of the way names operate often misreason, according to Aristotle in *On Sophistical Refutations*;[87] and since "a small error in the beginning becomes large in the end," according to the same [author] in Book One of *On the Heavens and the Earth*;[88] and since a large part of the errors pertaining to expressions and arguments arises from a faulty understanding of terms, as will become clear; there must first be given, according to the teaching of Boethius in his book *On the Training of Scholars*, a complete understanding of terms,[89] for "whoever spurns trifles will little by little fall," according to *Ecclesiasticus*, Chapter Nineteen.[90] And while there are many things to be considered about terms, I think the first to be considered pertains to the signification of terms.

CAPITULUM PRIMUM

[24] *Capitulum* ⟨*primum*⟩ *igitur est de ratione significandi generali.*

[25] Ad concipiendam igitur veritatem signorum oportet praemittere rationem signorum, quia aliter nihil dignum nec certum potest sciri de
5 significatione dictionum et vocum. Et, licet antequam vidi librum beati Augustini *De doctrina christiana*, cecidi per studium propriae inventionis in divisionem signorum, quam postea inveni in principio secundi libri *De doctrina christiana*, dico eius auctoritate, licet explico dicta eius ratione et exemplis, quod signum secundum ⟨eum⟩ est a natura vel datum ab
10 anima.

[26] Signum vero naturale oportet quod sit duobus modis: vel ex concomitantia naturali respectu sui signati, vel ex figuratione signi ad signatum, per quam potest naturaliter repraesentare signatum. Primus modus variatur per concomitantiam sive illationem et consequentiam
15 naturalem ⟨necessariam⟩ vel probabilem.

[27] Signum vero quod repraesentat signatum per illationem seu consequentiam naturalem et necessariam potest esse respectu praeteriti signati, ut ''Habet lac; ergo peperit''; vel respectu praesentis, ut ''Habet extremitates magnas; ergo est fortis''; vel respectu futuri, ut ''Aurora est
20 signum ortus solis cito venturi.''

[28] Si vero sit signum naturale per consequentiam probabilem, tunc potest esse respectu praeteriti, ut ''Terra est madida; ergo pluit''; vel respectu praesentis, ut ''Est mater; ergo diligit''; vel respectu futuri, ut est ''Rubedo in sero est signum serenitatis in crastino,'' et ''Rubedo in
25 mane est signum pluviae in illa die.'' Et sic universaliter currit locus a communiter accidentibus.

[29] Secundus modus signi naturalis est quod repraesentat per configurationem et expressionem similitudinis, ut vestigia rerum et imagines, et ea quae aliis sunt similia. Ut vestigium pedis in nive
30 significat illud cuius est, et imago Nicholai vel alterius. Et filius similis patri est signum quod genitus est ab eo. Et sic omnia artificialia repraesentant artem in mente artificis.

---

2 est] dest   9 datum] dūt   14 concomitantiam] concomitativam

[CHAPTER ONE]

[24] *The [first] chapter is on the general notion of signifying.*[91]

[25] In order to conceive the truth [conveyed] by signs it is first necessary to say a few words about the notion of signs, otherwise nothing worthwhile or certain can be known about the signification of words and vocal sounds.[92] Granted that before I saw the book of blessed Augustine *On Christian Doctrine* I fell upon a classification of signs by dint of my own discovery (which I later found in the beginning of the second book of *On Christian Doctrine*), I say with his authority, granted I explicate his statements with reasons and examples, that according to [him] a sign is either from nature or given by a soul.[93]

[26] A natural sign must be in two modes, [arising] either from natural concomitance with its significate or from configuration of the sign to its significate, through which it can naturally represent the significate.[94] The first mode is distinguished [from all others by the fact that the relation of signification here arises] through natural, [necessary] or probable concomitance or inference and consequence.[95]

[27] A sign which represents its significate through natural and necessary inference or consequence can be [a sign] of a significate in the past, as [in the inference] "She has milk; therefore she has given birth"; or [it can be a sign] of something present, as is the case with "It has large limbs; therefore it is brave"; or [it can be a sign] of something in the future, as in "Dawn is a sign that sunrise is about to occur."[96]

[28] If the sign is natural through probable consequence, then it can be [a sign] of something in the past, as [in the inference] "The ground is wet; therefore it has rained"; or [it can be a sign] of something present, as in "She is a mother; therefore she loves"; or [it can be a sign] of something in the future, as in "A red [sky] in the evening is a sign of a pleasant day tomorrow" and "A red [sky] in the morning is a sign of rain that day."[97] And thus throughout [these probable signs] runs the topic from concomitant accidents.[98]

[29] The second mode of a natural sign is [one wherein the sign] represents [something] by configuration and an expression of likeness, as in the case of the traces of things and images and those things that are like other things. For example, a footprint in the snow and an image of [St.] Nicholas or some other signifies the one whose it is; a son [who looks] like his father is a sign that he was begotten by him.[99] And all artifacts represent in this way art in the mind of an artist.[100]

[30] Sed obicitur: signum differt a causa et effectu, ut habere magnas extremitates nec est causa fortitudinis nec effectus, et ideo dicitur ab Aristotele signum. Similiter, habere lac est signum partus, non causa nec effectus, et sic de aliis. Ergo, cum artificialia sint opera artis et effectus, 5 non erunt signa. Et dicendum quod artificiale et est factum et opus artis et signum. In quantum est opus, sic est effectus; in quantum vero configuratur arti et conformatur, sic est signum repraesentans. Unde eadem res potest habere diversas rationes, et sic diversimode nominari.

[31] Secundus modus principalis signi est signum datum ab anima, et 10 hoc est duplex: unum est quod dicitur naturaliter significare apud Aristotelem, ut latratus canum ⟨et⟩ gemitus infirmorum; aliud ad placitum et per impositionem voluntariam, ut partes orationis.

[32] Sed obicitur quod sic latratus canis et huiusmodi erunt ⟨f. 79vb⟩ signa naturalia pluribus modis. Et dicendum quod aliter sumitur hic 15 'natura' quam prius, quia signum naturale priori modo dicebatur a natura quae est rei essentia inferens naturaliter ⟨necessario vel⟩ secundum probabiliter suum signatum, vel figurata ei. Sic enim essentia rei dicitur natura secundum Boethium libro *De duabus naturis*. Sic hic sumitur natura pro virtute dante rationem significandi sine deliberatione. Distin- 20 quendum, secundum quod Aristoteles secundo *Physicorum* dividit, agens in naturam et intellectum agentem ex proposito et deliberatione.

[33] Si ad hoc curialiter obiciatur quod artifex operatur imagines et cetera artificialia per intellectum agentem ex deliberatione et proposito, ergo erunt signa data ab anima agente per deliberationem, dicendum 25 quod, in quantum sunt opera, sic sunt facta ab anima ex proposito et deliberatione; sed, in quantum sunt signa, sic dividuntur naturalia ab eorum essentia configurata arti.

[34] Si dicatur quod potest statuere et statuit pro signis, ut vult ex deliberatione quod talis imago sit Nicholai, et talis alterius sancti, con- 30 cedo quod tunc est signum, ⟨sed signum⟩ dividitur uno modo naturale ab essentia configurata alii, alio modo ad placitum et per impositionem.

[35] Haec sunt signa naturalia, ut latratus canis significat iram, ⟨quae⟩ dici possunt esse naturalia a natura specifica quae est communis

---

3 Similiter] simul   4 opera] opus   19 Distinguendum] dcē

[30] But it is objected: a sign is different from a cause and an effect, for to have large limbs is neither a cause nor an effect of bravery, and for this reason it is called by Aristotle a sign. Similarly, to have milk is a sign of birth, but it is neither a cause nor an effect [of birth], and so for the other [examples]. Therefore, since artifacts are works of art and effects, they will not be signs.[101] [In response] it must be said that an artifact is something made and a work of art and a sign. Inasmuch as it is a work, it is an effect; but inasmuch as it is configured and conformed to art, it is a sign that represents. Hence, the same thing can be understood differently and thus be called by different names.[102]

[31] The second principal mode of a sign is a sign given by the soul, and it is twofold:[103] one is that said by Aristotle to signify naturally, as in the case of the barking of dogs [and] the groans of sick people,[104] the other is [a sign given] at pleasure and through voluntary imposition, as is the case with the parts of speech.[105]

[32] But it is objected that, if one speaks this way, the bark of a dog and the like will thus be natural signs in more than one mode. [In response] it must be said that 'nature' is taken here in a different sense than before, because a natural sign in the previous mode was said [to arise] from nature taken as the essence of a thing, naturally inferring its significate [necessarily or] with probability or configured to it,[106] for the essence of a thing is called a nature in this way according to Boethius in his book *On Two Natures*.[107] Thus nature is here taken for the power giving the characteristic of signifying without deliberation. One must distinguish, as does Aristotle in the second [book] of the *Physics*, between something acting according to nature and an intellect acting for a purpose and with deliberation.[108]

[33] If one were to object courteously to this that an artist fashions images and other artifacts by means of an intellect acting from deliberation and for a purpose, [and that] therefore [such things] will be signs given by a soul acting with deliberation, one should say [in response] that, inasmuch as they are works, they are made by a soul for a purpose and with deliberation; but inasmuch as they are signs, they are classified as natural from their essence which is configured to art [in the mind of an artist].[109]

[34] If it be said that [an artist] can and does make a determination for his signs, as in the case where he deliberately decides that a certain image be of Nicholas and some other of another saint, I concede that then there is a sign, [but a sign] is distinguished in one mode as natural, configured by its essence to another thing, [and] in another mode at pleasure and through imposition.[110]

[35] These [that follow] are natural signs, like a dog's bark [that] signifies anger.[111] They can be said to be natural [because they arise]

omnibus individuis unius speciei, per quam operatio speciei convenit naturaliter individuis; sic enim sumitur natura in quinto *Ethicae* ab Aristotele. Et sic est de vocibus omnium brutorum, quod sic significant naturaliter, et multae voces hominum. Et universaliter verus gemitus et
5 naturalis non fictus significat dolorem in omni homine, et multa alia similiter naturaliter significant, quae possunt fieri etiam ab intellectu in quantum naturaliter agit et sine proposito deliberandi.

[36] Beatus tamen Augustinus libro memorato dubitat an huiusmodi voces animalium fiant cum aliqua intentione animae. Sed mihi videtur
10 quod ex intentione fiant, quia animalia et aliam vocem proferunt in uno casu, et aliam in alio. Ut gallina, cum docet pullos cavere a milvo, profert aliam vocem quam quando invitat eos ad escam.

[37] Non solum vero anima sensitiva facit et dat signa et voces naturaliter significantes, sed anima intellectiva, quae proferuntur sine
15 deliberatione sed quodam instinctu naturali. Et sic fiunt voces gaudii et laetitiae et doloris et spei et timoris, tamquam subito ex naturali instinctu sine deliberatione. Sed haec consideratio multum attendenda est in originali peccato, et in primis motibus aliorum peccatorum, qui motus praecedunt omnem deliberationem, et similiter de mora infra vel ante
20 deliberationem plenam.

[38] Ex incidenti volo arguere, non dare sententiam, contra opinionem magistri *Sententiarum* et aliorum, qui aestimant peccatum originale fieri ex maculatione animae per carnem corruptam ex peccato primorum parentum, et ponunt exemplum de pomo proiecto in lutum,
25 quod maculatur ex contaginatione luti. Si anima sic ex unione cum carne macularetur, esset macula suae substantiae, et sui exterioris, non suae voluntatis; sed omne peccatum est voluntarium. Constat etiam quod corruptio quam traxit caro ex primis parentibus non est peccatum, quia caro non est subiectum peccati. Et ideo ex proprietate corruptionis ipsius car-
30 nis non fit macula peccati nec voluntatis; sed ⟨est macula⟩ substantiae animae cui caro unitur, sicut patet per simile quod dicunt de luto.

[39] Ex quo ulterius arguitur quod peccatum videtur fieri ex motu purae voluntatius. Si igitur non fiat per deliberationem voluntatis, fiet ex motu naturali voluntatis in ventre matris, cum unitur carni ante delibe-

---

2 *Ethicae*] eñte   3 significant] significat   7 deliberandi] deliberanti   9 aliqua] alia 11 milvo] muluo   12 quando] ante   17 in] quae   22 aestimant] est iniuuat 25 Si] in *add.*   31 caro] tibi || patet] patet *add.*

from the nature of a species (which is common to all individuals of one species) through which the [nondeliberative] activity of the species is natural to its individuals; for nature is considered in this way by Aristotle in the fifth [book] of the *Ethics*.[112] And such is the case with the cries of all brutes that they signify naturally, as do many human cries. Everywhere a genuine, natural, unfeigned groan signifies pain in every human. And likewise many other things signify naturally, which can also be brought about by an intellect whenever it acts naturally and without purposeful deliberation.[113]

[36] However, blessed Augustine in the book mentioned is uncertain as to whether cries like these of animals occur because of some intent of their souls.[114] But it seems to me that they would come from intent, because animals utter one kind of cry in one situation and a different [kind] in another.[115] For example a hen utters one type of cry when she teaches her chicks to guard against a hawk and another when she calls them for food.

[37] But not only does a sensitive soul make and give signs and cries that signify naturally, but [so also] does the intellectual soul, which are uttered without deliberation, yet from a kind of natural instinct. In this way arise the cries of joy and happiness, of grief and hope and fear, suddenly from a natural instinct without deliberation. But this point must be looked at closely in regard to original sin and the first inclinations to other sins—those inclinations which precede any deliberation—and similarly in regard to the delay before and prior to full deliberation.[116]

[38] Having entered upon this topic I want to argue a point [but] not render a judgment against an opinion of the Master of the *Sentences* and others.[117] These contend that original sin occurs from a soiling of the soul by flesh corrupted through the sin of our first parents, and they give the example of an apple thrown into the dirt which is soiled by the dirt's pollution. If a soul were in this way polluted by its union with flesh, then there would be a pollution of the substance [of the soul] and its exterior, [but] not by its own will; yet every sin is voluntary.[118] It is also the case that the corruption which flesh contracted from our first parents is not sin, since flesh is not subject to sin.[119] What this means is that a stain of sin does not arise from the property of corruption which flesh itself has nor because of [an act of] a will; but [there is a stain of sin] on the substance of a soul to which flesh is united, as is clear from the similar way in which they speak of dirt.[120]

[39] From this it is further argued that the sin seems to arise by an act of pure will. If therefore it would not come about through the deliberation of a will, it will come about by a natural inclination of the will in the mother's womb when [the soul] is united with the flesh, [but] before

rationem, quia constat quod anima embrionis non deliberat, nec etiam in
nativitate nec cito post nativitatem. Ad oppositum est quod peccatum
originale est mortale, et nunc videtur quod motus naturalis fit mortalis;
tunc enim vid⟨f. 80ra⟩eretur quod motus omnis voluntatis in hominibus
5 naturalis esset peccatum mortale, quod non conceditur.

[40] Sic igitur arguo ad utramque partem propter motus naturales
animae intellectivae. Sed determinari non potest sententia hic, cum dif-
ficillimae quaestiones sint de peccato originali et motibus naturalibus
animae rationalis, quae magis ad tertium tractatum pertinent, qui erit de
10 pure theologicis. In hoc quidem secundo tractatu explicabo solum principaliter philosophica quae sunt in usu quaestionum sumptarum ex
philosophia, licet indico materialiter quomodo haec quae tractabo
valeant ad puras theologicas quaestiones.

[41] Habet autem anima rationalis signa ex deliberatione facta et a
15 proposito, et ab Aristotele dicuntur signa ad placitum, ut voces quae sunt
partes orationis et ipsa oratio et argumenta et narrationes et similiter
nutus mutorum et signa monachorum.

[42] Sed tamen de partibus orationis distinguendum, quod omnia
praeter interiectionem significant ex pura deliberatione et perfecta. In-
20 teriectio vero non significat ex perfecta deliberatione, quia significat conceptum ex aliqua deliberatione, sed tamen per modum affectus, non per
modum conceptus; sicut etiam voces interiectionum imperfectae sunt et
absconditae.

[43] Sic igitur per viam certae considerationis, et narrationem purae
25 veritatis, expressae sufficienter per auctoritatem et exempla, cui nescio
contradicere, patet intentio sine superfluitate sophismatum ad utramque
partem, solum inducens et solvens quasdam obiectiones quarum solutiones necessariae fuerunt. Aliter enim fecissem magnum tractatum, si
ad utramque partem singulorum processissem.

_____

12 indico] in unicam   24 narrationem] narratione

deliberation, because it is a fact that the soul of an embryo does not deliberate, not even at birth nor soon after birth. But in opposition to this is the fact that original sin is mortal. And now it seems that a natural inclination becomes mortal, for it would seem that every natural inclination of the will in men would be a mortal sin, which is not granted.[121]

[40] In this way, therefore, do I argue on both sides [of these *questions*] because of [the nature of] the natural inclinations of an intellectual soul.[122] But final judgment cannot be rendered here because there are extremely difficult *questions* on original sin and the natural inclinations of a rational soul, which are more pertinent to the third treatise which will concern itself with purely theological matters.[123] In this second treatise I shall explain only primarily philosophical things which are of use [in resolving] *questions* taken from philosophy, granted I indicate concretely just how the things of which I shall treat will be useful for purely theological *questions*.

[41] Now the rational soul has signs made with deliberation and for a purpose, and these are called by Aristotle signs at pleasure: like vocal sounds which are parts of speech, speech itself, arguments, narratives, and similarly the nods of mutes and signs of monks.[124]

[42] However one must make a distinction in regard to the parts of speech because everything other than interjections signifies from pure and full deliberation. But an interjection does not signify from full deliberation because it signifies something conceived from deliberation in the way of a feeling, not in the way of a concept. For the same reason even the vocal sounds of interjections are imperfect and ill-formed.[125]

[43] Therefore, by way of a sound analysis and an exposition of pure truth sufficiently expressed through authority and examples, which I know not how to contradict, [my] intention [to write] on both sides without an excess of sophisms is thus revealed. I am introducing and resolving only certain objections whose solutions were necessary; for otherwise I would have turned out a large treatise had I proceeded [to write] on both sides of each [*question*].[126]

CAPITULUM SECUNDUM

[44] *Capitulum secundum de significatione vocis in particulari quoad quattuor: an scilicet vox ante impositionem significet aliquid; secundo an sibi possit imponi et significare se ipsum; tertio quomodo imponitur rebus extra animam;* ⟨*quarto*⟩ *quid significat?*

[45] Circa significata vocis in speciali multa consideranda sunt, et primo iuxta sententiam supradictam, "Qui spernit minima paulatim tendit ad ima," exponam tria minima, quae tamen multum valent ad sequentia.

[46] Et primum est an ante impositionem vox significet aliquid. Quod sic, probo: quia vox prolata habet speciem suam in anima proferentis, quae consequitur ad eam consequentia naturali, ergo significativa erit primo modo signi naturalis.

[47] Item, conformatur ei et configuratur; ergo secundo modo signi naturalis significat, et ⟨haec⟩ concedenda sunt.

[48] Si vero obiciatur quod signum differt a causa et effectu, et alia est ratio signi et causae et effectus, et vox est effectus proferentis, ergo non erit signum, solutio patet ex praedictis, quia idem potest esse signum et effectus diversimode. In quantum enim vox infert suam speciem naturali consequentia, vel configuratur ei, est signum; sed in quantum est opus proferentis, sic est effectus.

[49] Sed secundo quaeritur an aliter significet quam sic ante impositionem. Dicendum est quod non.

[50] Si vero caute obiciatur quod vere potest dici quod buba est buba, et nulla oratio est verior illa in qua idem de se praedicatur, ergo est pars orationis, et ita significat, ⟨...⟩.

[51] Similiter, cum dicitur "Buba est vox," item haec vox 'buba' ante impositionem, non considerata significatione naturali, aut est vox significativa aut non significativa; de quolibet enim affirmatio vel

---

7 Qui] quae   8 tamen] *corr. ex* tantum   12 erit] eam   26 ...] *apod. omit.*

[CHAPTER TWO]

[44] *Chapter two [treats] specifically of the signification of a vocal sound in regard to four [questions], namely, does a vocal sound signify anything before imposition; second, can it be imposed for itself and signify itself; third, how is it imposed for things outside a mind; [and fourth], what does it signify [at pleasure]?*[127]

[45] In regard to things that are signified by a vocal sound much must be considered in detail. And first, in accord with the statement mentioned above, "Who spurns trifles little by little falls to the depths," I shall present three trifles which, however, are very helpful for what follows.[128]

[46] The first is [this]: "Does a vocal sound signify anything prior to imposition?" That [the answer is] "Yes" I prove [in the following way]: because a spoken vocal sound has its own species in the mind of the speaker, which [sound] accompanies [the species] by natural consequence, therefore it will signify [its own species] in the first mode of a natural sign.[129]

[47] Likewise, [a vocal sound] is conformed and configured to it; therefore it signifies [its own species] in the second mode of a natural sign, and [these things] ought to be granted.[130]

[48] If, however, it be objected that a sign differs from a cause and an effect, that the notion of a sign is different from that of a cause and an effect, that a vocal sound is an effect of the one who utters it, [and that] therefore it is not a sign, the solution is clear from what has already been said, because the same thing can be in different ways both a sign and an effect. For inasmuch as a vocal sound infers its species by natural consequence or is configured to it, it is a sign; yet inasmuch as it is a work of the one who utters [it], it is an effect.[131]

[49] But secondly it is asked whether [a vocal sound] signifies in any way other than this before imposition. It must be said that [the answer is] "No."[132]

[50] Suppose, however, it be cautiously objected that it can truthfully be said that buba is buba (and no expression is more true than one in which the same [notion] is predicated of itself), [and that] therefore ['buba'] is a part of speech and thus signifies [at pleasure].[133]

[51] Similarly, when "Buba is a vocal sound" is spoken, again this vocal sound 'buba', before imposition [and] prescinding from [its] natural signification, either is a vocal sound that signifies [at pleasure] or [one] that does not, for of anything [there is] either affirmation or denial

negatio. Si 'buba' est vox significativa, habetur propositum. Si non, haec oratio erit vera: "Buba est vox non significativa." Ergo haec oratio est significativa; ergo partes eius omnes significant.

[52] Dicendum quod haec vocum congeries non facit orationem signi-
5 ficativam et nihil significat, quia prima pars huius sermonis, scilicet, 'buba', est vox non significativa ante impositionem; ergo tota oratio est non significativa ab una parte non significativa. Sicut si scribantur hae duae dictiones 'est' et 'vox', et praeponatur eis lapis vel lignum vel pomum in eodem pergameno in quo illa duo vocabula sequuntur, tota
10 congeries posita in pergameno nihil significaret. ⟨f80rb⟩ Sic nec cum haec vox 'buba' scribitur vel dicitur cum hoc verbo 'est', et cum hac dictione, vox erit oratio significativa. Et per hoc patet aliud, quod, cum dicitur 'buba' ante impositionem, aut est vox significativa aut non significativa; de quolibet affirmatio vel negatio. Dico quod non est hic af-
15 firmatio vel negatio, nec alia oratio significativa, nec veritas nec falsitas, sed congeries vocum ad invicem non significativarum; ab una enim parte non significativa est tota congeries vocum haec non significativa. Quod enim possint tales orationes esse verae et significativae, non potest fieri, nisi post impositionem huius ⟨vocis⟩ 'buba' sibi ipsi.

20 [53] Et tertio quaeritur an vox potest sibi ipsi imponi, ut fiat significativa et pars orationis significativae. Quod sic, concedendum est: voces sunt ad placitum instituentis; ergo possunt imponi sibi sicut aliis.

[54] Item, dicit Aristoteles primo *Elenchorum* quod 'album' et res et nomen est, volens quod nomen et 'album' potest significare res et ipsas
25 voces.

[55] Item, Augustinus in *Dialectica* sua dicit quod haec oratio potest esse vera: "'Tullius' est pes dactilicus." Ergo partes eius omnes sunt significativae; ergo 'Tullius' significat ibi aliquid. Sed nihil potest

---

4 facit] faciunt   5 et] sed   11 scribitur] scribatur   24 quod] et *add.*   27 omnes] omnis

[but not both]. If 'buba' is a vocal sound that signifies [at pleasure], the objection is granted. If not, this expression will be true: "Buba is a vocal sound that does not signify [at pleasure]." Therefore this expression signifies [at pleasure]; therefore all its parts signify [at pleasure].[134]

[52] [In response] it must be said that this aggregate of vocal sounds does not form a significative expression and it signifies nothing because the first part of the "statement," namely, 'buba', is a vocal sound that does not signify [at pleasure] before imposition; therefore the whole "expression" does not signify [at pleasure] because of one part that does not signify at pleasure.[135] If the two words 'is' and 'a vocal sound' would be written and a rock or [a piece of] wood or fruit would be placed before them on the same parchment in which those words follow, the whole aggregate placed on the parchment would have signified nothing.[136] So neither if the vocal sound 'buba' would be written or spoken with the verb 'is' will the vocal sound ['Buba is'] be an expression that signifies [at pleasure], even with this "word."[137] And because of this another [point] is clear [in regard to the second objection that contended] that, when 'buba' is spoken [in an "expression"] prior to imposition, either it is a vocal sound that signifies [at pleasure] or one that does not signify [at pleasure], [for] of anything [there is] either affirmation or denial [but not both]. I say that here there is neither affirmation nor negation nor another [kind of] expression that signifies [at pleasure]. Neither [is there here] truth nor falsity, but [rather] an aggregate of vocal sounds that do not signify [at pleasure] in virtue of their relation to one another, for from one part not signifying [at pleasure] the whole aggregate of vocal sounds does not signify [at pleasure]. That such expressions be able to be true and significative [at pleasure] cannot happen except after imposition of the [vocal sound] 'buba' for itself.

[53] Thirdly it is asked whether a vocal sound can be imposed for itself with the result that it becomes significative [at pleasure] and a part of speech that signifies [at pleasure].[138] That [the answer is] "Yes" should be conceded: vocal sounds are at the pleasure of the one who institutes [them]; therefore they can be imposed for themselves just as for other things.[139]

[54] Similarly, Aristotle says in the first [chapter] of *On Sophistical Refutations* that 'white thing' is both a thing and a name, intending that the name and [vocal sound] 'white thing' can signify both [white] things and the vocal sounds themselves.[140]

[55] Likewise, Augustine in his *Dialectics* says that this expression can be true: "'Tullius' is a dactyl foot." Therefore all its parts are ones that signify [at pleasure]; hence 'Tullius' there signifies something [at pleasure]. But it cannot signify [at pleasure] anything but a vocal sound

significare nisi vocem habentem longam unam et duas breves; ergo potest significare se.

[56] Si obiciatur quod signum est quod se offert sensui, aliud relinquens intellectui, ut communiter affirmatur, ergo vox non significabit se sed aliud, ⟨...⟩.

[57] Iterum, panis in fenestra non est signum substantiae panis, sed in quantum venalis, et ideo servatur alietas signi a significato; ergo vox non significabit se ipsam, nisi sub alia ratione, quam non contingit dare, ut videtur.

[58] Ad hoc dicendum quod alietas in substantia non requiritur hic, sed in modo et conditione, et hoc sufficit, sicut dictum est de pane quod significat se in quantum venalis est, et non secundum se absolute. Unde vox considerata ut sensibiliter prolata vel audita est significativa. Ut vero concipitur ab intellectu per speciem suam potest ex libertate intellectus fieri nomen sui et ⟨sibi⟩ imponi, et sic sub alia proprietate est signum et signatum.

[59] Sed quartum non est de minimis, sed quasi de illis quae maximam habent prolixitatem et contrarietatem opinionum, scilicet, postquam vox imposita est rei alicui extra animam, quid per vim impositionis significet principaliter? Et statim do sententiam levi et plana ratione, cui nullus prudens potest contradicere. Dico ergo quod vox imposita ad significandam rem extra animam significat solum eam rem secundum rationem impositionis; nam non recipit sic rationem nominis et signi nisi propter impositionem factam tali rei. Qua propter solum significabit rem illam cui imponitur, quantum est de proprietate impositionis.

[60] Si obiciatur secundum Aristotelem quod voces sunt notae passionum quae sunt in anima, et hae passiones sunt species rerum et habitus cognitivi et non res extra, ergo vox significabit tales passiones, dicendum est quod vox imposita rei non habet comparationem ad speciem et habitum, nisi quia imponitur rei. Nec rationem nominis habet nisi propter impositionem. Sed non imponitur speciei nec habitui, sed solum rei, et ideo secundum hanc rationem nominis non significabit ea

---

5 ...] *apod. omit.* 13 significativa] significatum 15 et sic] et et sic 19 vim] viam

having one long and two short [syllables]; therefore it can signify itself [at pleasure].[141]

[56] [But] suppose it be objected that a sign is something which offers itself to a sense faculty, leaving the other, [i.e., what it signifies,] for an intellect, as is commonly held, [and that] therefore a vocal sound will not signify itself [at pleasure] but the other.[142]

[57] Similarly, bread in a [bakery] window is not a sign [at pleasure] of the substance of bread, but [it is a sign at pleasure of bread] inasmuch as it is for sale, and thus a difference between the sign and what is signified is maintained. And therefore a vocal sound will not signify itself [at pleasure] except in virtue of another character which, it seems, it does not happen to have.[143]

[58] To this it must be said that a difference in substance is not required here except in mode and condition, and this suffices, just as it was said of bread that it signifies itself [at pleasure] inasmuch as it is for sale and not simply [as bread]. Hence an [imposed] vocal sound, considered as audibly uttered or heard, is [something] that signifies [at pleasure]. As conceived by an intellect through its species, it can become a name of itself in virtue of the freedom of an intellect and be imposed [for itself], and in this way are a sign and what is signified under a different attribute.[144]

[59] However, the fourth [issue] is not about trifles, but rather about those [matters] which generate the greatest excess and divergence of opinion, namely, after a vocal sound has been imposed for some thing outside a mind, what does it principally signify by force of the imposition?[145] And immediately I render a judgment [supported] by an uncomplicated and clear reason which no prudent person can contradict. I say, therefore, that a vocal sound imposed to signify a thing outside a mind signifies only that thing by reason of the imposition, for [a vocal sound] does not thus receive the character of a name and sign [at pleasure] other than through an imposition made for that particular thing. Because of this it will signify only that thing for which it is imposed, so far as the nature of imposition is concerned.[146]

[60] If it be objected in accord with Aristotle that vocal sounds are the marks of affections which are in a mind, and these affections are the species of things and cognitive habits and not things outside [a mind], [and that] therefore a vocal sound will signify such affections [at pleasure], it is to be said that a vocal sound imposed for a thing is not related to [the latter's] species and [cognitive] habit except in virtue of being imposed for the thing. Nor does it have the character of [being] a name except in virtue of imposition. But it is not imposed for the species or [cognitive] habit, but only for the thing, and hence according to this

quae sunt in anima. Sed quia species rei et habitus cognitivus de re sequuntur naturali consequentia ad rem et nomen rei—eo quod res non
potest intelligi sine illis, nec nomen reciperet nisi intelligeretur—ideo vox
rei imposita comparatur ad speciem et habitum sicut vox significativa
5 naturaliter, et primo modo signi naturalis, non sub ratione nominis quae
est vox significativa ad placitum.

[61] Et sic solvitur quod Boethius dicit in commentario super hunc
locum, scilicet, quod vox significat speciem rei in anima, sed non per impositionem, sed primo modo, et ideo illud quod dicit prius, "Quid est
10 aliud esse partem orationis, nisi mentis conceptum significare?" et pars
orationis significat ad placitum et per impositionem. Dicendum quod ibi
non accipit mentis conceptum qui est habitus cognitivus, sed mentis
⟨f. 80va⟩ conceptum, id est, rem conceptam a mente.

[62] Cum autem dicit Aristoteles septimo *Metaphysicae* quod domus in
15 anima est causa domus extra, et ita hoc nomen 'domus' significat aliquid
in anima et per impositionem, quia est pars orationis et subiectum in oratione et propositione, dicendum quod sic. Hoc nomen 'domus' in subiecto significat speciem domus in anima per impositionem et ad placitum,
sed aequivoce et nova impositione quam facit mens ad placitum, sicut
20 imponit vocem rei extra. Sed per unicam impositionem factam rei extra
numquam fieret 'domus' subiectum in oratione tali, nisi iterum imponitur speciei domus in anima.

[63] Cum vero dicat Augustinus libro *De magistro* quod haec dictio
'nihil' significat affectum animi, quia nullam ⟨rem⟩ potest significare ex-
25 tra animam, ut dicit, dicendum est quod imponitur non enti secundum
quod nos intelligimus non ens per privationem entis, quia quod bene
possumus facere. Et sic impositum est hoc nomen 'nihil', et est sufficienter loco reali extra animam, quantum ad intellectum imponentem et
quantum ad impositionem. Unde cum dicit quod significat affectum vel
30 affectionem, sumit affectum pro re affectata a voluntate imponente, sicut
expositum est illud Prisciani quod pars orationis significat conceptum
mentis.

[64] Et si dicatur quod, cum non ens non potest esse nisi in conceptione et consideratione intellectus, tunc erit conceptus mentis, et dicen-

---

19 facit] fuit   26 privationem] praenomen

understanding of [what] a name [is] it will not signify those things which are in a mind. But because the species of the thing and the cognitive habit of the thing accompany the thing and the name of the thing by natural consequence—inasmuch as a thing cannot be understood without them and would not receive a name unless it were understood—thus a vocal sound imposed for a thing is related to the species and [cognitive] habit as a naturally signifying vocal sound and in the first mode of a natural sign, not in virtue of [its] character as a name, which is a vocal sound that signifies at pleasure.[147]

[61] And in this way is made clear what Boethius says in his commentary on this point, namely, that a vocal sound signifies the species of a thing in a mind, not through imposition, but in the first mode,[148] and likewise what he says earlier, "What other is it to be a part of speech but to signify a *conceptum* of a mind?" and a part of speech signifies at pleasure and through imposition. [However] it must be said that, there, he does not mean a concept of a mind (which is a cognitive habit), but a *conceptum*, that is, a thing conceived by a mind.[149]

[62] When, however, Aristotle says in the seventh book of the *Metaphysics* that a house in a mind is a cause of a house outside [a mind], and [that] thus the name 'house' signifies something in a mind and through imposition because it is a part of speech and a subject in an expression and proposition, it must be said that [this is] so. The name 'house' in a subject [position] signifies the mental species of a house through imposition and at pleasure, but [it does so] equivocally and by a new imposition which a mind makes at pleasure, just as it imposes a vocal sound for a thing outside [a mind]. But 'house' would never become a subject in such an expression through the one imposition made for a thing outside [a mind] unless it is again imposed for the mental species of the house.[150]

[63] But since Augustine says in his book *Concerning the Teacher* that the word 'nothing' signifies an affect of a mind because, as he says, it can signify no [thing] outside a mind, it must be said that ['nothing'] is imposed for a nonentity in virtue of the fact that we understand a nonentity through a privation of an entity, since we are able to do this quite readily. In this way is the name 'nothing' imposed, and [what it signifies] is sufficiently in a real place outside a mind as far as an imposing intellect [is concerned] and as far as imposition [is concerned].[151] Hence when he says that it signifies an affect or affection, he is considering an *affectum* as a thing affected by an imposing will, as was explained that [statement] of Priscian that a part of speech signifies a thing conceived by a mind.[152]

[64] And if it be said that, since a nonentity cannot be but in a conception and consideration of an intellect, [and that] it will then be a concept

dum est quod non oportet, quia esse in consideratione et conceptione intellectus potest esse dupliciter: vel ut species et habitus intelligendi in ipso
intellectu existentes, sicut accidentia in subiecto, vel ⟨ut⟩ res prout est actu concepta et considerata. Sicut enim quodam modo est in intellectu, et
sic non est solum ens, sed non ens potest intelligi et esse in consideratione
et conceptione mentis. Sed quae sunt illo modo primo in consideratione
intellectus sunt species et intellectus; quae secundo modo sunt intelli-
gibilia, sive ens sive non ens.

of a mind, it must be said that this need not be so, for to be in a consideration and conception of an intellect can occur in two ways: either as a species and habit of understanding existing in an intellect itself like attributes in a subject, or [as] a thing as it is actually conceived and considered. For just as in a certain sense [a thing] is in an intellect, so not only an entity but also a nonentity can be understood and be in a consideration and conception of a mind. But those things which are in a consideration of an intellect in the first way are species and concepts; those in the second way are intelligible things, whether an entity or a nonentity.[153]

CAPITULUM TERTIUM

[65] *Capitulum tertium de connotatis et cointellectis* ⟨*per res quibus nomina imponuntur*⟩.

[66] Deinde diligenter considerandum est ulterius quod nomen impositum alicui rei soli extra animam potest multa simul significare extra animam, et haec vocantur in philosophia cointellecta, et apud theologos connotata. Omne enim quod naturali et necessaria consequentia sequitur ad nomen alicuius, cointelligitur et connotatur in eo, quia aliter non sequeretur ad ipsum necessario, ut "Creatura; igitur Creator" et "Creator; igitur Deus," quia solus Deus creat. Et omne accidens proprium connotat suum subiectum, ut "Risibile; ergo homo." Et omne universale connotat particulare vagum; et particulare vagum et signatum connotant speciem; et species genus; et relatum connotat alterum correlativorum; et aggregatum connotat materiam et formam. Et sic de infinitis aliis est quod naturali consequentia concomitantur alia; ergo connotantur et cointelliguntur per ea, quapropter nomen significabit ea.

[67] Si obiciatur quod non univoce potest significare plura, quia uni tantum imponitur, nec aequivoce, quia non est nisi unica impositio, et aequivocatio non est sine pluribus impositionibus, dicendum quod univoce et aequivoce significare referuntur ad modum significandi per impositionem et ad placitum, et sic dictio non significat nisi illud cui imponitur. Sed in praedicto modo significandi per concomitantiam naturalem est primus modus significandi naturaliter, qui prius expositus est.

[68] Si etiam obiciatur quod nomen quodlibet potest poni in oratione pro significato suo, sed numquam pro aliquo dictorum quae vocantur connotata, igitur non significabuntur per nomina, quod patet, quia, cum dicitur "Animal currit," vel "Socrates est animal," non potest nomen stare pro anima nec pro corpore. Et sic de aliis dicendum est quod, cum nomina sint partes orationis, et pars orationis significat ad placitum—et

[CHAPTER THREE]

[65] *The third chapter [treats] of things connoted and co-understood [through the things for which names are imposed].*[154]

[66] Next one should diligently consider further that a name imposed for some thing outside a mind can signify at the same time many things outside a mind, and in philosophy these are called "things co-understood" and among theologians "things connoted." Every thing which accompanies the name of something by natural and necessary consequence is co-understood and connoted in it, since otherwise [the connoted thing] would not necessarily accompany [the name], as exemplified in [the inferences] "[There is] a creature; therefore [there is] a Creator" and "[There is] a Creator; therefore [there is] God," because only God creates.[155] And every proper attribute connotes its subject, as [can be seen in] "[It is] capable of laughing; therefore [it is] a man."[156] And every universal connotes an indeterminate particular; an indeterminate particular and a determinate one connote a species; species [connotes] genus; a related entity connotes the other of the correlatives; and a composite connotes matter and form. And such is the case with an unlimited number of others that they accompany others by natural consequence; therefore [the latter] are connoted and co-understood through them and because of this a name will signify them.[157]

[67] If it be objected that [one name] cannot signify more than one thing univocally because it is imposed for only one thing, nor equivocally because there is but one imposition and equivocation is not had without more than one imposition, it must be said that to signify univocally and equivocally pertain to the mode of signifying by imposition and at pleasure, and a word does not signify [anything] in this way except that for which it is imposed. But [to signify] in the mode mentioned above of signifying through natural concomitance is the first way of signifying naturally, which has already been described.[158]

[68] If it also be objected that any name can be placed in an expression for its significate but never for one of the things [previously] mentioned which are called "things connoted," [and that] therefore they will not be signified [at pleasure] by the names, [it must be said] that this is so because, when "An animal runs" or "Socrates is an animal" is spoken, the name cannot stand for a soul or a body.[159] And likewise for other [cases] it must be said that, since names are parts of speech and a part of speech signifies at pleasure—and this is [to say that it signifies at

hoc est solam rem cui imponitur—numquam stabit pro alio, et ideo non pro connotatis, nisi fiat eis nova impositio, quod pluries fit. Et ideo non sequitur nisi quod pro illo cui imponitur stabit in oratione, nec significabit nisi illud per impositionem. Sed tamen alio modo significandi poterit aliud significare, ut etiam multa, ut nomen aggregati per impositionem significat illud tantum, simul tamen connotat ⟨f. 80vb⟩ materiam et formam, et proprium accidens, et multa alia quae intelliguntur per illud naturali consequentia.

[69] Sed tunc est gravis dubitatio Aristotelis in 8 *Metaphysicae* et gravior Commentatoris de nomine aggregati. Nam Aristoteles quaerit utrum nomen aggregati significet aggregatum vel formam; vel utrum hoc nomen 'domus' significet cooperimentum, quod est formale, an totum compositum ex lapidibus et lignis, quod est aggregatum; et utrum hoc nomen 'linea' significet duo puncta, quae sunt formalia, an totam longitudinem terminatam ad illa duo puncta; et an 'animal' significet aggregatum an animam. Et Aristoteles solvit quod utrumque significat, sed non secundum unam definitionem significationis, et unum per alterum. Sed qualiter diversimode non dicit, nec cui nomen debetur per alterum.

[70] Et dicendum quod nomen aggregato impositum significat ipsum primo et principaliter, et formam et materiam mediante aggregato. Et diversus est modus significandi, quia nomen aggregati ipsum significat ad placitum et per impositionem; materiam vero et formam primo modo significandi naturaliter. Sed quia Aristoteles hoc non exprimit, ideo Commentator conatur exponere, et dicit contrarium ei, quod non dixi. Propter quod necessarium est discutere illud.

[71] Commentator vero docet quod forma magis est et prius et dignius et principalius, et aggregatum secundario, et ad hoc ponit suam rationem, dicens quod nomen ⟨non⟩ significat rem nisi secundum quod est in actu; et causa actus in composito est forma; et cum duo fuerint quorum alterum est causa reliqui, illud quod est causa dignius habebit nomen, quia illud est nomen secundi propter primum, ut res calidae participant nomen caloris, sed ignis participat nomen caloris per prius.

---

6 tamen] tantum   14 an] ad   17 unum] uni   19 nomen] nomini

pleasure] the thing alone for which it is imposed—[a name] will never stand for something else, and thus not for things connoted, unless a new imposition is made for them, which often happens. And thus it does not follow except that [a name] will stand in an expression for that for which it is imposed, and it will not signify [anything] but that through imposition.[160] But, however, [a name] will be able to signify something else in another mode of signification, and indeed many things, just as the name of a composite signifies it alone through imposition, but at the same time connotes matter and form, a proper attribute, and many other things which are understood through [the composite] by natural consequence.

[69] But then there is the serious doubt of Aristotle in [Book] Eight of the *Metaphysics* and the more serious one of the Commentator about the name of a composite.[161] For Aristotle asks whether the name of a composite signifies the composite or [its] form; or whether the name 'house' signifies a shelter, which is [its] formal [element], or a whole composed of stones and wood, which is the composite; whether the name 'line' signifies two points, which are [its] formal [elements], or the whole length terminating in the two points; and whether 'animal' signifies a composite or [its] soul. Aristotle offers the solution that it signifies both but not through one definition of signification, and [that it signifies] the one through the other.[162] But [how it does this] in different ways he does not say, nor to which one the name belongs by reason of the other.

[70] And [so] it must be said that a name imposed for a composite signifies it first and principally and [its] form and matter by means of the composite.[163] And the mode of signifying is different because the name of a composite signifies it at pleasure and through imposition [and its] matter and form in the first mode of natural signification. But because Aristotle did not [expressly] state this the Commentator tries to explicate [Aristotle's remarks] and says the contrary of him, which I have not said. Because of this it is necessary to discuss that [point of view which the Commentator holds].

[71] The Commentator teaches that form is more [existent], prior, more worthy, and more important and that the composite is second, and in support of this he gives his reason, saying that a name does [not] signify a thing except inasmuch as [the thing] is in act and [that] the cause of act in a composite is [its] form. And [he says that] whenever there may have have been two things of which one is the cause of the other, that which is the cause will more properly bear the name because that [name of the first] is a name of the second in virtue of [being the name of] the first, as hot things have the name of heat, but fire has the name in a prior sense.[164]

[72] Haec est sententia Commentatoris. Sed in prima parte huius operis ostendi universali sermone, quod eius doctrina respuenda est ab omni sapiente propter certissimas causas, et quia destruxit philosophiam Aristotelis. Nunc vero et deinceps descendam in particulari ad eius opi-
5 niones efficaciter destruendas, et ostendam quod illi qui adhaerent ei turpiter decipiuntur, et philosophiae nesciunt veritatem. Dico ergo quod nec sententia principalis eius est vera nec verba nec rationes nec exempla quae inducit sunt vera nec propria nec ad propositum.

[73] Prius ideo ostendo quod nomen aggregato impositum non sit for-
10 mae, nam nomen est vox significativa ad placitum, secundum definitionem nominis datam ab Aristotele, et hoc est quod significat per impositionem rem cui imponitur ex intentione imponentis. Sed nomen impositum aggregato ea ipsa impositione non imponitur formae, licet nova impositione possit imponi et per aequivocationem ad placitum imponen-
15 tis. Igitur nomen aggregati non est nomen formae aliquo modo, cum nomen non sit nomen alicuius, nisi imponatur ad placitum ei cuius debet esse nomen. Ideo omne nomen potest subici et praedicari in oratione pro eo cuius est nomen, ut patet inductive. Sed nomen impositum aggregato, nisi iterum imponatur formae, non potest aliquo modo verificari pro for-
20 ma, ut cum dico, "Homo currit," non verificatur pro anima. Unde non est sensus quod anima currat, ut cum dicitur, "Socrates est homo," non verificatur pro anima. Igitur hoc nomen 'homo' non est nomen animae.

[74] Item, nomen aggregati non habuit respectum ad formam in significando eam, nisi per impositionem et post impositionem factam ag-
25 gregato. Igitur, si nomen aggregati est significativum formae, vel nomen, oportet ad minus quod sit primo et principaliter aggregati et nomen eius, quia unumquodque propter quod, illud magis.

[75] Et hoc allegat pro se Averroes, licet falso, cum dicit, "Quando duo fuerint quorum alterum est causa reliqui, illud quod est causa
30 dignius habebit nomen." Dico igitur quod nomen aggregato impositum non est nomen formae, quia nomen est vox significativa ad placitum, non naturaliter. Sed concedo quod significat formam et similiter materiam tamquam significans naturaliter, quia primo 〈modo〉 signi naturalis nomen aggregati significat formam et materiam. Et secundum hoc non

19 iterum] rationem   21 ut] nec   28 pro] per

[72] This is the judgment of the Commentator. But in the first Part of this work I pointed out in an unrestricted statement that his doctrine is to be rejected by any knowledgeable person for reasons that are clearly certain and because he has destroyed the philosophy of Aristotle.[165] At this point and henceforward I shall become more specific in effectively destroying his opinions, and I shall show that those who adhere to him are basely deceived and are ignorant of the truth [arrived at] by philosophy. I say, therefore, that neither his principal judgment is true nor [his] words nor his reasons, and [that] the examples he uses are neither true nor appropriate or to the point.

[73] Therefore I am pointing out first that a name imposed for a composite would not be [a name] of [its] form, for a name is a vocal sound that signifies at pleasure according to the definition of a name given by Aristotle, and this is that which signifies through imposition the thing for which it is imposed by intent of the one who imposes. But a name imposed for a composite is not imposed for [its] form by that particular imposition, granted it could be imposed [for the form of the composite] by a new imposition and by equivocation at the pleasure of the impositor. Hence the name of a composite is not in some way or other a name of [its] form, since a name is not a name of something unless it be imposed at pleasure for that of which it ought to be a name. Thus every name can be made a subject and be predicated in an expression for that of which it is a name, which follows by induction.[166] But a name imposed for a composite, unless imposed again for [its] form, cannot in any way be verified of [its] form, as when I say "A man runs," [to run] is not legitimately said of a soul. Hence the sense is not that a soul would run, as when "Socrates is a man" is said, [to be a man] is not legitimately said of a soul. Therefore the name 'man' is not the name of a soul.

[74] Again, a name of a composite did not refer to [its] form in signifying it except through an imposition and after an imposition made for the composite. Therefore, if a name or the name of a composite signifies a form, at the very least it must first and principally be [a sign] of the composite and [be] its name, because "whatever exists for something exists more for it than for anything else."[167]

[75] And Averroes alleges this in his own behalf, granted, falsely, when he says, "Whenever there will have been two things of which one is the cause of the other, that which is the cause will more properly bear the name."[168] I say, therefore, that a name imposed for a composite is not a name of [its] form, because a name is a vocal sound that signifies at pleasure, not naturally. But I concede that it signifies form and similarly matter as that which signifies naturally, because a name of a composite signifies [its] form and matter in the first [mode] of a natural sign.[169] And

est nomen, quia ⟨f. 81ra⟩ nomen est vox significativa ad placitum. Et per hoc ulterius patet quod primo et principaliter et proposito ac principali modo significandi in vocibus et nominibus nomen aggregati significat aggregatum, et secundario significantur forma et materia per nomen ag-
5 gregati.

[76] Et ut verba eius reddantur impropria et falsa cum dicit, ''Nomen aggregati est dignius formae,'' addo quod nomen cuilibet rei impositum dignius est eius quam alterius cui non imponitur, ut patet in omnibus nominibus. Et etiam dignius est ut aggregatum habeat nominationem
10 propriam quam ⟨forma⟩ suam, quia quidquid dignitatis est in forma, aggregatum habet, et ultra hoc, materiae dignitatem. Unumquodque sicut se habet ad esse sic ad intellectum, ut Aristoteles dicit primo *Metaphysicae*. Sed aggregatum habet verius esse quam forma, quia praeter esse formae habet esse materiae. Quapropter verius et dignius potest intelligi, quan-
15 tum est a parte sua, igitur et nominari.

[77] Item, quantum est a parte nostra, quia secundum Aristotelis *Priora* et ut experimur, nata est via nobis cognoscendi a confusis ad distincta, et ideo ab aggregato ad formam et materiam. Igitur, cum facilius et citius et melius intelligimus aggregatum, facilius a nobis et
20 verius recipit nomen quam forma.

[78] Item, cum differentiae generales rerum sint ignotae nobis, ut Aristoteles dicit quarto *Meteororum*; sed hae differentiae substantiales sunt formae rerum substantiales, ⟨et⟩ longe minus notae sunt formae quam aggregata.
25 [79] Haec autem omnia convincunt Averroem in hoc quod dicit quod nomen dignius est formae quam compositi, quia non solum mentitur de nomine aggregati, sed de nominatione propria ipsius formae et aggregati, quia dignius est aggregatum nominari quam forma propria denominatione, quam forma sua propria nominatione. Et ideo multo fortius est ag-
30 gregatum dignius suo nomine quam forma nomine aggregati.

[80] Nec Averroistae impedire possunt haec, licet sentiunt cum eo quod forma dat esse aggregato, nam non solum forma dat esse aggregato, sed materia, licet forma plus. Materia enim non nihil est, sed vera natura

11 dignitatem] et; *spatium c. 4 lit. sec.*   16-17 Aristotelis *Priora*] Aristotelem *Priorum*

in this sense it is not a name, for a name is a vocal sound signifying at pleasure. And because of this it further follows that a name of a composite signifies the composite first, principally, by rational intent, and in the principal mode of signification of vocal sounds and names and that form and matter are signified secondarily through the name of a composite.[170]

[76] And that his words may be recognized as improper and false when he says, "The name of a composite is more worthy of [its] form," I add that a name imposed for any thing is more worthy of it than of the other for which it is not imposed, as is clear in [the case of] all names. And it is also more fitting for a composite to have its own proper naming than for [a form to have] its, because a composite has whatever is of worth in a form and beyond this the worth of matter.[171] Just as each thing bears itself in relation to [its] being, [it presents itself] to an intellect in the same way, as Aristotle says in the first [book] of the *Metaphysics*.[172] But a composite has a more complete [type of] being than form, since it has the being of matter in addition to the being of form.[173] Because of this it can more truly and properly be understood, as far as it is concerned, and therefore be named.

[77] Likewise, [the same follows when looked at] from our part, for according to Aristotle's *Prior* [*Analytics*] and as we know from experience there is innate in us a way of knowing [that proceeds] from the confused to the distinct, and thus from a composite to [its] form and matter.[174] Therefore, since we understand a composite more readily, more quickly, and better, it receives a name from us more readily and accurately than [its] form.

[78] Similarly, [this follows] because the general differences of things are unknown to us, as Aristotle says in the fourth [book] of the *Meteorology*; but these substantial differences are the substantial forms of things, [and] forms are far less known than composites.[175]

[79] All these things, however, convict Averroes when he says that a name is more worthy of the form than the composite,[176] because he lies not only about the name of a composite but also about the proper naming of the form itself and the composite, since a composite is more worthy of being named with proper denomination than form, than form with [its own] proper naming.[177] And thus a composite is more worthy of its name with much more justification than [its] form [is worthy] of the name of a composite.

[80] Nor can the Averroists prevent these [conclusions] since they agree with him that form gives being to a composite, for not only does form give being to a composite but [so does] matter, granted form [gives being] more. For matter is not nothing, but true nature and essence, hav-

et essentia, habens esse suae essentiae. Et ideo cum cedat in essentiam
compositi, essentia compositi et esse eius dependent essentialiter a
materia, licet forte magis a forma.

[81] Cum autem arguit Averroes quod nomen debetur aggregato
5 secundum quod est in actu, sed est in actu per formam, ergo nomen
debetur formae et magis, quia est causa esse actualis, nam cum aliquid
debetur duobus quorum unum est causa reliqui, magis debetur causae
quam causato, dicendum est quod vile sophisma facit, quia non debetur
alicui rei propter eius esse actuale, nec propter causam illius esse, quia
10 tunc naturaliter significaret. Sed debetur cuilibet rei non ex se, sed ex
voluntate instituentis, quia nomen est vox significativa ad placitum. Et
ideo, licet forma sit causa rei, et materia similiter, non sunt causa
nominationis compositi, nec nominationis propriae, sed liberum ar-
bitrium imponentis nomen secundum suae beneplacitum voluntatis.

15 [82] Quod etiam inducit exemplum de calido in igne, et in aliis calidis.
Licet exemplum verum sit secundum se, tamen nihil est ad propositum,
et falso applicatur. Concedendum enim est quod nomen calidi dignius et
principalius dicitur de calido in igne quam de aliis calidis, quorum
caliditatis ignis causa est. Sed hoc nihil est utile ad propositum Commen-
20 tatoris, quia nomen aggregati non causatur a forma, sed a beneplacito instituentis. Nec hoc nomen habet comparationem aliquam ad formam
ante impositionem factam aggregato, sed solum per impositionem factam
aggregato et secundario. Propter quod forma, si participat aliquo modo
nomen aggregati, habebit hoc ab aggregato et non e converso. Et tamen
25 forma non participabit nomen aggregati, ut dicatur nomen eius ad
placitum, et ideo non in ratione nominis, quod est vox significans ad
placitum. Sed solum erit ⟨signum⟩ eius tamquam vox significativa
naturaliter primo modo signi naturalis, ut saepe dictum est. Sic igitur
patet insania Averrois et multiplex eius fatuitas, quae stultos cogit multi-
30 pliciter in errorem.

[83] Nunc ⟨f. 81rb⟩ in fine istius capituli innuo et excito lectorem, ut
consideret qualiter vox significet multa in figurativis locutionibus, quibus
maxime sacer textus plenus est, cum praeter sensum literalem potest vox
significare tres alios sensus, scilicet, allegoricum et tropologicum et
35 anagogicum. Sed haec consideratio propria est in tertio tractatu qui ap-
propriatur textui sacro; similiter quomodo sacramenta significant, et alia

---

19 utile] simile   33 plenus] plenius

ing the being of its essence.[178] And thus when it plays its part in the essence of a composite, the essence of a composite and its being depend essentially on matter, granted more thoroughly on form.

[81] Averroes, moreover, argues that a name belongs to a composite inasmuch as [the latter] is in act; but it is in act through form; therefore the name belongs to a form all the more because it is the cause of actual being: when something belongs to two things of which one is a cause of the other, it belongs more to the cause than to that which is caused.[179] [To this] it must be said that he engages in a vile sophism, because [a name] does not belong to any thing because of its actual being, nor because of the cause of that being, for then it would signify naturally. But it belongs to some thing not of itself but in virtue of the will of the one who institutes it, because a name is a vocal sound that signifies at pleasure. And hence, granted that form be a cause of a thing, and matter likewise, they are not a cause of the naming of a composite nor of the proper naming. Rather, [the cause is] the free will of the one imposing the name in accord with the good pleasure of his own will.[180]

[82] He also introduces the example of heat in fire and in other hot things.[181] Granted the example be true in itself, yet it offers no support for his claim and it is inaccurately applied, for one must concede that the name of a hot thing is more appropriately and more principally said of heat in fire than of other hot things of whose heat fire is the cause. This is not like the Commentator's claim because the name of a composite is not caused by a form but by the good pleasure of the one who institutes it. Nor does this name have any relation to a form before imposition for the composite, but only through an imposition made for the composite and secondarily. Because of this a form, if it shares in some way in the name of a composite, will do this through the composite and not conversely. And yet a form will not share in the name of a composite to the effect that [the name of the composite] would be said [to be] its name at pleasure, and thus not as a name, which is a vocal sound that signifies at pleasure. But it will only be [a sign] of it as a vocal sound that signifies naturally in the first mode of a natural sign, as has often been stated. In this way, therefore, is made clear the madness of Averroes and his multifaceted nonsense which drives foolish ones in many ways into error.

[83] Now at the end of this chapter I alert and summon the reader to consider how a vocal sound signifies many things in figurative expressions, of which the holy text is full, since besides a literal sense a vocal sound can signify three other senses, namely, an allegorical and tropological and anagogical.[182] But this consideration is appropriate for the third treatise which is reserved for the sacred text; likewise, how sacraments and other signs in the sacred text signify. However, let him

signa sacri textus. Advertat tamen prudens considerator et inveniet quod secundus modus signi naturalis in his specialiter operetur.

who would prudently consider these things be aware and he will discover that the second mode of a natural sign is especially operative in them.[183]

CAPITULUM QUARTUM

[84] *Capitulum quartum primae distinctionis duo principia logicae et meta-physicae exponit, scilicet, quod vox non potest significare aliquid commune enti et non enti, et quod vox imposita possit cadere a sua significatione.*

5   [85] His praedictis adnexa sunt principia duo communia metaphysicae et logicae maxime necessaria, propter quorum ignoran-tiam gravissimi errores contingunt in tota disputatione tam theologica quam philosophica. Primum istorum est quod vox non potest significare aliquid commune univocum enti et non enti, licet huius contrarium sit

10 vulgatum, et obstinate gaudeat multitudo studentium hoc errore. Secun-dum est magis necessarium, scilicet, quod vox potest cadere a sua significatione, cuius contrario non solum obstinate sed obstinatissime omnes fere detinentur, ut fingant non solum errores innumerabiles, sed haereses detestandas. Ex ignorantia istorum duorum problematum tenet

15 multitudo quod Caesar mortuus sit homo, et quod homo mortuus sit animal, et quod Christus in triduo fuit homo, et alia infinita falsissima et stultissima circa restrictiones et ampliationes in propositionibus, et circa necessitates et contingentias et alia, de quibus omnibus disputandum est per ordinem suis locis. Et duobus modis procedam pro veritatibus

20 stabiliendis, probando, scilicet, quod verum est, et dando oppositum, omnia volo solvere quae possunt obici in hac parte. Nam in his erroribus maxime vigent auctoritas fragilis et indigna, et consuetudo longa, et sen-sus damnabilis multitudinis stultae, quae sunt causae errorum omnium in vita et studio, sicut copiose et efficaciter declaratum est in prima parte

25 huius operis et probatum est.
    [86] Et optime novi pessimum et stultissimum istorum errorum ⟨auc-torem⟩, qui vocatus est Richardus Cornubiensis, famossissimus apud stultam multitudinem. Sed apud sapientes fuit insanus et reprobatus Parisius propter errores quos invenerat ⟨et⟩ promulgaverat quando

30 solemniter legebat *Sententias* ibidem, postquam legerat *Sententias* Oxoniae ab anno Domini 1250. Ab illo mccl. igitur tempore remansit multitudo in huius magistri erroribus usque nunc, scilicet, per quadraginta annos et amplius, et maxime invalescit Oxoniae, sicut ibidem incepit haec demen-tia infinita.

---

14 haereses] haerese   18 contingentias] contingendas   26 errorum] errorem   27 Cornu-biensis] Cornibiensis   28 insanus] insanis   30 legerat] legeret

[CHAPTER FOUR]

[84] *The fourth chapter of the first distinction sets forth two principles of metaphysics and logic, namely, that a vocal sound cannot signify something common to an entity and a nonentity and that an imposed vocal sound would be able to fall away from its signification.* [184]

[85] To the preceding are coupled two extremely important principles common to metaphysics and logic, because of lack of awareness of which the most serious errors occur in all the types of disputation, both theological and philosophical. The first of these is that a vocal sound cannot signify something univocally common to an entity and a nonentity, granted its contrary be widespread and the student horde obstinately rejoices in the error. [185] The second is more important, namely, that a vocal sound can fall away from its signification, by the contrary of which practically all are held bound not only obstinately but very obstinately [and] with the effect that they fabricate not only innumerable errors but [also] heresies that ought to be detested. Because of ignorance in regard to these two problems the multitude holds that dead Caesar is a man, that a dead man is an animal, and that Christ was a man during the three days [in the tomb], and [it holds] another unlimited number of false and very foolish things about restriction and ampliation in propositions and about necessities and contingencies and other things, all of which are to be disputed in an orderly way in their proper places. [186] And I shall proceed in two ways to establish the truth, [i.e.,] I wish to resolve all things that can be objected in this Part by proving what is true and presenting the opposite. For weak and unworthy authority, time-honored custom, and the damnable opinion of the foolish multitude thrive on these errors, [all of] which are the causes of all errors in life and scholarship, as has been copiously and effectively pointed out in the first Part of this work and has been proven. [187]

[86] And I knew well the worst and most foolish [author] of these errors, who was called Richard of Cornwall, a very famous one among the foolish multitude. [188] But to those who knew, he was insane and [had been] reproved at Paris for the errors which he had invented [and] promulgated when lecturing solemnly on the *Sentences* there, after he had lectured on the *Sentences* at Oxford from the year of the Lord 1250. [189] From that [year of] 1250 up till now the multitude has remained in the errors of this master, i.e., for forty years and more, and it is currently gaining strength at Oxford, just where this unlimited madness began.

[87] *Prologum igitur istum praemisi ante distinctionem istorum problematum cum suis corollariis propter maximas stultitias, non solum per disputationem evacuandas, sed prius in prooemio denuntiandas, fore dignissimas detestari.*

[88] Primo igitur ostendo quod nomen non potest significare aliquid
5 commune univocum enti et non enti, sive praesenti, praeterito, et futuro. Aristoteles enim dicit secundo *Metaphysicae* quod nihil est commune praeterito et futuro et ei quod habet potentiam iam essendi, hoc est, rei praesenti; nec aliqua definitio communis est eis.

[89] Item, ubi non est convenientia relata, impossibile est quod sit ab-
10 soluta; sed entis ad non ens non est comparatio, ut Aristoteles dicit capitulo de vacuo; igitur non convenient in aliquo absoluto nec communi eis.

[90] Item, illud commune futurum aut est ens aut non ens, quia de quolibet affirmatio vel negatio. Si vero sit ens, non conveniet non enti; si
15 vero sit non ens, non conveniet enti; igitur non est commune.

[91] Item, illud commune, si est sic, cum declinat in ⟨f. 81va⟩ praeteritum, non est; similiter, cum in futurum descendit, non est; igitur solum ⟨est⟩ dum est in presenti, quapropter erit tantum commune praesentibus.

20 [92] Item, illa quae distant infinita distantia et diversimode non possunt convenire in aliquo; sed ens et non ens sunt huiusmodi, quia superare hanc distantiam non potest nisi potentia infinita, ut in creatione quae fit a nihilo in aliquid; igitur, etc.

[93] Item, plus conveniunt omnia entia quam ens et non ens; sed nihil
25 potest esse commune univocum x predicamentis quae dividunt ens aequivoce vel analogice; igitur multo fortius nec poterit aliquid esse commune univocum enti et non enti.

[94] Item, plus distat et differt Creator a nihilo quam a creatura; sed nihil commune univocum est Creatori et creaturae; igitur nec enti et non
30 enti.

[95] Item, plus conveniunt materia et forma et compositum quam ens et non ens; sed nihil est commune univocum istis tribus, sed aequivoce, scilicet, hoc nomen 'substantia' quod praedicatur de his tribus; cuius probatio erit quod substantia praedicata de his non est genus

---

1-3 *Prologum...detestari.*] *In margine alia manu scribitur:* Id quod hic scribitur minio est litera et non rubrica.   16 est] esse   22 superare] super   25 ens] en   28 nihilo] uo   33 quod] qui

[87] *I have therefore first set forth this Prologue before a division of these problems with their corollaries because of the excessive follies which ought not only be eliminated through disputation but first be decried in a Prologue so that they may be highly worthy of being detested.*

[88] First, therefore, I show that a name cannot signify anything univocally common to an entity and a nonentity, whether present, past, or future. For Aristotle says in the second [book] of the *Metaphysics* that nothing is common to a past and future thing and to that which already has the power of being, that is, to a thing present; nor is there any definition common to them.[190]

[89] Likewise, where there is no relational agreement it is impossible that there be an absolute one; but there is no comparison between an entity and a nonentity, as Aristotle says in a chapter on the void; therefore they do not agree in something absolute or common to them.[191]

[90] Similarly, that future common thing is either an entity or a nonentity, because of anything [there is] either affirmation or denial. If indeed it is an entity, it will not agree with a nonentity; but if it is a nonentity, it will not agree with an entity; therefore it is not common.

[91] Again, that common thing, if it is such, does not exist when it fades into the past; likewise, it does not exist when it moves into the future; therefore it only [is] while it exists in the present, [and] for this reason it will be common only to things present.

[92] Similarly, those things which are distant [from each other] by an infinite distance and in [an infinite number of] different ways cannot agree in something; but an entity and a nonentity are such because [nothing] but an infinite power can overcome this distance, as [happens] in creation which comes about [through a transition] from nothing into something; therefore, etc.

[93] Again all entities agree more [among themselves] than an entity and a nonentity; but nothing can be univocally common to the ten predicaments which divide being equivocally or analogically; therefore with all the more reason will something not be able to be univocally common to an entity and a nonentity.[192]

[94] Likewise, the Creator is more distant and different from nothing than from a creature; but there is nothing univocally common to the Creator and a creature; therefore neither to an entity and a nonentity.[193]

[95] Similarly, matter, form, and a composite are more in agreement than an entity and a nonentity; but there is nothing univocally common to these three, though [there is something] equivocaly [common], i.e., the name 'substance' which is predicated of these three.[194] The proof of this will be that substance predicated of these is not the most general

generalissimum, quia illud erit compositum ex materia et forma, sicut Boethius dicit super *Praedicamenta*, et Augustinus similiter in commentario suo super *Praedicamenta* Aristotelis, et hoc satis patebit inferius; igitur multo minus erit aliquid commune enti et non enti.

5   [96] Item, quia maxime inconvenienter fingunt quod 'Caesar' significat aliquid commune enti et non enti, et univoce, et una impositione, arguo: hoc nomen 'Caesar' non potest significare aliquid commune univocum pluribus Caesaribus existentibus nec univoce nec unica impositione, sed pluribus impositionibus et aequivoce, ut patet omnibus; igitur multo minus erit hoc nomen 'Caesar' commune enti et non enti univoce.

[97] Sed tamen quaerunt subterfugia diversa, et loco rationis falsas cavillationes inducunt, dicentes quod nomen imponitur essentiae rei, abstrahendo ab omni differentia temporis. Sed hoc patet materialiter esse falsum, quia omnia nomina quae imponimus rebus imponimus ut sunt praesentia nobis, ut de nominibus hominum in baptismo. Et similiter quando imponimus nomina animalibus, fertur intentio nostra ad rem presentem nobis, ut manifestum est consideranti. Numquam enim homines, quando imponunt nomina infantibus vel animalibus suis, respiciunt nisi ad res praesentes sensui, et ideo non abstrahunt a presenti tempore, nec ab esse actuali. Propterea potest obici sicut prius quaerendo an sit ens, et tunc non conveniet non enti.

[98] Item, essentia praeterita non est essentia, sicut nec essentia mortua vel homo mortuus. Similiter nec essentia futura est essentia, sicut nec essentia in potentia vel ens in potentia, quia hoc est secundum quid, et ideo non infert essentiam simpliciter. Igitur sola essentia praesens sub esse actuali est essentia; igitur, si nomen significat essentiam, significat ⟨eam⟩ praesentem sub esse actuali.

[99] Sed ad hoc cavillant dicentes quod nomen significat rem sub esse essentiae, quod non est esse actuale, sed commune praesenti, praeterito ac futuro. Contra quod procedendum sicut contra essentiam, quia commune essentiae non est sine essentia, et ideo quaerendum est ab eis an res sub isto esse sit aliquid vel nihil, sicut prius. Et res sub isto esse, si est praeterita, nihil est; si est futura, similiter nihil est; igitur solum erit praesens si est quod est in esse actuali. Et planum est quod nomina im-

---

8 Caesaribus] Caesar ibi scilicet || unica] univoca   30 quod] quae   31-32 commune] communi

genus because that will be a composite of matter and form, as Boethius says [in his commentary] on the *Predicaments* and similarly Augustine in his commentary on the *Predicaments* of Aristotle, and this will become sufficiently clear below. Therefore much less will there be something univocally common to an entity and a nonentity.[195]

[96] Again, because they most inappropriately imagine that 'Caesar' signifies both univocally and by one imposition something common to an entity and a nonentity I argue: the name 'Caesar' cannot signify something univocally common to many existing Caesars, neither univocally nor by one imposition, but by many and equivocally, as is clear to all; therefore much less will this name 'Caesar' be univocally common to an entity and nonentity.

[97] But, however, they seek various subterfuges, and in place of reason introduce false quibbles saying that a name is imposed for the essence of a thing, abstracting from every difference of time.[196] Yet this surfaces to be materially false because all the names which we impose for things we impose inasmuch as they are present to us, as [in the case of] names of people in Baptism. And similarly, when we impose names for animals, our intent is directed to a thing present to us, as is clear to one who considers [these cases]. For people, when they impose names for infants or animals, never regard [anything] but things present to the senses and thus do not abstract from present time nor actual being.[197] Because of this it can be objected as before, asking whether [the essence of the thing for which a name is said to be imposed] be an entity, and [if the answer is "Yes,"], then it will not agree with a nonentity.

[98] Again, a past essence is not an essence just as a dead essence [is] not [an essence] or a dead man [a man]. Similarly, a future essence is not an essence just as neither is an essence in potency or an entity in potency, for this exists [only] in a certain sense and thus does not infer essence [taken] simply.[198] Therefore, only a present essence under actual being is an essence, [and] therefore, if a name signifies an essence, it signifies [one] present under actual being.

[99] But they quibble about this, saying that a name signifies a thing under a being of [its] essence which is not actual being but [being] common to the present, past, and future. Against this one must proceed as [was argued] against essence [considered in abstraction from being] because [that which is] common to essence is not without essence, and hence it must be asked of them whether the thing under this being is something or nothing, as [was asked] before.[199] And the thing under this being, if it is a past thing, it is nothing; if it is a future thing, likewise it is nothing; therefore it will only be a present thing if it is that which is in actual being. And it is clear that names are imposed for infants and all

ponuntur infantibus et omnibus sub esse praesenti. Et etiam esse actuale
aut erit idem quod essentia, ut aliqui concedunt, aut erit propria passio
essentiae, ut alii sentiunt. Sed impossibile est quod essentia sit sub esse
essentiae, nisi concomitetur esse actuale et praesens; quia si est idem cum
5 essentia aut concomitans ⟨illam⟩ sicut propria passio, manifestum est
quod non potest essentia sine illo esse manere, et ideo essentia semper est
praesens sub esse actuali.

[100] Item, essentia in rebus compositis fit ex vera unione materiae
cum forma, ut patet in homine et individuis eius et in animalibus et aliis
10 similiter; igitur, cum non sit unio materiae cum forma, non est essentia
compositionis. Quapropter, cum anima separatur a corpore, vel pereat,
non erit essentia talis rei. Igitur, cum in morte separatur ⟨f. 81vb⟩ anima
a corpore, vel in brutis corrumpatur—et in aliis rebus forma corrumpi-
tur—non manebit, nec erit essentia nec esse essentiae. Et ideo insaniunt
15 qui dicunt Caesarem esse vel hominem, anima a corpore separata.

[101] Sed cum mendacia multiplicantur semper, et iterum fingunt
unum esse quod numquam a philosophia nec a sapientibus fuit inventum
nec receptum, et dicunt illud esse habituale. Et hoc dicunt esse commune
praesenti, praeterito, et futuro, et commune enti actualiter et non enti ac-
20 tualiter. Nec intelligunt quid dicunt, nec sciunt dicere quid sit hoc esse,
sed ob hoc solum fingunt ut evadant et sermone contradicant veritati.
Arguendum est igitur contra hoc esse fictum sicut prius: res vel essentia
habens tale esse aut est ens aut non ens, et sic ultra sicut prius. Et iterum,
cum est praeterita, non est futura vel praesens; et ideo solum erit ens, et
25 artabitur ad ens tantum et esse actuale. Item, possumus arguere contra
eos ex propriis philosophiae, et auctoritate Aristotelis secundo *De anima*,
ubi vult quod habitus est actus primus et forma; igitur esse habituale est a
forma praesente in materia; igitur in separatione vel corruptione formae
a materia non erit esse habituale; et ideo nec homo nec Caesar habet esse
30 habituale postquam anima separata est a corpore.

[102] Item, adhuc insaniunt contra veritatem dicentes quod 'ens' participium licet significet esse praesens et esse actuale in praeterito, tamen
'ens' nomen significat abstracte ab esse actuali et cum communitate
quadam ad ens et non ens actu. Et contra hoc procedendum est sicut

2 essentia] essentiae || concedunt aut] concedunt et   3 Sed] cor quod   9 ut] et
15 Caesarem] cessarem   21 sermone] *spatium c. 5 lit. seq.*   29 habet] hunc
31-32 participium] parcipium

things under present being. And also, actual being either will be the same as essence, as some contend, or it will be a proper passion of essence, as others believe. But it is impossible that an essence be under the being of [this] essence unless (the essence) accompany actual and present being; because if (actual being) is one with an essence or accompanies [it] as [its] proper passion, it is clear that an essence cannot remain without it, and hence an essence is always present under actual being.[200]

[100] Again, essence in composites arises from a true union of matter with form, as is the case with [the universal nature] man and its individuals and with animals and other things likewise; hence, when there would be no union of mater with form, there is no essence [resulting from] composition. For this reason when a soul is separated from [its] body, or should it perish, there will be no essence of such a thing. Therefore, when a soul is separated in death, or should it corrupt in the case of brutes—and form corrupts in other things—it will not remain and there will be neither an essence nor the being of an essence. And hence they are insane who say that Caesar exists or [that he is] a man once [his] soul has separated from [his] body.[201]

[101] But since lies are always multiplied, they again fabricate a type of being which was never discovered or accepted by philosophy nor by people of wisdom, and they say that it is habitual. This, they say, is common to the present, past, and future and common through act to an entity and through act to a nonentity. They neither understand what they are saying nor do they know how to say what this being is, and because of this they simply fabricate [it] so as to escape and contradict truth with their words. One must argue against this fictional [type of] being just as before: a thing or essence having such being either is an entity or [is] a nonentity, and so on, as before.[202] And again, when it is a past [thing or essence], it is not [a future] or a present one; and thus it will only be an entity and will be restricted only to an entity and to actual being.[203] Likewise, we can argue against them on the basis of [principles] proper to philosophy and on the authority of Aristotle in the second [book] of *On the Soul* where he indicates that habit is first act and form; therefore habitual being is from form present in matter; therefore in the separation or corruption of form [respectively] from [or] by matter there will be no habitual being; and thus neither man nor Caesar have habitual being after the soul is separated from the body.[204].

[102] Similarly, they still rave against truth when they say that, granted the participle 'being' would signify present being and actual being in the past, nevertheless the name 'being' signifies in abstraction from actual being and with some kind of communality in act with an entity and a nonentity.[205] And against this one must proceed as before: either

prius: aut illud commune est ens aut non ens, et patet processus. Item, si
illud est praeteritum vel futurum, nihil est; igitur tantum significabit
praesens. Item, ex participiis potest argui contra hoc, quoniam nomen et
participium non differunt in re significata sed in modo significandi, ut
5 dicit Priscianus, ut 'amans illius' nomen est ⟨et⟩ 'amans illum' est participium. Et ideo eamdem rem significant, propter quod res significata
per hoc nomen 'amans' et per hoc participium 'amans' eadem est, et ideo
similiter de 'ente'.

[103] Quapropter, si 'ens' participium significat rem praesentem et
10 actualem, et hoc nomen 'ens' similiter, his reprobatis patet quod esse in
potentia vel in aptitudine non possunt allegari, licet aliqui stulti evadant
verba stultorum. Sed sapientes sciunt quod esse in aptitudine non est
esse, ut caecus aptus natus est ad videndum, non tamen potest dici quod
videt; sed eius contradictorium non est verum. Similiter, esse in potentia
15 vere non est, quia indiget producente ipsum in esse, ut "Filius est in
potentia, igitur non est." Sed adhuc cavillant de esse habitudinis, sed hoc
in propositione habet locum, et ideo destruetur postea, cum de propositionibus fiet sermo.

[104] Mira igitur fatuitas est puram et planam veritatem contemnere
20 gratis, et declinare ex maxima superbia ad stultissimas falsitates. Ad oppositum pro eis sunt fantasticae eorum praedicationes quae, in quantum
destructae sunt, pertinent ad priorem partem problematis, sed, in quantum solutae sunt, pertinent ad secundam.

[105] Sed tamen aliquae cavillationes sunt rationabiles, et solvi pos-
25 sunt veraciter. Una est quod nomen significat sine tempore, ut
Aristoteles dicit; igitur abstrahit a praesenti, praeterito, et futuro. Dicendum quod hoc est quantum ad modum significandi, non quantum ad
rem, ut impossibilia et vacuum et infinitum et talia. Sic possumus im-
ponere illis nomina, sed alia impositione et alia quam illa quae entibus
30 fit, et aequivoce; ut 'Caesar' potest per novam impositionem significare
Caesarem praeteritum vel futurum vel mortuum, sed aequivoce enti et
non enti.

[106] Item, Aristoteles dicit in libro *Perihermenias* quod a praedicato
privativo vel a nomine infinito sequitur nomen negativum, ut "Est
35 iniustum vel non iustum; igitur non est ⟨iustum⟩," licet non e converso.
Igitur, cum dicit quod bene sequitur "Hic est iniustus; igitur non est

7 eadem est] idem significat   8 similiter] sumiter   15 vere] vera   17 propositione] pro-
nomine ‖ ideo] non   20 falsitates] falli; *spatium c. 11 lit. seq.*   21 praedicationes quae]
praedicatione quod   25 sine tempore] sive rem   28 et vacuum] ut vacuum

that which is common is an entity or [it is] a nonentity, and the procedure is clear. Again, if it is a past or future thing, it is nothing; therefore it, [a name], will only signify a present thing. Likewise, it can be argued against this [insane theory] on the basis of [the signification of] participles since a name and a participle do not differ in the thing signified but in the way they signify [it], as Priscian says, 'amans illius' is a name [and] 'amans illum' is a participle. And thus they signify the same thing, because of which the thing signified through the name 'amans' and through the participle 'amans' is the same thing, and thus similarly in regard to 'being' [which is both a name and a participle].[206]

[103] Wherefore, if the participle 'being' signifies a present and actual thing, and the name 'being' likewise, it is clear in regard to these reprobates that potential or aptitudinal being cannot be alleged, granted some foolish ones travel on the words of the foolish.[207] But those who are wise know that aptitudinal being is not being. For example, a blind man is born with a capacity for seeing, yet it cannot be said that he sees; but the contradictory of this is not true.[208] Similarly, potential being does not really exist, because it needs something producing it into being, as [can be seen in the inference] "A son is in potency; therefore he does not exist." Yet they still quibble about habitual being, but this [issue] has its place in [a discussion of] propositions and will thus be destroyed later when there will be talk of propositions.[209]

[104] It is therefore a strange foolishness to hold pure and plain truth freely in contempt and to fall from excessive pride into very foolish errors. In opposition to them are their fanciful predications which, inasmuch as they have been destroyed, pertain to the first part of the problem, but, inasmuch as they have been resolved, pertain to the second.[210]

[105] But yet some quibbles are reasonable and can be truthfully resolved. One is that a name signifies without time, as Aristotle says; therefore it abstracts from the present, past, and future.[211] [In response] it must be said that this is [the case] in regard to [its] mode of signifying, not in regard to the thing [signified], as [can be seen when one considers things like] impossibles, the void, an infinite, and the like.[212] Thus we can impose names for them, but [only] by another imposition and one other than that which occurs for entities, and [when we do this, we impose names] equivocally. For example, through a new imposition 'Caesar' can signify a past, future, or a dead Ceasar, but [it signifies] an entity and a nonentity equivocally.[213]

[106] Again, Aristotle says in [his] book On Interpretation that a negative name follows from a privative predicate or from an infinite name, as [in] "It is unjust or not-just; therefore it is not [just]," granted the converse [does] not [follow].[214] Therefore when he says "This man is

iustus," et non sequitur, "Homo non est iustus; igitur est iniustus vel
non iustus," oportet quod 'homo' sit commune enti et non ⟨enti⟩ sicut
'non esse iustum'; vel oportet quod consequentia teneat, "Homo non est
iustus ⟨f. 82ra⟩; igitur est iniustus." Rationalis vero est haec obiectio,
5 quam cum sequente inveni ante quadraginta ⟨annos⟩ quando difficultatis huius ⟨solutionem⟩ ventilavi. Dicendum est igitur quod duplici
de causa potest intelligi quod non sequitur a negativo praedicato ad infinitum vel privativum: aut quia terminus subiectus tali praedicato
negativo sumitur commune enti et non enti univoce, et hoc est falsum,
10 vel quod subiectus ⟨terminus⟩ potest aequivoce significare ens et non
ens, sive quod subiectum potest esse ens vel non ens. Quod in idem redit,
quia praedicatum est commune enti et non enti propter negationem esse
sub tali praedicato, quia negatio plus tollit quam affirmatio affirmet, ut
'non esse iustum'. Propter quod potest dici de Sorte existente quod non
15 est iustus, si est iniustus, et de Sorte mortuo quod non est iustus, sed non
quod sit iustus. Similiter, de homine vivo potest dici quod non sit iustus,
si est iniustus; et de homine mortuo quod non est iustus. Et ideo hoc
nomen 'homo' vel 'Sortes' sumatur aequivoce pro homine ente et non
ente; vel 'Sortes' oratio est multiplex pro ente et non ente, et aequivoce,
20 non univoce, nec unica impositione. Quoniam praedicatum negativum
potest verificari de subiecto aliquo ente et de alio non ente, numquam
tamen sequitur ex hoc, quod de eodem subiecto et univoco praedicetur,
⟨nec⟩ quod sit univoce commune enti et non enti, sed aequivoce.

[107] Item, argui potest sic per hoc quod Aristoteles loquitur de
25 subalternis in libro praedicto. Dicit enim, "Aliquis est pulcher,"
"Aliquis non est pulcher," et negativam probat dupliciter dicens, "Si
enim est foedus, non est pulcher," et "Quod fit pulchrum non est
pulchrum, quia quod fit non est." Similiter: aliquid fit, ut domus per
artem, ut homo vel animal in generatione naturali; igitur aliquid non est;
30 et constat quod aliquid est; igitur hae sunt verae, "Aliquid est,"
"Aliquid non est."

[108] Magna videtur perplexitas eo quod hoc videatur sequi ex dictis
Aristotelis. Sed tamen non dicit hoc, nec loquitur de his subcontrariis,
"Aliquid est," "Aliquid non est," sed videntur posse assumi per simile

---

5 annos] q; *spatium c. 4 lit. seq.*   10 subiectus] subiectum   11 subiectum] subiectus terminus   14 Sorte] Socrate   17 ideo] si *add.*   20 negativum] necessarium   27 fit pulchrum]
sit pulchrum   28 fit non] sit non ‖ aliquid fit] aliquis sit   30 quod] per

unjust; therefore he is not just" correctly follows and that "A man is not just; therefore he is unjust or not-just" does not follow, [either] it is necessary that 'man' be [taken as] common to an entity and a non[entity], as [is likewise the case with] 'not to be just', or it is necessary that [this] consequence hold: "A man is not just; therefore he is unjust."[215] But this objection is reasonable which, along with the following, I came across forty [years] ago when I aired [the solution] to this difficulty.[216] It must be said, therefore, that for two reasons it can be understood that an infinite or privative does not follow from a negative: either because a term subject to that kind of a negative predicate is taken [to signify something] univocally common to an entity and a nonentity, and this is false, or because the subject [term] can equivocally signify an entity and a nonentity, or because the subject is able to be an entity or a nonentity. [And] this results in the same thing since the predicate [in "A man is not just"] is common to an entity and a nonentity because of the denial of being under such a predicate, since a denial takes away more than an affirmation would affirm, as [is seen in] "not to be just."[217] Because of this it can be said of an existing Sortes that he is not just, if he is unjust, and of a dead Sortes that he is not just, but not that he be just. Similarly, it can be said of a living man that he is not just, if he is unjust, and of a dead man that he is not just. And thus would the name 'man' or 'Sortes' be taken equivocally for man the entity or nonentity, or, [to put it another way], 'Sortes' is an ambiguous expression for an entity and a nonentity, and [it is this] equivocally, not univocally, nor by one imposition.[218] While a negative predicate can be verified of a subject entity and of another nonentity, nevertheless it never follows from this that it may be predicated of the same subject and univocally, [nor] that it be univocally common to an entity and a nonentity, but [that it may be predicated] equivocally.

[107] Again, one can argue in this way on the basis of what Aristotle says of subalternates in the previously mentioned book.[219] He says, "Some [man] is handsome," "Some [man] is not handsome," and he proves the negative [proposition] in two ways when he says, "For if he is ugly, he is not handsome" and "What is coming to be handsome is not [yet] handsome, because what is coming to be is not."[220] Similarly [one could argue]: something is coming to be, like a house through art [or] like a man or an animal in natural generation; therefore something does not exist; and [yet] it is a fact that something is; therefore these two [subcontraries] are true: "Something exists," "Something does not exist."[221]

[108] There seems to be great confusion because this would seem to follow from Aristotle's words. And yet he does not say this nor does he speak of these subcontraries, "Something exists" [and] "Something does

ex hoc dicto, "Quod fit non est, sed aliquid fit; igitur aliquid non est." Et
ideo dicendum quod haec est falsa, "Aliquid non est," quia 'aliquid'
sumptum simpliciter significat ens in actu, et sic non significat ens in
potentia. Et ideo similiter haec est falsa, "Aliquid fit," quia simpliciter
5 sumptum dicit ens actu; sed ens actu est iam in facto esse; quapropter
falsa est haec "Aliquid non est."

[109] Si dicatur quod addiscens aliquam scientiam non solum est in
potentia sciens sed quodam modo actu, ut Aristoteles vult nono
Metaphysicae, dicendum est secundum partem aliquam vel aliquas potest
10 habere scientiam, secundum partem sed non totam. Nec denominabitur
sciens talem scientiam, ut, licet aliquis puer didicerit alphabetum, et
sciverit ipsum, non tamen scit grammaticam nec dicitur grammaticus,
sed dicetur in potentia scire grammaticam. Et est potentia essentialis,
quae indiget agente et generante scientiam in puero. Et ideo non dicetur
15 actu grammaticus sed in potentia, quia est in fieri; et quod sit hoc modo
non est in facto esse, nec in actu.

[110] Si dicatur quod motus et tempus sunt vere aliquid, et constat
quod non sunt aliquid nisi in fieri, sed quod fit non est, igitur aliquid non
est, dicendum quod esse in fieri est dupliciter: vel quod tendit in factum
20 esse ut sit permanens in actuali esse, et sic quod fit non est; aliter dicitur
esse in fieri quod non requirit aliud esse quam fieri, sicut successiva, et
tale fieri non tollit esse debitum talibus rebus. Sed de his rebus est multiplex difficultas de quibus non est ad praesens inquirendum.

[111] Ex hac igitur radice patet quod non potest homo esse animal,
25 nullo homine existente, nec Caesar poterit esse homo, quia nomina
huiusmodi significant essentias rerum praesentes et actuales, ⟨et⟩ quia
nomen ⟨non⟩ significat aliquid commune praesenti, praeterito, et futuro.
Sed tamen multas alias cavillationes fingunt circa huiusmodi propositiones, et faciam rationabiles ⟨responsus⟩ cum veniam ad propositiones per
30 leges necessariarum propositionum et per se verarum. Sed in tantum dictum sit nunc de hac radice.

3-4 ens in potentia] ens ens in potentia   5 facto] sicō   22-24 multiplex...animal] *in mar-*
gine eadem manu

not exist,'' but they seem to be able to be assumed because of [their] similarity to this saying: "What is coming to be does not exist; but something is coming to be; therefore something does not exist." And thus it must be said that this is false, "Something does not exist," because 'something', taken simply, signifies an entity in act, and thus it does not signify an entity in potency.[222] And thus likewise this is false, "Something is coming to be," because ['something'] taken simply, bespeaks an entity in act; but an entity in act is already in completed being; wherefore this is false, "Something does not exist."[223]

[109] If it be said that one who is learning some science not only is one who is knowledgeable in potency but [also one who is] in a certain sense actually [knowledgeable], as Aristotle intends in the ninth [book] of the *Metaphysics*, it must be said that he has partial knowledge, partial but not total.[224] Nor is he denominated one who knows such a science, as [in the case where], granted, some boy would have learned the alphabet and known it, he does not, however, know grammar nor is he said [to be] a grammarian, but will be said to know grammar potentially. And the potency is [the type called] essential, that which requires something acting and generating knowledge in the boy. And thus he will not be said [to be] actually a grammarian but [one] in potency, because he is in [a state of] coming to be [a grammarian]; and what exists in this way is not in completed being nor [is it] in act.

[110] If it be said that motion and time are truly something, and it is a fact that they are not something [except that which is] in [a state of] coming to be, but what is coming to be does not exist, therefore something does not exist, it must be said that there are two ways of being in [a state of] coming to be: either that which is tending toward completed being in order to be permanent in actual being, and in this sense what is coming to be does not exist; otherwise that is said to be in [a state of] coming to be which does not require any being other than coming to be, like successives, and this way of coming to be does not remove the being proper to such things.[225] But there are many difficulties with these things about which one ought not inquire at the present.[226]

[111] From this approach, therefore, it is clear that man cannot be animal if no man exists, nor will Caesar be able to be a man, because names like these signify present and actual essences of things [and] because a name does [not] signify something [univocally] common to the present, past, and future.[227] Nevertheless, they fabricate many other quibbles about propositions of this type through [a consideration of the] laws of necessary and *per se* true propositions.[228] But let this much suffice for now from this approach.

CAPITULUM QUINTUM

[112] *Capitulum quintum huius primae distinctionis de hoc quod vox potest cadere a sua significatione, quod negant cavillando obstinatissime.*

[113] Boethius quidem libro *Divisionum* dicit, "Si nulla alia sit res
5 quam significet, vox designificativa esse non dicitur."

[114] Item, perempto uno relativorum, perimitur ⟨f. 82rb⟩ et relativum alterum. Si enim non est pater, non est filius, nec e contrario; sed signum et signatum sunt relativa; igitur, perempto signato, non erit vox significativa.

10 [115] Item, nihil quod venit ⟨ab⟩ extra et ab extrinseco nec de natura rei potest esse necessarium ei et perpetuum; sed significatio non est de natura vocis, sed accidit ei ab extrinseco, et aliquando ⟨sine⟩ illa habuit suam materiam et formam in esse completo naturae suae; igitur significatio non est ei necessaria nec perpetua; igitur potest deleri ab ea.

15 [116] Item, quod solum recipere potest aliquid ad placitum nostrum potest ad placitum nostrum perdere illud; sed nomina imposita rebus sunt signa ad placitum nostrum; ergo possunt amittere rationem signi, cum placeat nobis. Et hoc patet per experientiam quasi infinitorum nominum et verborum quae antiquitus significabant, sed nunc apud nos
20 nihil significant. Quae si quis proferret, reputaremus voces non significativas, nec aliquid intelligeremus per eas, ut si dicerem, "Faxo domum," "Faxis arcam," "Faxit ecclesiam," nullus nunc in usu communi intelligeret; nec alicui significarent ista verba aliquid, licet antiquitus 'faxo', 'faxis', 'faxit' significabant 'faciam', 'facies', 'faciet',
25 testante Prisciano, et sic de infinitis.

[117] Item, hoc possumus videre in aliis signis, nam, quando notum est hominibus quod vinum est in taberna, circulus expositus pro signo tenet rationem signi vini. Quando ⟨autem⟩ sciunt quod vinum non est in taberna, licet exponatur circulus, nullus tamen recipit circulum pro
30 signo, quia, illo viso, non intrent pro vino, scientes quod non est signatum. Igitur iam cecidit a ratione signi eadem voluntate hominum qua fuit prius signum factum.

---

3 negant] negat   4 nulla] nullam   10 extra] exin; *spatium c. 10 litt. seq.*   12 illa] illo
17 sunt] secundum   19 significabant] signabant   28 Quando] quam *praeponit.*   30 intrent] irent

[CHAPTER FIVE]

[112] *The fifth chapter of this first distinction [is] on this, [namely], that a vocal sound can fall away from its signification which, quibbling quite obstinately, they deny.*[229]

[113] Boethius says in [his] book *On Division*, "A vocal sound is not said to be signifying if there be no other thing which it signifies."[230]

[114] Likewise, if one of [two] relatives is destroyed, [the other] relative is also destroyed, for if there is not a father there is not a son, though not the contrary; but a sign and a significate are relatives; therefore if a significate is destroyed, there will be no signifying vocal sound.[231]

[115] Similarly, nothing which comes [from] without and extraneously and [is] not of the nature of a thing can be necessary and eternal to it; but signification is not of the nature of a vocal sound but accrues to it from without, and at one time [a vocal sound] had its matter and form in the completed being of its nature [without] it; therefore signification is not necessary nor eternal to it; therefore it can be removed from it.[232]

[116] Again, that which can receive something only at our pleasure can lose it at our pleasure; but names imposed for things are signs at our pleasure; therefore they can lose the character of a sign should it please us. And this is clear from experience of a more or less infinite [number] of names and verbs which in days gone by were signifying but now signify nothing among us. Were someone to utter them [now], we would deem the vocal sounds [to be] nonsignifying and would not understand anything through them. For example, were I to say "*Faxo* a house," "*Faxis* a coffer," "*Faxit* a church," no one would understand [these expressions to be] in common usage; nor would these verbs signify anything to someone, granted in days gone by, as Priscian bears witness, '*faxo*', '*faxis*', '*faxit*' signified "I shall make," "you will make," he will make," and so on for innumerable [other examples].[233]

[117] Similarly, we can see this in [the case of] other signs, for when it is known to men that there is wine in a tavern, a circle set forth as a sign has the character of a sign of wine. [But] when they know that there is no wine in the tavern, granted a circle be set forth, no one takes the circle for a sign because, having seen it, they would not enter in search of wine, knowing that it has not been signified. Therefore it has already lost its character of a sign by the same will of men by which it was formerly constituted a sign.[234]

[118] Sed rationabiles obiectiones possunt fieri hic: licet res non sit praesens cui nomen impositum est, illa tamen eadem est praeterita; igitur potest significare illam adhuc, sed ut praeteritam; et ita idem significabit cui imponebatur. Dicendum est quod non, quia non im-
5 ponebatur nisi sub ratione praesentis et esse actualis, ut patet ex priori probatione; et ideo cum periit res, et sic non est, nomen non significabit illud.

[119] Item, si dicatur ⟨quod⟩, licet praeterita res non sit, et ita nihilo-minus tamen potest esse significatum vocis, ut patet de vacuo et infinito,
10 et de hoc nomine 'nihil', et de nominibus infinitis ut 'non homo' et aliis huiusmodi, dicendum est quod vox quae significabat rem praesentem per impositionem, aliquando non significabit rem illam praeteritam sub eadem impositione et univoce. Sed bene potest imponi ei nova impo-sitione, licet sit nihil, quia possumus per privationem entis intelligere non
15 ens, et sicut intelligimus non ens, sic possumus dare nomen. Sed nova erit impositio, et aequivoce respectu prioris signati.

[120] Si obiciatur illud Augustini in *Dialectica*, "Cum dico 'Tullius est orator,' 'Tullius stat in capitolio deauratus,' 'Tullius iacet in sepulcro,' 'Tullius est pes dactylicus,' omnia haec dicuntur aequivoce,"—cum
20 igitur transumit nomen ad statuam Tullii et ad cadaver et pedem, multo fortius ad personam Tullii cui nomen imponebatur—et dicendum quod non significat illa nisi per novas impositiones. Et sic concedendum est quod postquam cecidit vox a significatione, propter rem cui imposita fuit mortuam, sic potest imponi illi praeteritae.

25 [121] Item, cum dicitur "Tullius est orator," aut stat pro eodem significato quo prius in vita, et habetur propositum, aut non, sed pro statua, vel cadavere, vel persona mortua, et sic erit oratio tota falsa. Sed Augustinus dicit quod sit vera. Dicendum est quod stat pro persona prae-terita, et similiter 'orator' pro oratore praeterito, et aliter non habet veri-
30 tatem.

[122] Si dicatur: "Caesar est Caesar" et "Homo est homo" sunt semper verae, quia nulla propositio verior illa in qua idem de se prae-dicatur, et oratio vel propositio est vox significativa, igitur partes eius

5 ratione] re   10 et aliis] ut aliis   19 dactylicus] dactulis   20 statuam] fortuam
31-32 sunt...verae] est....vera

[118] But reasonable objections can arise here. [For example], granted the thing not be present for which a name was imposed, yet [the thing] is the same as the thing of the past; therefore [its name] can still signify it, but as a thing of the past; and thus it will signify the same thing for which it was imposed. It must be said that [this is] not [the case] because [the name] was not imposed except [for something] under present and actual being, as is clear from the preceding proof, and thus when the thing perishes and hence does not exist, the name will not signify it.

[119] Likewise, should it be said [that], granted a thing of the past would not exist, nevertheless it can be a significate of a vocal sound, as is clear [in the case] of the void, an infinite, the name 'nothing', infinite names like 'not-man', and others suchlike, it must be said that a vocal sound, which signified a thing of the present through imposition, at one time or other will not signify that thing of the past by the same imposition and univocally.[235] But [a name] can well be imposed for it by a new imposition, granted [the thing] be nothing, because we can understand a nonentity through the privation of an entity, and just as we understand a nonentity so can we give [it] a name.[236] But the imposition will be new and [it will function] equivocally in regard to the former significate.

[120] Suppose that of Augustine in [his book] *On Dialectics* be objected: "When I say 'Tullius is an orator,' 'Tullius stands in gold on the Capitoline [Hill],' 'Tullius lies in a grave,' [and] 'Tullius is a dactyl [metric] foot,' all these things are said equivocally"—when, therefore, he transfers the name ['Tullius'] to a statue of Tullius, to [his] corpse, to [a metric] foot, and, much more importantly, to the person of Tullius for whom the name was imposed.[237] And [to this] it must be said that ['Tullius'] does not signify these things except through new impositions. And thus it is to be conceded that, after a vocal sound has fallen away from [its] signification because the thing for which it was imposed is dead, it can be imposed in this way for a thing of the past.

[121] Again, [one could object that] when "Tullius is an orator" is spoken, either ['Tullius'] stands for the same significate as before in [his] life, and the objection is granted, or [it does] not, but [rather it stands] for the statue, or the corpse, or the dead person, and in this sense the whole expression will be false. But Augustine says it is true. [To this] it must be said that it stands [equivocally] for the dead person, and likewise 'orator' for an orator in the past; otherwise it is not truthful.[238]

[122] Suppose it be said [by way of objection that] "Caesar is Caesar" and "Man is man" are always true because no proposition is more true than that in which the same is predicated of itself, and an expression or proposition is a signifying vocal sound; therefore its parts always signify

semper significant postquam semel significabant, ergo sive res sit
praesens sive praeterita semper significat, ⟨...⟩.

[123] Item, cum dico "Caesar est Caesar," hoc nomen 'Caesar' est
pars huius orationis, et oratio est vox significativa ad placitum, ergo
5 partes eius significant ad placitum. Dicendum est, sicut superius
⟨f. 82va⟩ dictum est, quod vox ante impositionem non est pars orationis,
quia non est significativa ad placitum. Et similiter, cum cadit a significatione vel per voluntatem nostram vel per hoc quod res cui imposita fuit
non est, et ideo tunc nihil significat ad placitum, nisi casu imponatur. Et
10 ideo cum haec vox 'Caesar' fuit imposita rei praesenti et sub actuali esse,
re pereunte, manet non significativa semper, nisi iterum imponatur. Et
ideo ante impositionem renovatam nihil significat. Et propter hoc haec
vox "Caesar est Caesar" nihil significabit: nec est oratio nec propositio,
nec verum vel falsum significat, quia ab una vel duabus partibus non
15 significativis est totus sermo non significativus. Et per hoc patet secundum, quod talis oratio non est vox significativa ad placitum, quia partes
eius nihil significant.

[124] Et ideo si obiciatur: 'Caesar' est vox significativa vel non est
significativa, de quolibet affirmatio vel negatio; si igitur est vox signifi-
20 cativa, habetur propositum; si non est vox significativa, haec oratio est
vera: "Caesar nihil significat"; sed oratio vera est vox significativa ad
placitum; igitur partes eius significant, tam subiectum quam
praedicatum—sed illud per consimile in secunda quaestione primi
capituli huius distinctionis.

25 [125] ⟨Obicitur:⟩ si aliquis in morte alicuius nominans eum exclamet
pro dolore, "Johannes est mortuus," tam ipse proferens quam audientes
intelligunt vocem sine impositione nova, quia nullus dicit, "Imponatur
hoc nomen 'Johannes' cadaveri, vel praeterito"; igitur significabit sicut
prius. Dicendum est quod licet haec obiectio maxime occultat veritatem,
30 tamen considerandum est quod dupliciter fit impositio nominum: uno
modo sub forma imponendi vocaliter expressa, ut communiter imponuntur nomina infantibus et aliis rebus, et sic non est hic impositio facta; sed
aliter potest fieri apud solum intellectum cogitantem de voce et
significato, et sic proferens hanc orationem "Johannes est mortuus" im-

---

2 ...] *apod. omit.*

after they once were signifying; therefore whether the thing [signified] be present or past, [its name] always signifies.[239]

[123] Similarly, when I say "Caesar is Caesar," the name 'Caesar' is a part of this expression and an expression is a vocal sound signifying at pleasure; therefore its parts signify at pleasure. [To these objections] it must be said, as was stated above, that before imposition a vocal sound is not part of an expression because it does not signify at pleasure.[240] And likewise, when it falls from [its] signification either by our will or because of the fact that the thing for which it was imposed no longer exists, then it signifies nothing at pleasure, unless it be imposed by chance.[241] And thus when this vocal sound 'Caesar' was imposed for a thing present and under actual being, once the thing perished, it remains nonsignifying always, unless it be again imposed. And thus before a renewed imposition it signifies nothing. And because of this the "vocal sound" "Caesar is Caesar" will signify nothing: neither is it an expression nor [is it] a proposition nor does it signify either what is true or false, for the whole "statement" does not signify because of one or two [of its] parts that do not signify.[242] And because of this a second [point] is clear, [namely], that such an "expression" is not a vocal sound that signifies at pleasure because its parts signify nothing.[243]

[124] And thus suppose [the following] be objected: 'Caesar' is [either] a vocal sound that signifies or [one] that does not signify—of anything [there is either] affirmation or denial; if, therefore, it is a vocal sound that signifies, the objection is granted; if it is not a vocal sound that signifies, [then] the expression "Caesar signifies nothing" is true; but an expression [that is] true is a vocal sound that signifies at pleasure; therefore its parts signify, both the subject and the predicate.[244] But [one must reply to this] in a way similar [to what was said by way of response] in the second *question* of the first chapter of this distinction.[245]

[125] [It is objected that,] if on the occasion of someone's death one should cry in anguish "John is dead," naming him, both the speaker and those hearing understand the vocal sound ['John'] without a new imposition, because no one says, "Let this name 'John' be imposed for the corpse or the thing of the past"; therefore it will signify as before. It must be said that, granted this objection obscures the truth very greatly, yet it should be noted that imposition of names occurs in two ways. [It happens] in one way under a vocally expressed form of imposing, as [occurs] commonly [when] names are imposed for infants and other things, and the imposition made here is not of this type. But it can occur in another way, [namely], within the intellect alone thinking about a vocal sound and a significate, and in this way the one uttering the expression "John is dead" imposes a name for the thing of the past or the corpse, and thus

ponit nomen rei praeteritae vel cadaveri, et ideo de necessitate renovatur, quam recipiunt audientes sicut proferens intelligit.

[126] Sed ⟨si⟩ contra hoc dicatur quod nec proferens nec audiens percipiunt impositionem renovatam nec de illa cogitant, dicendum est quod
5　ante orationem hanc prolatam, "Johannes est mortuus," necessario datur nomen praeterito vel cadaveri. Sed non percipitur actualiter in illa exclamatione, quia maior occupatio animi occultat minorem, sicut maior lux occultat minorem visui, ut patet de luce solis quod occultat lucem stellarum die. Et ideo, cum animus proferentis occupetur principaliter
10　circa sensum plenae orationis exprimentis dolorem, non percipit expresse renovationem impositionis, cum omnibus accidat. Et quilibet experitur quod homines faciunt vel dicunt aliqua, et illa non percipiunt propter fortiorem animi occupationem, ut nimium gaudentes vel admirantes vel dolentes ⟨vel⟩ timentes vel studio magno circa aliquod occupati faciunt et
15　dicunt alia circa quae, iterum occupati, non advertunt propter maiorem occupationem circa alia.

[127] Si etiam obiciatur quod viator extraneus, videns circulum, vadit ad tabernam vini, et, licet non sit ibi vinum, tamen circulus fuit ei signum, igitur sive sit vinum sive non, circulus remanet in ratione signi,
20　igitur similiter erit de voce, dicendum est quod non manet eadem significatio, nec impositio. Sed viator, ignorans absentiam vini, imaginetur vinum in taberna, et, vino imaginato, licet falso, facit sibi circulum pro signo nova institutione sua; et ideo ratio signi renovatur. Et sic est de voce et omnibus signis.

25　[128] Sed nunc considerandum est quanta insania feruntur qui negant veritatem istius problematis, auctoritate falsa inventoris huius mendacii seducti. Et tamquam tempestate delati ad saxum inhaerescunt. Et consuetudine alteratam habentes mentem non possunt consentire rationi, et a veritate se nudos profitentur qui ⟨in⟩ multitudine, pessima interprete
30　veritatis, se armant. In prima parte huius operis ⟨f. 82vb⟩ per sententias declaratum est omnium sapientium, ex quibus causis ducti fingunt quod non discutiunt nec disputant de hoc ad utramque partem, ⟨et⟩ probant quod vox non potest cadere a sua significatione. Sed hoc supponunt tamquam radicem infinitorum quae estimant verissima, cum sint falsissima,
35　ut quod homo est animal, nullo existente, et quod Caesar sit homo, et

3 hoc] *in margine eadem manu*　12 dicunt] dicant　14 circa] orca　15 occupati] occupi; *spatium c. 3 lit. seq.* ‖ non] quae non　22 facit] scit　29 interprete] interpreti

[the name] is necessarily renewed, which those hearing [the expression] receive with the same sense as the speaker understands [it].[246]

[126] But [if] against this it be said that neither the speaker nor [anyone] listening perceives the renewed imposition nor thinks about it, it must be said that the name ['John'] is necessarily given to the thing of the past or the corpse before the uttered expression "John is dead."[247] But it is not actually perceived in that exclamation because a greater preoccupation of a soul obscures a lesser just as a brighter light hides a dimmer [one] from sight, as is clear [in the case] of the light of the sun which hides the light of stars by day. And thus since the soul of the speaker is principally occupied with the sense of a highly charged expression communicating grief, it does not clearly perceive the renewal of the imposition, since [this type of imposition] happens to everyone.[248] And anyone experiences [the fact] that people do and say certain things and are not aware of them because of a more intense preoccupation of the soul, just as those who rejoice or are astonished or grieve [or] are fearful or are preoccupied with an intense study of something too much do and say other things of which, again, [I say], being preoccupied, they do not take notice because of a greater preoccupation with other things.[249]

[127] Suppose the following also be objected: a foreign traveller, seeing a circle, goes to a wine shop and, granted there would be no wine, yet the circle was a sign for him.[250] Therefore whether there be wine or not, the circle remains in the character of a sign; therefore it will be similar in regard to a vocal sound. [To this] it must be said that the signification does not remain the same, nor the imposition. Rather, the traveller, unaware of the absence of wine, would imagine wine in the shop and, once, granted, false wine is imagined, he constitutes the circle a sign for himself by his new institution; and hence the character of a sign is renewed. And this is the case with a vocal sound and all signs.[251]

[128] But now one should consider by what madness they are carried away who deny the truth of this problem, seduced by the false authority of the inventor of this lie.[252] And they cling to a rock as though tossed about in a storm. Having a mentality conditioned by custom they cannot consent to reason, and [being people] who arm themselves [with] the rabble, the worst interpreter of truth, they acknowledge themselves [to be] divested of truth.[253] In the first part of this work it was declared through the judgments of all who are wise by what causes they [are] led [who] imagine what they do not discuss nor dispute on both sides [and] prove about this, [namely], that a vocal sound cannot fall away from its signification.[254] But they suppose this as the basis for an unlimited [number of] things which they consider quite true, though they be quite false, for example, that man is animal when no [man] exists and that

quod Christus in triduo fuit homo, et alia innumerabilia erronea; sicut ex praecedenti radice sua falsissima, quod nomen significat aliquid commune enti et non enti, eliciunt mendacia paene infinita, quorum reprobatio deinceps per totum corpus istius libri evidenter patebit.

Caesar be a man and that Christ was a man during the three days, and innumerable other erroneous things; just as they draw an almost infinite [number of] lies from their preceding, very false principle, [namely], that a name signifies something [univocally] common to an entity and a nonentity, whose reprobation, henceforth, will be made evidently clear throughout the whole body of this book.

CAPITULUM SEXTUM

[129] *Capitulum sextum huius distinctionis primae de aequivocis et analogicis,*
scilicet, de modis aequivocationis et analogiae.

[130] Expositis difficultatibus circa univoca, quomodo significant, in
5 hoc capitulo dicendum est de significatione aequivocorum et analogorum
⟨et⟩ de modis eorum, in quorum assignatione magna est utilitas tam in
theologia quam in philosophia, et maximae difficultates solvuntur. Et
non oportet magnam disputationem facere ad utramque partem, quia,
certificata veritate in his levi declaratione, excluditur omnis dubietas
10 simul cum superfluitate. Aristoteles autem pluries loquitur de aequivocatione et analogia, sed numquam colligit omnes modos simul, quamvis ex dictis eius in diversis locis suae philosophiae eliciam omnia hic
necessaria. Scimus igitur quod in omni aequivocatione est diversitas
significatorum: quot modis igitur est diversitas, tot modis potest esse
15 aequivocatio, secundum quod dicit in *Topicis*, "Quamcumque differentiam invenimus, manifestum est quoniam multipliciter dicitur."

[131] Potest igitur diversitas inveniri ubi nulla est convenientia absoluta nec relata, ut inter ens et non ens, ut probatum est in capitulo
quarto. Quapropter, cum haec sit maxima diversitas, maxima est aequi-
20 vocatio, et ideo hic est primus modus et principalis aequivocatio.

[132] Secundo considerandum quod potest esse diversitas absoluta
penitus inter aliqua, et tamen est aliqua convenientia in relatione, ut inter Creatorem et creaturam. Nihil enim commune absolutum participant, sed tamen creatura habet comparationem ad Creatorem, et est
25 vestigium eius et effectus. Et sic illa quae praedicantur de Creatore et
creatura, ut 'ens' et 'unum' et 'bonum' et 'verum' et 'substantia' et
'essentia' et huiusmodi multa, dicuntur isto modo aequivoca.

[133] Et ad hunc modum reducuntur alia exempla, ut illa quae dicuntur de decem praedicamentis, sicut quaedam praedictorum, ut 'ens' et
30 'unum' et 'aliquid' et 'res' et 'creatura' et 'bonum', et 'verum' et
'finitum', et 'limitatum in natura', et huiusmodi, quia x praedicamenta

---

5 aequivocorum] aequivocarum   10 superfluitate] firtate   14 significatorum] significativorum   15-16 differentiam] differentia   18 nec] ut   19 maxima est] maxime est
20 aequivocatio] aequivocationis   21 considerandum] considerando

[CHAPTER SIX]

[129] *The sixth chapter of this first distinction [treats] of equivocals and analogicals, i.e., of the modes of equivocation and analogy.*[255]

[130] Now that the problems about how univocals signify have been revealed one must speak in this chapter about the signification of equivocals and analogicals [and] about their modes [of signification], in the assignment of which there is great utility both in theology and philosophy [and through which] very serious problems are resolved. And there is no need to have a great disputation on both sides [of the issue] because, once truth has been certified in these matters by a simple declaration, all doubt is precluded along with [any] excess. Moreover, Aristotle speaks on many occasions about equivocation and analogy, but he never gathers all the modes together at one time, though I shall select everything necessary here from his words in the different places of his philosophy. Hence we know that in every equivocation there is a difference of significates: in as many ways as there is difference, in so many modes can there be equivocation, according to what he says in the *Topics*, "Whatever difference we find, it is clear that it is spoken of in many ways."[256]

[131] Therefore a difference can be found where there is no absolute nor relative agreement, like between an entity and a nonentity, as was proven in the fourth chapter.[257] Wherefore, since this is the greatest difference, there is the greatest equivocation, and thus this is the first mode and the principal equivocation.[258]

[132] Secondly, one should consider that there can be a wholly absolute difference among some things and yet [at the same time] there is some agreement in relation, as between the Creator and a creature, for they share in nothing absolutely common, but yet a creature does have a relation to the Creator and is both a sign of Him and [His] effect. And thus those things which are predicated of the Creator and a creature, like '*ens*', '*unum*', '*bonum*', '*verum*', 'substance,' 'essence', and many suchlike, are called equivocals in this mode.[259]

[133] And other examples are reduced to this mode, like those which are said of the ten predicaments, just as certain ones of those previously mentioned, e.g., '*ens*', '*unum*', '*aliquid*', 'thing', 'creature', '*bonum*', '*verum*', '*finitum*', '*limitatum in natura*', and the like, because the ten predicaments do [not] agree in anything absolutely [and] univocally common to them, but yet they do have an order among themselves: attributes

⟨non⟩ conveniunt in aliquo absoluto communi eis univoce, sed tamen ordinem habent ad invicem: et accidentia sunt effectus, et insunt substantiae, et praedicantur de ea, et insunt ei, et in multis modis comparantur
ad eam. Et sumo hic 'ens' et 'unum' et huiusmodi pro significatis secun-
5 dis, scilicet, pro re subtracta unitati et entitati, quia primum significatum
in his, quod est unitas et entitas, est commune substantiae et accidenti,
sicut accidentia sunt communia multis subiectis, ut 'album' et 'nigrum'
possunt accipi quantum ad qualitates ipsas vel quoad rem subtractam.
Sed hic est difficultas magna et prolixitas vehemens, et copiosa discus-
10 sione ⟨digna⟩, quae in sequentibus capitulis explicabuntur.

[134] Sunt etiam alia exempla istius modi aequivocationis, ut in
aequivocatione 'sani', quod formaliter dicitur de animali, ostensive vel
indicative de urina, effective de medicina, conservative de dieta. Et sic de
multis quae dicuntur diversis modis, ubi omnia referuntur ad unum,
15 sicut hic tria referuntur ad primum. Et sunt diversa significata secundum
se, sicut in omnibus ubi dicitur aliquid formaliter vel effective, sicut
homo dicitur calidus formaliter, sed piper et zin⟨f. 83ra⟩ziber effective, et
alia infinita. Similiter sol dicitur calidus a naturali potentia in secunda
specie qualitatis, et ignis calidus dicitur ab habitu in prima specie vel ter-
20 tia. Et similiter homo dicitur piger formaliter; et tempus turbidum et
hiemale dicitur fixum effective, quia facit pigros, saltem occasionaliter; et
mors dicitur pallida quia facit pallorem. Et inter cetera unitas dicitur
una, et bonitas bona, et veritas vera, sed homo dic tur bonus et unus et
verax sub alio sensu. Unum tamen ad aliud reducitur: homo enim dicitur
25 unus formaliter, unitas dicitur una quia facit unitatem in rebus, et sic de
aliis. Si tamen alius sensus possit et debeat esse, patebit in sequentibus
capitulis evidenter.

[135] Adhuc est speciale exemplum de voce quae dicitur de materia et
forma. Impossibile enim est quod aliquid sit commune univocum illis,
30 quia Aristoteles dicit secundo *Metaphysicae* ⟨quod⟩ materia est alia ab
essentia cuiuslibet formae et non est differentia perfecta in creaturis nisi
inter formam et materiam. Omnes enim formae accidentales et substantiales aliquo modo conveniunt in ratione generali formae; sed materia
non communicat cum aliqua forma. Et omnes aliae compositae substan-
35 tiae communicant in genere generalissimo, et ideo solum est perfecta
diversitas in creaturis inter materiam et formam. Propter quod nulla convenientia absoluta potest esse. Relata tamen convenientia est inter illas,
quia materia est in potentia ad formam, et forma est actus materiae, et
ideo mutuo ad se referuntur, et inferunt se mutuo; ut, si materia est, for-

---

3 et praedicantur] et et praedicantur   6 est commune] sunt communia   16 formaliter]
formatur   17 zinziber] inziber   28 voce] v̄   31 perfecta] persidam   35 perfecta] persidam

both are the effects of and are in substance; they are predicated of it, inhere in it, and are related to it in many ways.[260] And here I am taking '*ens*' and '*unum*' and the like for [their] second significates, namely, for a thing having unity and entity, because the first significate of these [terms], which is unity and entity, is [univocally] common to a substance and an attribute, just as attributes are common to many subjects, as '*album*' and '*nigrum*' can be taken in regard to qualities themselves or in regard to a thing having [them].[261] But here there is a serious problem and vehement long-windedness [worthy] of an extended discussion which will be explained in the chapters that follow.[262]

[134] There are other examples of this mode of equivocation, as in the equivocation of 'healthy', which is formally said of an animal, ostensibly or indicatively of urine, effectively of medicine, [and] preservingly of diet.[263] And such is the case with many things that are spoken of in different ways where all refer to one thing, just as these three refer to the first. And the significates are different of themselves, just as in all cases where something is said formally or effectively, like man is called hot formally but pepper and ginger [are called hot] effectively, and innumerable others.[264] Similarly, the sun is called hot from a natural power in the second species of quality, and fire is called hot from a habit in the first and third species.[265] And likewise man is called lazy formally; stormy and wintry weather is called fixed effectively because it makes [people] lazy, at least occasionally; and death is called pale because it causes pallor. And among the others oneness is called one, goodness good, and truth true, but man is called good and one and truthful in another sense. However, the one is reduced to the other: man is called one formally, oneness is called one because it causes oneness in things, and so on for the others. If, however, there may be able and ought to be another sense, it will surface clearly in the chapters that follow.[266]

[135] Still there is a special example in regard to a vocal sound that is spoken of matter and form. It is impossible that something be univocally common to them because Aristotle says in the second [book] of the *Metaphysics* [that] matter is other than the essence of any form and there is no perfect difference among creatures except [that] between form and matter.[267] All accidental and substantial forms in some way agree in the general notion of form; but matter does not communicate with any form. And all other composed substances communicate in a most general genus, and thus alone between matter and form is there a perfect difference among creatures. Because of this there can be no absolute agreement. There is, however, a relational agreement between them because matter is in potency to form and form is the act of matter, and hence they are mutually referred to themselves and mutually infer themselves.[268] For

ma est, et e contrario, quia nec materia potest esse per se, nec forma aliqua in creaturis. Nam forma accidentalis requirit materiam subiectam;
forma substantialis similiter, quia nulla substantia creata est pura forma
nec pura materia ut demonstrabitur inferius, licet aliquis de fictis auc-
5 toribus, licet famosus, estimat substantias spirituales ut angelos et
animas esse puras formas, cuius positiones et modi ponendi et rationes
evacuabuntur posterius suis locis.

[136] Hi igitur duo modi aequivocationis praedicti nullam convenientiam absolutam habent, licet primus nec habeat convenientiam relatam,
10 sicut nec absolutam; sed secundus habet convenientiam relatam, ut expositum est. Possumus invenire differentiam minorem cum aliqua absoluta convenientia, ubi tamen nihil commune a parte rei praedicatur
univoce de significatis, ut substantia praedicatur de materia et forma et
composito. Convenit enim materia omni composito, et forma similiter,
15 quia sunt partes eius et de sua essentia. Et tamen sola vox sine aliquo
communi praedicatur de eis et composito, quia substantia quae est genus
generalissimum praedicatur de composito, sed non de materia nec forma,
quia illud genus est compositum ex materia et forma, ut probabitur inferius. Compositum vero nomine suo non potest praedicari de simplici, et
20 ideo sola vox est communis composito et simplicibus partibus eius.
Solum vero est vox aequivoca ad partem essentialem et totam, et totum
universale et partem subiectivam; hoc eodem modo aequivocationis, ut
relatio est genus generalissimum in hoc praedicamento, et species
specialissima oppositionis dicitur relatio. Et impossibile est quod aliqua
25 res communis univoce ⟨sit generi⟩ generalissimo et alicui speciei; tunc
esset aliud genus generalius quam sit generalissimum, quod est impossibile. Et similiter potest esse in multis aliis, quia voces sunt ad
placitum.

[137] Quarto possumus videre iterum aliam maiorem convenientiam
30 absolutam quam prius, ut latent aequivocationes in genere, sicut
Aristoteles dicit septimo *Physicorum*, ubi significata communicant in aliqua natura radicali, licet illa descendens in illa varietur secundum esse
varia. Ut essentia generis secundum se est una radix variabilis in diversas
species, non secundum differentias accidentaliter completas, sed etiam

---

11 aliqua] alia   21 et totum] sed totum   23 relatio] eius *add.*   26 generalius] generalissimum   29 iterum] inter   33 variabilis] uniabilis   34 secundum] per *add.*

example, if there is matter, there is form, and conversely, because among creatures neither matter can be by itself nor some form. Accidental form requires matter [as its] subject; substantial form likewise, because no created substance is pure form nor pure matter (as will be proven below), granted one of the so-called authors, though he be famous, considers spiritual substances like angels and [human] souls to be pure forms, whose positions, ways of stating the case, and reasons will be eliminated later in their proper places.[269]

[136] These two previously mentioned modes of equivocation, therefore, represent no absolute agreement [among the significates in each], granted the first would not reflect [even] a relational agreement, just as [it would not reflect] an absolute [one]; but the second reflects a relational agreement, as has been pointed out. [Nevertheless] we can find a lesser difference with some absolute agreement where, however, nothing common in regard to the thing is predicated univocally of the significates. For example, substance is predicated of matter and form [on the one hand] and a composite [on the other], for matter agrees with every composite, and likewise form, because these are its parts and [they pertain to] its essence.[270] And yet a vocal sound alone, without anything [else univocally] common, is predicated of them and a composite because substance, which is a most general genus, is predicated of a composite but not [univocally] of matter or form, since that genus is composed of matter and form, as will be proved later.[271] Indeed, a composite cannot be [univocally] predicated through its own name of [something] simple, and hence a vocal name is common to a composite and its simple parts.[272] But the vocal sound is exclusively equivocal [when predicated in regard] to an essential part and a whole and [in regard to] a universal and its particulars; [whatever is said of these is predicated] in the same mode of equivocation. For example, relation is the most general genus in the predicament [of "Relation"] and the most determinate species of opposition is called a relation. And it is impossible that some thing [be] univocally common to a most general [genus] and to one [of its] species, [for] then there would be a genus more general than the most general, which is impossible.[273] And [the case] can be similar in regard to many other things because vocal sounds are at [our] pleasure.[274]

[137] Fourthly, we can again find another absolute agreement greater than before, like the equivocations [that] lie hidden in genus, as Aristotle says in the seventh [book] of the *Physics*, [i.e.,] where significates share in some root nature, granted that it would be differentiated in accord with its different beings when it descends into them.[275] Thus the essence of genus of itself is one root capable of being differentiated into different species [that would] not [be] accidentally complete because of [their] dif-

antequam intelligitur in illas. Ut essentia similis in semine equi producta et in semine asini est una radicalis essentia, sed tamen esse varia habet antequam deducatur haec essentia in differentias; et ita esse sunt essentialia. Propter quod essentialiter variatur haec radicalis essentia generis.
5 Quod attendens naturalis philosophus dicit quod genus est aequivocum, sed logicus, considerans non ita profunde, quia antecedens relatio radicalis est essentia absque illa essentia varia, dicit quod genus dicitur univocum.

[138] Et quintus modus quando adhuc maior est identitas, quoniam
10 eadem res potest significari diversis modis, ut 'amans illius' nomen est ⟨et⟩ 'amans illum' participium est, docente Prisciano. Sed constat quod eadem res significatur per hoc nomen 'amans' et per hoc participium 'amans' ⟨f. 83rb⟩ et per hoc verbum 'amo', quia partes orationis cognatae significationis non distinguuntur penes significata, sed penes
15 modos significandi, ut dicit Priscianus, sicut ita de quo exemplificatum est. Et tamen aequivoca est, quando vox eadem significat ⟨ut⟩ participium et nomen.

[139] ⟨Est etiam⟩ quod praedicatur per sextum modum aequivocationis, ubi maxima est identitas significatorum quae potest esse, quia
20 idem nomen potest sumi aequivoce per casuum diversitatem, vel aliorum accidentium, quia accidentia sunt modi significandi accidentales, ut ''Quicumque sunt episcopi sunt sacerdotes; isti asini sunt episcopi; ergo isti asini sunt sacerdotes.'' Nullus puer qui summulas suas audierit ignorat quod hic est aequivocatio penes casus. Si ergo potest fieri ae-
25 quivocatio penes modos accidentales significandi, multo fortius penes modos essentiales significandi. Quia maior est diversitas penes modos essentiales significandi per quas distinguuntur partes orationis, igitur maior ratio aequivocationis. Et ideo inter 'amans' nomen et participium est aequivocatio in quinto modo aequivocationis.
30 [140] De modis vero aequivocationis impossibile est quod ulterius inveniatur alius modus proprius, quia sextus modus minimam habet differentiam quae potest inveniri. Et ideo, cum minor non potest esse differentia, non est ulterius aequivocatio. Et hoc est verum de modis propriis aequivocationis. Potest tamen unus modus esse improprius, ut
35 in transitive positis et figurativis, ut ''Pratum ridet'' et ''Quid faciat laetas segetes,'' ut *Georgica* Virgilii incipiunt. Sed transponuntur vocabula ad bonitatem et fecunditatem et pulchritudinem pascui segetum.

---

6 quia] sed   10 diversis] diversi   14 cognatae] cognitae   19 ubi] ut   24 quod] quando
35 in...figurativis] intransitive positus et figuratus   36 transponuntur] transponitur

ferences, but even before [the essence of genus] is understood in [the differences].[276] For example, the similar essence produced in the seed of a horse and in the seed of a donkey is one root essence, but yet it has various beings before this essence would be led down into the differences; and thus the beings are essential. Because of this the root essence of genus is esentially differentiated. A natural philosopher considering this says that genus is equivocal, but a logician, not considering [the issue] so deeply, says that genus is called univocal because the antecedent root relation is an essence without that differentiated essence.[277]

[138] And a fifth mode [occurs] when the identity [between significates] is even greater, since the same thing can be signified in different ways.[278] For example, as Priscian teaches, ['*amans*' in] '*amans illius*' is a name [and '*amans*' in] '*amans illum*' is a participle. But the fact is that the same thing is signified by the name '*amans*' and by the participle '*amans*' and by the verb '*amo*', because the parts of an expression of cognate signification are not distinguished in regard to [their] significates but in regard to their modes of signifying, as Priscian teaches [and] just as [was the case] with that given as an example.[279] And yet, when the same vocal sound signifies [as] a participle and as a name, it is equivocal.

[139] [Finally, there is] that which is predicated through a sixth mode of equivocation, where the identity of the significates is the greatest that can be, because the same name can be taken equivocally throughout a diversity of [grammatical] cases or other attributes, since attributes are accidental modes of signification, as in "*Quicumque sunt episcopi sunt sacerdotes; isti asini sunt episcopi; ergo isti asini sunt sacerdotes.*"[280] No boy who would have heard [lectures on] his textbooks does not know that here there is equivocation in regard to case. If, therefore, there can come about equivocation in regard to accidental modes of signifying, so much the more in regard to essential modes of signifying. Because there is a greater difference in regard to the essential modes of signifying through which the parts of speech are distinguished, therefore the character of equivocation is greater.[281] And thus the equivocation between the name and the participle '*amans*' is in the fifth mode of equivocation.

[140] In regard to the modes of equivocation it is impossible that another proper mode be found beyond [these] because the sixth mode represents the least difference that can be found. And thus, when there cannot be a lesser difference, there is no equivocation beyond [them]. And this is true of the proper modes of equivocation. However, one mode can be improper as in things transitively imposed and [in] figurative [expressions] like "The meadow smiles" and "What makes the crops joyous?" as the *Georgics* of Virgil begins.[282] But the words are transposed to the goodness, fertility, and beauty of the crops of the field.[283]

[141] De modis vero analogiae expediam breviter, dicens quod omnes modi aequivocationis sunt modi analogiae praeter primum modum aequivocationis; quia, cum 'analogia' graece sit 'proportio' et 'comparatio' latine, ut ait Tullius et notum est scientibus aliquid de graeca, ideo, cum in primo modo aequivocationis non sit aliqua comparatio significatorum, ut expositum est, non est aliquis modus analogiae. Sed cum in omnibus aliis modis est comparatio et proportio significatorum, ut patet ex dictis, in omnibus illis est analogia.

[142] Est etiam analogia ubi non est aequivocatio, ut in 'ente' et 'uno' sumitur, si considerentur secundum significata prima, ut significet ⟨'ens'⟩ existentiam actualem et 'unum' unitatem, nam per prius conveniunt substantiae quam accidenti. Sed illud patebit in sequentibus capitulis. Et secundum metaphysici considerationem in decimo libro omne genus dicitur per prius de specie nobiliori quam de alia, ut animal de rationali quam irrationali. "⟨Per⟩ prius" dico quantum ad dignius esse et dignitatem naturae, licet secundum naturalem philosophum aequivocatio est similis cum hoc et secundum logicum univocatio, secundum diversas eorum considerationes.

---

2 praeter] *post cor. ex* secundum   4 graeca] graece   6 significatorum] significativorum
7 significatorum] signifivativorum   9 Est etiam] et etiam   13 capitulis] capituli

[141] I shall settle [the question] of the modes of analogy briefly, saying that all modes of equivocation are modes of analogy except the first mode of equivocation because, since 'analogy' is 'proportion' in Greek and 'comparison' in Latin, as Tully says and as is known to those who know something about Greek, [and] since there is not a comparison of significates in the first mode of equivocation, as has been pointed out, thus there is no mode of analogy.[284] But since there is a comparison and proportion of significates in all the other modes, as is clear from what has been said, there is analogy in all of them.

[142] And [there is] also analogy where there is no equivocation as is found in the case of 'ens' and 'unum', if they be considered according to their first significates, with the result that ['ens'] signifies actual existence and 'unum' unity, for they agree more with substance than attribute. But this will become clear in the following chapters.[285] And according to the view of the metaphysician in the tenth book [of the *Metaphysics*] every genus is said more of [its] more noble species than of [any] other, as animal [is said more] of rational [animal] than of irrational [animal].[286] I say [''more''] because of the more worthy being and the dignity of the nature, granted equivocation is similar to this according to a natural philosopher and univocation according to a logician because of their different points of view.[287]

NOTES TO THE TRANSLATION

1. This paragraph and all those below printed in italics are rubrics, i.e., parts of the manuscript written in red ink that provide instructions regarding the material that follows.

   The principal divisions of this work are called by Bacon either Parts (*pars*) or Treatises (*tractatus*). (See below, #16 and #72, and #43 and #83, respectively.) But the rubricist uses the terms 'Part' and 'Distinction (*distinctio*'). (See here and below, #3, and #84, #112, and #129, respectively; the latter group is clearly an anomaly.) The whole work is twice referred to as a book, once by Bacon (see below, #128) and once in a rubric, though in a later hand (below, #15). Subdivisions, however, are consistently spoken of as chapters by Bacon (#83, #130, #133-134, and #142) and the rubricist. The translation divides the work into Parts and Chapters. For a comment on the use of the term 'treatise' in this work see "Introduction," p. 9, n. 39.

2. See Cicero *Tusculanae disputationes* 1. 12. 26, ed. and transl. J.E. King, *Cicero: Tusculan Disputations*, Loeb Classical Library (Cambridge, Mass.: Harvard University Press; London: Willaim Heinemann, 1927; revised 1945), pp. 32 and 33. Bacon's version varies slightly from the present standard edition, as will be the case with almost all his quotations in this work. Henceforth such will not be noted except where a substantial variation has occurred.

3. See Pliny *Naturalis historia* Prologue 21, ed. and trans. H. Rackham, *Pliny: Natural History* 1, Loeb Classical Library (Cambridge, Mass.: Harvard University Press; London: William Heinemann, 1938; revised 1949), pp. 14 and 15.

4. At the beginning of the 12th century theology exercised itself principally in the form of commentaries and glosses (notes) on the sacred text, considerable space being alloted to the opinions of the Church Fathers. But by mid-century the re-discovery of Aristotles's *Topics, Prior* and *Post Analytics* and *On Sophistical Refutations* as well as innovative methodological successes in the field of Canon Law had moved people like Peter Lombard (+ 1142) to approach theological issues by casting them in the form of single questions to each of which arguments pro and con would be given along with a determination or solution and response to objections. This method or format became quite popular and by the end of the century supplanted commenting on Scripture as the principal way of doing theology, becoming itself an oral and literary genre. A *question* then, as Bacon uses the term here, is not just a question but the whole process just described. By the time Bacon was a university student a principal tool of the educational process was the disputation on *questions*, i.e., a formal debate on a question in which a bachelor was required to take either the affirmative or negative and defend it against challenges from anyone in attendance, a final determination or solution being given on the following day by the master who had presided over the disputation. The use of philosophical concepts and logic—all arguments had to be presented in syllogistic form—heavily influenced the development of theology as a science and Bacon resented the introduction of

these tools into theology, considering it the first of his seven problems with the educational system of his time. (See, e.g., *Opus minus*, ed. Brewer, pp. 322.23-323.25.) Nevertheless he condemned people like Albert the Great and Thomas Aquinas for attempting to do this kind of theology without first becoming Masters of Arts. (See *Compendium studii philosophiae*, ed. Brewer, pp. 425.11-426-28.) For a brief history of the development of *questions* from method to genre within the discipline of theology, see Yves M.-J. Congar, *A History of Theology* (Garden City, New York: Doubleday, 1968), pp. 69-84. For a description of three types of disputations and their role in the medieval academic system see James Weisheipl, "Curriculum of the Faculty of Arts at Oxford in the early Fourteenth Century," *Mediaeval Studies* 26 (1964) 176-185. See also Ignacio Angelelli, "The Techniques of Disputation in the History of Logic," *Journal of Philosophy* 67 (1970) 800-815.

5. Throughout the Middle Ages and until the time of Erasmus the work from which the quotation was taken was thought to be Seneca's. However, see Publilius Syrus *Sententiae* 270, ed. R.A.H. Bickford-Smith (London: C. Clay and Sons, 1895), p. 17; transl. D. Lyman, J., *The Moral Sayings of Publius Syrus, A Roman Slave* (New York: Andrew J. Graham, 1862), p. 40, no. 406.

6. See *Proverbs* 13:12; I have not located the source for the quotation ascribed to Terence.

7. According to Rashall (Cst, p. 26, n. 4) this quotation is from the medieval poem "Vetula" thought in Bacon's time to have been written by Ovid but now ascribed to Richard de Fournival (fl. 1246-1260). However, Rashall also notes that Richard seems to have stolen the quotation from Statius' *Thebaid* where it is said with altered meaning of a son of Oedipus: "*spes mentem / extrahit et longo consumit gaudia voto* (fretful hope keeps his mind busy, and in far reaching prayers he tastes all his heart's desires)." See Statius *Thebais* 1. 322-323, ed. and transl. J.H. Mozley, *Statius* 1, Loeb Classical Library (London: William Heinemann; New York: G.P. Putnam's Sons, 1928), pp. 364 and 365.

8. See Seneca *De beneficiis* 1. 7. 2, ed. and transl. John W. Basore, *Seneca: Moral Essays* 3, Loeb Classical Library (Cambridge, Mass.: Harvard University Press; London: William Heinemann, 1935), pp. 26 and 27.

9. See ibid., 2. 1. 2, pp. 50 and 51.

10. Cf. ibid., 2. 1. 3, pp. 52 and 53.

11. Cf. ibid., 2. 1. 4, pp. 52 and 53.

12. See Sallust *Iugurtha* 64. 6, ed. and transl. J.C. Rolfe, *Sallust*, Loeb Classical Library (Cambridge, Mass.: Harvard University Press; London: William Heinemann, 1921; revised 1931), pp. 274 and 275.

13. See Publilius Syrus *Sententiae* 173, ed. R.A.H. Bickford-Smith (London: C.J. Clay and Sons, 1895), p. 11; transl. D. Lyman, Jr., *The Moral Sayings of Publius Syrus, A Roman Slave* (New York: Andrew J. Graham, 1862), p. 28, no. 229.

14. In Migne (*PL* 30. 294) there is a spurious letter from Jerome to Damasus, however, it does not contain this quotation.

15. See *Wisdom* 7:13.

16. The source for this quotation is unknown, though Bacon makes use of it (with slight variations) in at least two of his other works. See *Metaphysica Fratris Rogeri Ordinis Fratrum Minorum de viciis contractis in studio theologie*, ed.

Robert Steele, *Opera*, 1, p. 2.29-33, and F.A. Gasquet, "An Unpublished Fragment of a Work by Roger Bacon," *English Historical Review* 12 (1897) 500.4-8. In these works the King is identified respectively as Dindimus and Dindemus.

17. See Seneca *Epistulae* 6. 4., ed. and transl. Richard M. Gummere, *Seneca: Ad Lucilium epistulae morales* 1, Loeb Classical Library (Cambridge, Mass.: Harvard University Press; London: William Heinemann, 1917), pp. 26 and 27.

18. See Boethius *De hypotheticis syllogismis* 1. 1, ed. and transl. (Italian), Luca Obertello, *A. M. Severino Boezio De hypotheticis syllogismis, Testi Classici di Logica*, vol. 1, ed. Domenico Pesce (Brescia: Paideia, 1969), p. 204.

19. See *Ecclesiasticus* 20:32.

20. This chapter recapitulates the general theme of the sixteen chapters of Part One of Bacon's *Opus maius* of 1267 with principal focus on Chapters 1-5 and 7. The order of the issues is sometimes altered and selection is made among the previously stated quotations. (See ed. Bridges, 3, pp. 1-35; transl. Burke, *The Opus Maius of Roger Bacon*, 1, pp. 3-35.)

21. In the *Opus maius* a fourth cause is mentioned, namely, the hiding of one's own ignorance by a display of apparent wisdom. (See ed. Bridges, 3, pp. 2.18-19 and 18.17-25.33; transl. Burke, 1, pp. 4 and 19-26.) The omission here is curious in view of the fact that this cause is described as "the fount and origin of the three causes" and "more pernicious" than the others. (See ed. Bridges, 3, pp. 19.3-4 and 18.18 respectively, and transl. Burke, 1, pp. 20 and 19 respectively.)

22. Bacon elaborates on these three in the *Opus maius*:

> But yet however weak authority be it possesses a name of honor and custom inclines to sin more violently than it; however the opinion of the crowd is more impetuous than both of them. For authority only entices, custom binds, and the opinion of the crowd begets obstinate [people] and confirms [them].

(See ed. Bridges, 3, pp. 8.33-9.3; transl. Burke, 1, p. 10.)

How are these pitfalls to be avoided? Bacon responds:

> We cannot have protection for defense against these unless we follow the commands and counsels of God and His scriptures, of Canon Law, the saints, the philosophers, and of all wise men of old,

or, as he states it a little later,

> but there is not a remedy against these three unless with all courage we rely on insightful (*validos*) authors instead of the opinions of the crowd ...

(See ed. Bridges, 3, pp. 11.26-29 and 17.27-29 respectively; transl. Burke, 1, pp. 13 and 19 respectively.)

23. See Seneca *Epistulae* 123. 6, ed. and transl. Richard Gummere, *Seneca: Ad Lucilium epistulae morales* 3, Loeb Classical Library (Cambridge, Mass.: Harvard University Press; London: William Heniemann, 1925), pp. 426 and 427.

24. See Cicerco *Tusculanae disputationes* 3. 1. 2, ed. and transl. E. King, *Cicero: Tusculan Disputations*, Loeb Classical Library (Cambridge, Mass.: Harvard University Press; London: William Heinemann, 1927; revised 1945), pp. 226 and 227.

25. See *Nicomachean Ethics* 1.6. 1096a13-16. By 1292 Book One of the *Nicomachean Ethics* existed in three translations. (See below, #14, n. 63).

The *Ethica nova* reads: *"... ambobus enim entibus amicis, sanctum magis honorare veritatem."* (Ed. Renatus Gauthier, *Aristoteles Latinus*, vol. 26, fasc. 2 [Leiden: E.J. Brill; Brussels: Desclée de Brouwer, 1972], p. 71.12.) Grossetestes's translation (or that made under his supervision) and the revision ascribed to Moerbeke read: *"Ambobus enim existentibus amicis, sanctum prehonorare veritatem."* (Ibid., fasc. 3, p. 146.16, and fasc. 4, p. 379.24-25.) Bacon's first quotation squares with none of these three and his second reveals similarities and dissimilarities with all three. Hence it is unclear which two translations he has in mind.

26. For this and the succeeding remark see *Vita Aristotelis*, ed. Valentine Rose, *Aristotelis Qui Ferebantur Librorum Fragmenta* (1886; photoprint Stuttgart: B.G. Tuebner, 1966), p. 447.2-5.
27. See Ps.-Boethius *De disciplina scholarium*, 5.4 ed. Olga Weiers (Leiden; Cologne; E.J. Brill, 1976), p. 121.5-9. Cf. *Opus maius*, ed. Bridges, 3, p. 16.25-30; transl. Burke, 1, p. 18.
28. See Cicero *Academica* 2. 3, ed. and transl. H. Rackham, *Cicero: De natura deorum* [and] *Academica*, Loeb Classical Library (Cambridge, Mass.: Harvard University Press; London: William Heinemann, 1933; revised 1951, 1956), pp. 474 and 475. In the *Opus maius* Bacon offers an additional reason for discretion in accepting authority as a norm: the sacred writers and other learned men
    > have set forth many things with great authority which they retracted with greater humility later ... Moreover the saints vigorously fought with one another's positions with the result that we are disgusted to see [it] and are astonished beyond measure ...
    (See ed. Bridges 3, p. 27.5-15; transl. Burke, 1, p. 28. See also ed. Bridges, 3, pp. 14.9-16.9; transl. Burke, 1, pp. 15-17.)
29. See *Jeremiah* 13:23.
30. See *Proverbs* 22:6.
31. See Sallust *Iugurtha* 85. 41, ed. and transl. J.C. Rolfe, *Sallust*, Loeb Classical Library (Cambridge, Mass: Harvard University Press; London: William Heinemann, 1921; revised 1931), pp. 320 and 321, where, however, the text reads: *"... let them pass (agant) their old age."*
32. See Aristotle *Nicomachean Ethics* 2. 1. 1103b24-25.
33. See ibid., 10. 9. 1179b17. The Latin version used here by Bacon (as emended) is Grosseteste's. (See ed. Renatus Gauthier, *Aristoteles Latinus*, vol. 26, fasc. 3 [Leiden: E.J. Brill: Brussels: Desclée de Brouwer, 1972], p. 365.11-12.)
34. Presumably the Latin translation referred to is that called the *Ethica nova* as it is not the one ascribed to Moerbeke. However this cannot be verified since the quotation does not appear among the known fragments of Book Ten.
35. If Bacon is thinking of *Nichomachean Ethics* 10. 9. 1179b31-1180a4, then the meaning is that penalties provided by law for transgressions are necessary for those who because of habit are unable to be perusaded by arguments.
36. Cf. Aristotle *Metaphysics* 2. 3. 995a4-8.
37. See Cicero *Tusculanae disputationes* 1. 16. 38, ed. and transl. J.E. King, *Cicero: Tusculan Disputations*, Loeb Classical Library (Cambridge, Mass.: Harvard University Press; London: William Heinemann, 1927; revised 1945), pp. 44 and 45.

38. For the reference to Aristotle see *On Memory and Reminiscence* 2. 452a28.

39. I have not located the source for these quotations.

40. Of all the authorities on Aristotle known in the 13th. century two were preeminent and both Muslims. The first, Ibn Sina, known to the Latin West as Avicenna (980-1037), was called by Bacon "the leader and prince of philosophy," second only to Aristotle himself. (*Opus maius*, ed. Bridges, 3, p. 14.19-20; transl. Burke, 1, p. 16.) The second, Ibn Rushd or Averroes (1126-1198), often (as here) simply referred to as "the Commentator," enjoyed decreasing esteem in Bacon's eyes as time went on. In the *Opus maius* of 1267 he rates him just behind Avicenna, but at the same time acknowledges that others think more highly of him: "... in these times whatever he says enjoys the favor of the wise ... granted in some things he has spoken less well." (Ed. Bridges, 3, p. 21.7-12; transl. Burke, 1, p. 22.) In the *De signis* he is said to be, after Aristotle and Avicenna, a noble philosopher but one deficient in certain respects. (*Ds* 68.) Between then and the *Cst*, however, Bacon became quite severe in his judgment, at least on a certain issue: "In this way, therefore, is made clear the madness of Averroes and his multifaceted nonsense which drives foolish ones in many ways into error." (See below, #82; see also #72, #75-76, and #81.) For the references in the text cf. Aristotle *Metaphysica* 2. 3. 994b32-995a5 and see Averroes *Metaphysica* 2. 3, ed. Iuntina (Venice: 1562; reprinted Frankfort on the Main: Minerva, 1962), f. 35rC.

41. The quotation is possibly an extrapolation from remarks made by Chrysostom in Homily 69 of his *Commentarius in S. Matthaeum evangelistam* about the transfer of God's election from the Hebrews to the Christians. See *Matthew* 22:1-14 and Chrysostom, ed. Migne, *PG* 58. 647C-D.

42. Plato *Timaeus* 51E. The translation by Calcidius reads: "*Quid quod rectae opinionis omnis uir particeps, intellectus uero dei proprius et paucorum admodum lectorum hominum?* (What [is there] of right opinion that every man shares; understanding is proper to God and very few lettered people)" (ed. J.H. Waszink, *Timaeus a Calcidio translatus commentarioque instructus*, 2nd. ed., *Corpus Philosophicorum Medii Aevi: Corpus Platonicum*, vol. 4, ed. Raymond Klibanski [London: The Warburg Institute; Leiden: E.J. Brill, 1975], p. 50).

43. See Cicero *Tusculanae disputationes* 2. 1. 4, ed. and transl. J.E. King, *Cicero: Tusculan Disputations*, Loeb Classical Library (Cambridge, Mass.: Harvard University Press; London: William Heinemann, 1927; revised 1945), pp. 148 and 149.

44. See ibid., 2. 26. 63, pp. 218 and 219.

45. Ibid., 2. 26. 64, pp. 218 and 219.

46. See Seneca *De vita beata* 1. 3, ed. and transl. John Basore, *Seneca: Moral Essays* 2, Loeb Classical Library (Cambridge, Mass.: Harvard University Press; London: William Heinemann, 1932; revised 1935 and 1951), pp. 100 and 101.

47. Ibid., 2. 1, pp. 102 and 103.

48. See ibid., 2. 2, pp. 102 and 103.

49. See *Exodus* 23:2.

50. This paragraph and the next present a considerably more detailed foundation for this notion than is found in Part One of the *Opus maius*. (Cf. ed. Bridges, 3, p. 8.20-31; transl. Burke, 1, p. 10.)

51. See *Epistle of James* 2:17.
52. Cf. *Epistle of James* 2:19.
53. Cf. Josephus *Jewish Antiquities* 1. 2. 2, 1. 3. 9, and 1. 8. 2, ed. and transl. H.St.J. Thackeray, *Josephus* 8, Loeb Classical Library (London: William Heinemann; New York: G.P. Putnam's Sons, 1930), pp. 30 and 31, 32 and 33, and 82 and 83 respectively, and see *Secretum secretorum cum glossis et notulis Fratris Rogeri*, ed. Steele, *Opera*, 5, pp. 62.22-63.14 and 64.15-31. The latter work is a set of private instructions purportedly given to Alexander the Great by Aristotle and widely read in Latin and Muslim circles in the thirteenth century. Steele suggests that it had its origin "in the interaction between Persian and Syriac ideas which took place in the seventh to ninth centuries ..." (ibid., p. x). Philip of Tripoli made a Latin translation of one of the two Arabic versions around 1243 (ibid., p. x and xx) and it was this translation that Bacon glossed or annotated sometime between his return to Oxford (ca. 1250) and 1257 when he returned to Paris (ibid., p. viii). Bacon himself mentions having had a good copy of the work in Paris and his remarks indicate that he was writing his glosses at Oxford. (See ibid., p. 39.31-35.) For the singular impact of this work on Bacon's decision to shift his attention to the practical sciences see Easton, *Roger Bacon*, p. 73-86.
54. Presumably the quotation is from the *Secret of Secrets* but I have not found it. In the *Opus maius* the notion is stated in the third person and not as a quotation: "... and especially the Greeks because they were more studious." (See ed. Bridges, 3, p. 54.32-33; transl. Burke, 1, p. 53.)
55. The Stoics came after Aristotle's time.
56. Cf. *Vita Aristotelis*, ed. Valentine Rose, *Aristotelis Qui Ferebantur Librorum Fragmenta* (1886; reprinted Stuttgart: B.G. Teubner, 1966), pp. 449.3-8 and 450.5-6.
57. See Cicero *Topica* 1. 3, ed. and transl. H.M. Hubbell, *Cicero: De inventione, De optimo genere oratorum, Topica*, Loeb Classical Library (Cambridge, Mass.: Harvard University Press; London: William Heinemann, 1949), pp. 384 and 385.
58. Cf. Cicero *Tusculanae disputationes* 5. 37. 107, ed. and transl. J.E. King, *Cicero: Tusculan Disputations*, Loeb Classical Library (Cambridge, Mass.: Harvard University Press; London: William Heinemann, 1927; revised 1945), pp. 532 and 533, where, however, no mention is made of anyone going into exile with Aristotle. I have not found any place in the *Academics* where this issue is mentioned.
59. A good part of Aristotle's natural treatises was translated as early as the late 12th century by Gerard of Cremona (+1187), Henricus Aristippus (+1162), and various anonymous translators. *Metaphysics* 1-1.4 (*Metaphysica vetustissima*) and *Nichomachean Ethics* 2-3 (*Ethica vetus*) were also available at that time along with works by Alkindi, Alfarabi, Avicebron, Costa ben Luca, and Isaac Israeli. Even Avicenna's paraphrase of Aristotle, *al-Shifā* (*Book of Healing*), known to the Latins as *Sufficentia*, had been translated before 1200. Bacon's remarks, then, are probably meant to refer to the newer translations that occurred in the first half of the 13th century. The first Latin quotations from Averroes seem to be found in two works by William of Auvergne probably written between 1231 and 1236. (For further remarks on the translations of Aristotle's works see Bernard C. Dod, "Aristoteles Latinus" in *The Cambridge History of Later Medieval Philosophy*, Norman Kretzmann, Anthony Kenny, and Jan Pinborg, eds. [Cambridge,

London, New York, New Rochelle, Melbourne, Sydney: Cambridge University Press, 1982], pp. 45-79.) Lack of translations is also given in the *Opus maius* as one of the reasons why the learned men in the early Church failed to see the value of Aristotelian science. (See ed. Bridges, 3, p. 28.8-10; transl. Burke, 1, p. 29.) The consequence, Bacon says, is that later writers like Gratian (ca. 1140), the Master of the *Sentences* (Peter Lombard) (ca. 1100-1160), Hugh of St. Victor (d. 1141), and Richard of St. Victor (d. 1173) did not know how to evaluate the relation between philosophy and theology and hence often spoke prejudicially against the former. (See ed. Bridges, 3, pp. 33.5-12; transl. Burke, 1, pp. 33-34.)

60. In a Parisian provincial council of 1210 the books of Aristotle on natural philosophy, the *Metaphysics*, and writings on these by Avicenna and Averroes were forbidden to be lectured on at Paris either publicly or privately, a deed which Bacon ascribes to "dense ignorance." (For the decree see Lynn Thorndike, *University Records And Life in the Middle Ages* [New York: Columbia University Press, 1944], pp. 26-27; for Bacon's remark see his *Opus maius*, ed. Bridges, 3, p. 21.13-17; transl. Burke, 1, p. 22.) The decree was renewed in 1215 and on April 13, 1231, Pope Gregory IX reiterated the ban but added the proviso that they were not to be lectured on "until these shall have been examined and purged from all suspicion of errors." (Thorndike, University Records, p. 38.) Evidently, however, some lecturing (and surely private reading) did take place for on April 20 of the same year he gave the abbot of St. Victor and the prior of the Dominicans at Paris the authority to absolve those who had incurred excommunication in regard to the ban and three days later appointed a commission to review the works in question "so that, what are suspect being removed, the rest may be studied without delay and without offense." (Ibid., p. 40.) It is not clear that the commission ever completed its task and there is no record that the ban was ever officially lifted. For a thorough study of the ban and its consequences for the relations between the faculties of arts and theology see Fernand Van Steenberghen, *La philosophie au XIIIe siècle*, Philosophes Médiévaux 9 (Louvain: Publications Universitaires; Paris: Béatrice-Nauwelaerts, 1966), pp. 88-100.

Easton offers various reasons why Bacon's date of 1237 is premature, but it is clear that by the mid-1240s, when Bacon was lecturing on them at Paris, the ban was no longer officially observed. (See Easton, *Roger Bacon*, pp. 35-45.) He also suggests that Bacon has possibly confused what may have been a first invitation in 1237 (while the ban was still enforced) to lecture at Paris with a subsequent one (which he accepted), the ban no longer being enforced. (Ibid., p. 34, n. 1.)

I am not aware of any research that indicates that a faulty translation played any role in the condemnations of 1210 and 1215 or the more detailed proscriptions of 1270 and 1277. That works were "erroneously translated" is a recurrent complaint by Bacon from about 1250 on. For example, in his *Opus maius* (ed. Brewer, p. 327.22-23) he deridingly points out that a living scholar (whom Easton and Jeremiah M.G. Hackett argue is none other than Albert the Great) "did not know languages" and in the *Compendium studii philosophiae* ridicules the philological efforts of Papias, Hugutio, Brito, and Alexander Neckham. (See, respectively, *Roger Bacon*, pp. 210-231; "The Attitude of Roger Bacon to the *Scientia* of Albertus Magnus" in *Albertus Magnus And the Sciences: Commemorative Essays, 1980*, James A. Weisheipl, ed. [Toronto: Pontifical Institute of Medieval Studies, 1980], pp. 53-72; and ed. Brewer, pp. 446.29-464.3.)

61. While the reference is to Edmund of Abingdon the evaluation of the claim rests on three dates which are uncertain at this time: (1) the years intended by "in my times;" (2) when Edmund lectured at Oxford; and (3) the dates of two commentaries on *On Sophistical Refutations*, one by Robert Grosseteste and the other by a certain Anonymous Laudianus. Quite possibly both of these commentaries preceded the time when Bacon would have been a student at Oxford. For a discussion of Bacon's claim see Easton, *Roger Bacon*, pp. 10-12; Crowley, *Roger Bacon*, pp. 20-21; and Sten Ebbesen, "Jacobus Veneticus on the *Posterior Analytics* And Some Early 13th Century Oxford Masters on the *Elenchi*," *Cahiers de l'Institut du Moyen-Âge grec et latin*, 21 (Copenhagen: University of Copenhagen, 1977), pp. 4-9. Two years later Ebbesen adds: "... I am now fully convinced that *Anonymous Laudianus* cannot be dated later than the very early 13th century and I strongly believe in a 12th century date." (Anonymous Aurelianensis I: *Commentarium in Sophisticos Elenchos*," *Cahiers de l'Institut du Moyen-Âge grec et latin*, 34 [Copenhagen: University of Copenhagen, 1979], p. xlii.) Possibly Bacon intends to say only that Edmud was the first to lecture on that work after a lapse at Oxford. Unfortunately, even an evaluation of this more restricted claim must wait further research.

62. Nothing is at present known about this master.

63. The claim that the (*Nicomachean*) *Ethics* was "even more lately communicated" seems to be true. According to Bernard Dod the following translations existed: (1) a twelfth century anonymous one of Books Two and Three called the *Ethica vetus*; (2) an anonymous early thirteenth century translation of Book One called the *Ethica nova*. (Fragments of Books Two to Ten suggest the whole work was translated, but only the first Book was circulated in this version); (3) a translation of the complete work by Grosseteste around 1246-1247, which was given wide circulation, and (4) an anonymous revision, possibly by Moerbeke, in 1250-1260. (See Bernard C. Dod, "Aristoteles Latinus" in *The Cambridge History of Later Medieval Philosophy*, Norman Kretzmann, Anthony Kenny, and Jan Pinborg, eds., and Eleonore Stump assoc. ed. [Cambridge, London, New York, New Rochelle, Melbourne, Sydney: Cambridge University Press,1982], pp. 47, 49, 52, 61, 64.) An evaluation of the claim that it was "[only] recently and rarely lectured on" requires more data than present research reveals.

64. For the reference to the thousand volumes see above, #13.

65. One must look to Bacon's earlier works for a basis upon which to make nominations for the three held in such esteem, for no hint is given in the rest of this work. The first would certainly have to be Avicenna, "the highest and most important (*summus et praecipuus*) immitator and defender of Aristotle ... and the greatest of the philosophers after Aristotle himself" (*Ds* 57). And even given the decreasing regard with which Bacon may have held Averroes, I suspect that the judgment expressed in the *Opus maius* still held: Averroes is second only to Avicenna. (See above, #10, n. 40.) Third place is considerably more difficult to determine. Two whom Bacon highly esteemed and perhaps mentions favorably more than any others are Robert Grosseteste and Adam Marsh. They were of the old school (*antiqui*) and said to be "the greatest clerics of the world and perfect in divine and human wisdom." (*Opus tertium*, ed. Brewer, p. 75.2-4.) The influence of the

former on Bacon in matters scientific and the preceding references to translations could possibly have brought his name to mind, but advocacy of his candidacy must also take into consideration two things: (1) the statement in question refers to accurate judgments on works already translated, and (2) Bacon's remark in the *Compendium studii philosophiae* that Grosseteste "totally" neglected the books of Aristotle and their method [*vias eorum*]," preferring his own experiments and other authorities. (Ed. Brewer, p. 469.8-12). Against Marsh's nomination is the fact that he did not lecture in the faculty of arts from 1232 on (see Crowley, *Roger Bacon*, p. 27) and it is questionable that Bacon would be thinking of anyone so immersed in theology. Persons consistently praised by Bacon and who could qualify with some degree of plausibility are indeed few, and further research should not rule out the possibility that Bacon is making a veiled appeal for posterity to supply his own name here, or at least argue its merits.

66. For the notion of a *question* see above, #2, n. 4.

67. There is probably some confusion in the text here. Palladius is the source for the preceding maxim that you should take into account the kind of person to whom you are speaking—Palladius has "to whom you are about to instruct (*cui praecepturus es*)"—but I do not find the present quotation in his *Opus agriculturae*. For the previous quotation see Palladius, *Opus agriculturae* 1. 1, ed. Robert Rodgers, *Bibliotheca Scriptorum Graecorum Et Romanorum Teubneriana* (Leipzig: B.G. Teubner, 1975), p. 2.23-24.

68. See Aristotle *Physics* 1. 1. 184a16-20.

69. For the notion of a disputation see above, #2, n. 4. The latter part of this statement recalls Bacon's unveiled condemnation in the *Compendium studii philosophiae* of people like Albert the Great and Thomas Aquinas (explicitly named) who became theologians without first having become masters in philosophy. (See ed. Brewer, 426.1-28.)

70. A real disputation (*disputatio realis*) is one wherein the central thesis is a proposition that refers to actual things or states of affairs. For example, a disputation on the question whether all men are mortal would be a real disputation, where one on the question whether all propositions are either true or false would not be. Similarly, real truth (*veritas realis*) concerns truth about something actual and not about a logical entity.

71. Bacon's reference to likenesses and forces that come from agents in the world implies an account, given in great detail in his *De multiplicatione specierum*, of how we are able to know things outside our minds. (See David C. Lindberg, *Roger Bacon's Philosophy of Nature: A Critical Edition, with English Translation, Introduction, and Notes of De multiplicatione specierum and De speculis comburentibus* [Oxford: Clarendon Press, 1983], pp. 1-269.) In essence the theory is this. Objects in the world give off or generate forces (*virtutes*) variously called (pp. 4.42-6.70) likenesses (*similitudines*), forms (*formae*), intentions (*intentiones*), passions (*passiones*), or impressions (*impressiones*). In the context of cognition, he notes (p. 4.43-46), they are usually called species (*species*). We are able to have reliable knowledge of things outside our minds because their likenesses transform the medium between them and us in such a way that fidelity is maintained as they are propagated to our sensory faculties and through them on into the reaches of our souls (p. 4.48-49). Since only individual things exist, each object generates only one kind of species, but, where the object is composed in many ways (as are all things other than God), the likenesses reflect these various levels of com-

position. Hence Bacon speaks of the species of accidents and substance (pp. 20.1-24.58), matter and form (pp. 28.138-30.179), and particulars and universals (pp. 40.350-42.390). All of these are reflected in any one species generated by a composed entity. He will implicitly draw on this theory later when he talks about the relation between knowledge and speech. (See below, Chapter Two.)

72. I am indebted to an anonymous reviewer for pointing out that William of Moerbeke was the first (ca. 1265-1272) to include in his translation of the *Metaphysics* that part of the text now found in Book Eleven, inserting it between what were then Books Ten and Eleven, and causing the treatise on separated substances—the heavenly spheres and the first mover—to be found in the twelfth book. By 1292 this was the standard translation and division of that work, yet Bacon clearly adheres to the earlier numbering. Were this part of the Prologue a revision of material found, e.g., in the *De signis* or some other part of the *Opus maius*, one might assume that Bacon, in borrowing heavily from that earlier material, failed to make the appropriate correction; but I find no similarly detailed comparison between metaphysics and logic in any of his other works. Hence I suspect it may be more likely that in 1292, while fully aware of William's innovation and its acceptance by others, he continued to abide by the judgment he expressed in the *Compendium studii philosophiae* of ca. 1272, namely, that William's translations were the worst of all, and chose the earlier numbering as a kind of continuing protest. (For his evaluation of the various translators of his times see his *Compendium studii philosophiae*, ed. Brewer, pp. 471.13-472.24.) The quotation from Aristotle is not direct, but see *Metaphysics* 4. 2. 1004b22-25.

73. Avicenna offers various remarks on the similarity and difference between metaphysics and logic. (1) Both treat of being (*esse*) but the former considers only real being (corporeal or incorporeal) where the latter confines itself to intentional being. (2) The subject matter of metaphysics is being as being and not an aspect of being appropriate to one of the individual sciences such as *Topics* and *Sophistics*. (3) *Topics* results in opinion; metaphysics in certitude. And (4) a sophist seeks to appear wise in his utterances while a metaphysician seeks truth itself. (See Avicenna *Metaphysica* 1. 2, *Opera philosophica*, ed. Iuntina [Venice: 1508; reprinted Frankfort on the Main: Minerva, 1961], f. 70vAG.)

74. See Aristotle *Metaphysics* 1. 1. 980a23-981a5 and *Posterior Analytics* 2. 19. 99b34-100a9.

75. See 1. 1-3. 71a1-72b24 and 2. 19. 99b34-100a9.

76. The reference is too vague to point specifically to anything in the rest of this work.

77. This does not seem to be a direct quote, but the principle is stated in various ways throughout Book Four of the *Metaphysics*. For example see 4. 4. 1007b29, and 4. 7. 1011b24.

78. In *Metaphysics* 5. 1012b34-1025a34 Aristotle presents thirty terms and defines them according to their various meanings. Sometimes he speaks of a notion that is common to all meanings of a given term, as in 5. 3. 1014b14-15, but he also speaks of meanings by extension, as in 5. 4. 1015a11-12. It is not clear whether Bacon's distinction between ''*per se* modes and others'' is meant to refer to either of these.

79. Aristotle says that an accidental entity is "that which is neither always nor for the most part" (*Metaphysics* 6. 2. 1026b32, transl. W.D. Ross, *The basic Works of Aristotle*, ed. Richard McKeon [New York: Random House, 1941], p. 780).

80. See *Topics* 6-7. 139a24-155a39 and *Posterior Analytics* 2. 7. 92a34-92b38, and 2. 13. 96a20-97b39.

81. Possibly Bacon has in mind *On Interpretation* 13. 23a21-26.

82. See *Metaphysics* 10. 4. 1055a37-1055b29 and *Categories* 10. 11b15-18.

83. See above, #21, n. 73.

84. See *Topics* 1. 2. 101b4.

85. See Horace *Ars poetica* 335-337, ed. and transl. H. Rushton Fairclough, *Horace: Satires, Epistles, And Ars poetica*, Loeb Classical Library (Cambridge, Mass.: Harvard University Press; London: William Heinemann, 1947), pp. 478 and 479.

86. The metaphor here refers to the pro and con method of discussing *questions*.

87. 1. 165a14-16.

88. See *On the Heavens* 1. 5. 271b9.

89. See Ps.-Boethius *De disciplina scholarium* 1. 11, ed. Olga Weijers (Leiden; Cologne: E.J. Brill, 1976), p. 97.4-6.

90. 19:1.

91. An earlier presentation (ca. 1267) of most of the material in this chapter can be found in the *De signis* (3-15). The earlier work, however, opens with two sections for which no parallel text is found in the *Cst*. In *Ds* 1 Bacon points out that a sign is in the Aristotelian category of relation; that signification involves three elements: a sign, what is signified, and an interpreter; that something remains only potentially a sign so long as there is nothing for it to signify; and that (intelligible) nonentities can also be signified. In *Ds* 2 he defines a sign as "that which once presented to a sense faculty or intellect designates something to that intellect (... *illud quod oblatum sensui vel intellectui aliquid designat ipsi intellectui* ...)." This definition is remarkable for two reasons. First, it requires that the interpreter have an intellect and thereby precludes animals from being able to communicate among themselves by signs, which Bacon clearly does not intend. (See *Ds*. 8 and below, #36.) Secondly, the definition allows for the case where something imperceptible by a sensory faculty could also be a sign. The majority in his day, he tells us (see below, #56), rejected this feature, preferring one that seems to be dependent on the second definition given by Augustine in *On Christian Doctrine*:

> For a sign is a thing which of itself makes something other come into thought besides the impression it makes upon the senses (*Signum est enim res praeter speciem, quam ingerit sensibus, aliud aliquid ex se faciens in cognitionem uenire*).

(2. 1. 1, ed. Joseph Martin, *Corpus Christianorum, Series Latina* 32, p. 32.)

Bacon seeks justification for a broader notion of a sign by claiming that Aristotle says that mental representations (*passiones, habitus* [*cognitivi*], *species*) are signs of the things outside the mind they represent to us. He is clearly referring to *On Interpretation* 1. 16a3-8 and it reads:

> Now spoken sounds are symbols of affections (*pathêmaton symbola*) in the soul, and written marks symbols of spoken sounds. And just as written marks are not the same for all men, neither are spoken sounds. But

what these are in the first place signs of (*sêmeia*)—affections of the
soul—are the same for all; and what these affections are likenesses of
(*nomoiômata*)—actual things—are also the same.
(Transl. J. L. Ackrill, *Aristotle's Categories And De Interpretatione* [Oxford:
Clarendon Press, 1963; reprinted with corrections, 1966], p. 43. Ackrill
uses the Greek letters.) As one can see Aristotle distinguishes among sym-
bols, signs, and likenesses and calls mental affections (representations) of
things outside the mind likenesses, not signs. Further, Norman Kretzmann
cogently argues that 'affections' here refers only to mental images and not
to a broader range of mental entities. (See his "Aristotle on Spoken Sound
Significant by Convention," *Ancient Logic And Its Modern Interpretations*, ed.
John Corcoran *Synthese* 9 [Dordrecht; Boston: D. Reidel, 1974], pp. 8-9.)
Yet Bacon, along with the medieval tradition, uses 'species' to denote the
broader range which, among others, includes images, mental models for
speech, and concepts. (See above, #20, n. 71, and below, #46 and #60,
nn. 129 and 147.) Paradoxically, having broadened his definition of a sign
to include concepts as signs, he never pursues the point further nor does he
list them as an example in one of his classes of natural signs.

92. For the distinction between words and vocal sounds see Introduction, p. 29.

93. In the *De Signis* the foundation for this initial division of signs is expressed
more explicitly when Bacon writes:
Some signs, however, are natural; some are directed by a soul to signify
(*ordinata ab anima ad significandum*). [The former], moreover, are called
natural because they are constituted signs from their essence and not by
an intent of a soul (*non ex intentione animae*) (*Ds* 3).
In Bacon's principal division, then, signs are distinguished on the basis of
whether or not they come about by intent. Note that this is not a distinction
between inanimate and animate agents. A cock's crow signifying the time
of night is a sign given by an animate agent, but the cock does this by
nature, not by intent. Hence Bacon classifies such a sign as natural. (See *Ds*
4.) For an analysis of the claims pertaining to *On Christian Doctrine* see "Introduction," pp. 22-24; for Augustine's division of signs see his *De doctrina
christiana* 2. 1. 2-2. 2. 3, ed. Joseph Martin, *Corpus Christianorum, Series
Latina* 32, pp. 32.12-33.18; transl. D. Robertson, Jr., *St. Augustine: On
Christian Doctrine* (New York: The Liberal Arts Press, 1958), pp. 34-35.

94. While Bacon's choice of the term 'concomitance' to name the first subclass
of natural signs might suggest that he has in mind only those things or
events that are repeatedly recognized to be or occur at the same time, it is
clear from what immediately follows and throughout that he also includes
those things or events which are or occur in sequence. In fact more often
than not he will refer to this class by speaking simply of "signs that infer,"
a kind of archaic shorthand for "signs by which people infer." Also, he
speaks here of a two-fold division of natural signs. This represents a change
in his semiotics from that presented in the *De signis* (4). For further comment see "Introduction," p. 10.

95. This text is a little problematic. It is clear from the next sentence that the
word 'necessary' has been left out. Also, the connectives 'or' and 'and'
render the meaning somewhat ambiguous, as does the mention and position of the three notions of concomitance, inference, and consequence. The
first and third refer to a temporal relation that obtains between a sign and
what it signifies; the second refers to an act of a mind that constitutes one

thing a sign of another in this mode. Hence things are signs in this mode if and only if an interpreter is aware that in the past they have repeatedly (or often) occurred simultaneously or in sequence, by which one can rationally infer that the same relation now obtains, even though only one of them be in evidence at the moment. The parallel statement in the *De signis* is unambiguous: "And these [natural signs] are divided into three classes: the first occurs when something is said to be a sign because of the fact that it necessarily or probably infers [something else]" (*Ds* 4).

96. While the third example is simply a statement about a sign relation, the examples themselves and the fact that the first two are cast in the mode of an enthememematic argument are indications that Bacon is drawing on a tradition rooted in Aristotle's treatment of signs in the *Prior Analytics* (2. 27. 70a3-70b39). There the latter distinguishes between two types of events: those that are such that when one occurs another also occurs and those that only happen together for the most part. Bacon adopts this distinction for a division of natural signs based on necessary or probable inference. (However, it should be noted that Aristotle calls the former "signs" and the latter "probabilities.") Bacon's examples are also found in the *De signis* (4), but there he adds two others: to have knowledge is a sign that one can teach and a cock's crow is a sign of the time of night, the latter previously mentioned (ca. 1250) in his *Sumule dialectices* (p. 234.5-7). Bacon can consider the possession of knowledge as a (natural) sign of the ability to teach because his definition of 'sign' is not restricted, as Augustine's is, to things that are perceptible. (See above, #24, n. 91.)

97. In the *Prior Analytics* (2. 27. 70a3-6) Aristotle distinguishes these from signs and calls them probabilities. They refer to things or events that have been recognized to occur together often enough to ground a probable inference, but not a certain (necessary) one. *De signis* 4 has additional examples, some taken from the medical tradition where signs play an obvious role in diagnosis: red, aquatic, or black dreams are signs respectively of choleric (or sanguine), phlegmatic, or melancholic disorders; over-dressing is a sign of pride or lust; and nocturnal wandering a sign of a thief.

98. In his *Sumule dialectices* (p. 314.3-11) Bacon says that a topic (*topos, locus*) is either a maximal proposition (*maxima*) or the terms placed in it which differentiate one from another (*differentiae*) and he gives a description of the various maxims and their differences as established by Themistius. (Ibid., p. 324.24.) Thus a topic is a principle that can be used, as was the case with Aristotle, Cicero, and Boethius, though with varying degrees of emphasis, to help in discovering dialectical arguments for the purpose of disputation or, as seems to be the case here, to supply a missing premiss in an otherwise enthymematic dialectical argument. (Eleanore Stump, drawing on the research of Otto Bird, notes that Abelard was especially instrumental in bringing about this shift in purpose. See her *Boethius' De topicis differentiis* [Ithaca, New York; London: Cornell University Press, 1978], pp. 25-26.) These topics draw heavily on the predicables (genus, species, definition, difference, and accident) and Bacon is saying here that the topic needed to asess the correctness of his signs by probable inference is taken from accident and pertains to things that are concomitant; it is called the "topic from concomitant accidents." In his *Sumule dialectices* (p. 321.15) he adds that the maximal proposition derived from this is "Concomitant accidents are wont to accompany one another (*Communiter accidentia solent sese concomitari*)."

Thus, e.g., the enthymeme "The ground is wet; therefore it has rained" can be rendered valid by the addition of two premisses: "That the ground is wet and that it has rained are concomitant accidents" and "Concomitant accidents are wont to accompany one another." For the development of the treatises on topics see Otto Bird, "The Tradition of the Logical Topics: Aristotle to Ockham," *Journal of the History of Ideas* 23 (1962) 307-323, and for a translation and analysis of one of them, Boethius' *De topicis differentiis*, see Eleanore Stump, *op. cit.*

99. The parallel text in the *De signis* (5) is somewhat more specific and states explicitly how signification in this mode differs from that in the preceding:

> The second mode of a natural sign occurs when something is signified, not because of some inference, but because of a conformity and configuration of one thing to another in its parts and properties.

No inference is required; the sign is so similar in appearance to something else that, on seeing the sign, one is immediately led to think of the other. He also adds in this text that the species generated by all things, both substances and attributes, are signs of these things in this mode. For the notion of species see above, #20, n. 71.

100. The term 'art' in this sentence is somewhat difficult to interpret. On the one hand it would seem to refer to the skill an artist reveals through his or her finished product. Indeed, Bacon says in the *De signis* (17): "Likewise we can well say that an elegantly crafted artifact is a sign of a good artist." However he also states (earlier) in that work that artifacts signify in this mode "art, species, and the likenesses of things that exist in the mind of an artist" (*Ds* 5). 'Species' and 'likenesses' refer to the same thing, the mental representations or models after which an artist fashions his or her artifact. And since it is difficult to understand how one's skill is configurable, I suspect that all three terms refer to mental models in *De signis* 5 and that 'art' in the *Cst* is an abbreviated way of talking about all three. While Bacon never makes the point, it would be fully consistent with his semiotics to say that an elegantly crafted artifact is a sign by *necessary* inference of a good artist.

101. The objection recalls a distinction Aristotle makes in the *Posterior Analytics* (1. 6. 75a28-35) between knowing why something is true and simply knowing that it is true. The former, says Aristotle, draws on a knowledge of the essential causes of things where the latter contents itself with an awareness of accidents or appearances. To pursue Bacon's example, if one knew that lactation and childbirth were causally linked then one would have scientific knowledge based on a theory of cause and effect; but if one simply knows that the two always occur together, then one can infer only by drawing on a recollection of the past appearances of these two phenomena, and this is knowledge by signs. (The objection is implied but not explicitly stated in *Ds* 6.)

102. In saying that an artifact is "something made and a work" Bacon is granting that it is an effect and hence causally related to an artist. But this is not the only relation involved, for artifacts also look like the mental models from which they were fashioned, and this resemblance is also a relation. What is missing here is a reason for arguing that the two are different, though it is given in the *De signis*: causal relations obtain whether or not anyone is aware of them where sign relations require an interpreter. (See *Ds* 6.) In other words the former are dyadic; the latter triadic. Since, then,

every artifact is known to have (at least) the double characteristic of being related to something else causally and significatively, it can be called by the two names 'work' and 'sign' to reflect these differences.

103. The *De signis* describes a sign in this second principal class as "directed by a soul and receiving the characteristic of a sign from an intent of a soul (*ordinatum ab anima et ex intentione animae recipiens relationem signi*)" (*Ds* 7). As will be seen from the ensuing text the term 'soul (*anima*)' is deliberately used equivocally in both works to refer to the source of activities in animals and persons. Bacon's decision to divide all signs first and principally on the basis of the nature of the act by which they are given—without or with some kind of intent—is evidence of his originality. It marks a clear departure from the customary division found in the *summulae logicales* (textbooks on logic) of his time where the signs mentioned are divided on the basis of whether or not they are the product of rationally directed activity. The latter distinction has a venerable tradition that reaches back to Aristotle's *On Interpretation* (2. 16a19-29). Bacon's new division was first presented in his *Metaphysica* and that part of his *Communia naturalium* which, according to Stewart Easton, was possibly written between 1260-1267, though published shortly after the *Opus maius* (*De signis*) of 1267. (See above, Introduction, p. 10, n. 47.) For an example of the earlier division see Bacon's own *Sumule dialectices* (pp. 232.20-234.16).

104. The fact that Bacon describes these signs as natural gives evidence that he wants his semiotics to represent, not a clean, but a partial break with tradition. Since these signs, being given by nonrational intent, are called natural in the *summulae*, it is clear that he is superimposing that tradition on his new system. The result is that 'natural' and its cognates become equivocal terms in his semiotics, and he will attempt to unravel the ensuing confusion in responses to two objections that immediately follow. The introduction of this class in the *De signis*, while being more descriptive, involves the same equivocation:

> The other sign given by a soul is that which arises without the deliberation of reason and choice of the will, neither at pleasure nor for a purpose (*ex proposito*). On the contrary [it arises] as it were suddenly, without detectable delay (*per privationem temporis sensibilis*), by a kind of natural instinct, and by force of a nature and power acting naturally (*Ds* 8).

For further comment on the fusion of these two systems of classification see Introduction, pp. 19-20. Bacon leaves unstated whether a dog's bark signifies anger to us or to other animals or both. But see below, #36, n. 115.

105. 'Imposition' is the term medievals use to refer to the act by which spoken and written words or objects are freely chosen to stand for various other objects or notions. Bacon brings out in the *De signis* how imposition distinguishes itself from all other ways by which signs arise when he writes:

> The one [type of sign] is [that given] by a soul with the deliberation of reason and choice of the will, either at pleasure or for a purpose (*sive ad placitum, sive ex proposito*), and a sign instituted by an intellect is of this kind (*Ds* 7).

He goes on to give examples: languages, dialects (*idiomata*), and various marketable items used as advertisements of themselves. This class is variously referred to as signs at pleasure, or from deliberation, or for a purpose. While spoken and written words are good examples of signs in this mode, so too are the ciphers used in shorthand and secret codes. For further comment on the meaning of 'at pleasure' see Introduction, pp. 26-28.

106. Rashdall suggests that the last words here should read "as configured to art." (See *Cst*, p. 39, n. 2.) While I see no justification for this, the phrase 'necessarily or (*necessario vel*)' does need to be added since Bacon is clearly referring to the previous use of 'natural' and 'nature' in describing *all* signs that arise from nature, i.e., 'from the essences of things. One can also note that this sentence makes it clear that the terms 'from nature' and 'from their essence' as found respectively in this work and the *De signis* are intended to mean the same thing and consequently mark no development from 1267 to 1292 in the way Bacon understands this type of signification.

107. Perhaps Bacon is broadly interpreting Boethius' remark: "For if the word nature indicates substance, when we have described nature we have also given a description of substance." See Boethius *Contra Eutychen et Nestorium* 1, ed. and transl. H.F. Stewart, E.K. Rand, and S.J. Tester, *Boethius: The Theological Tractates*, Loeb Classical Library (London: William Heinemann; New York: G.P. Putnam's Sons, 1918), pp. 79 and 81.

108. The referent of the term 'here' in the preceding sentence is ambiguous. It could refer to the way 'nature' is taken in regard to the cause of natural signs by inference and configuration or to its use in speaking of signs in the first submode of those given by a soul like a dog's bark. The context calls for a contrast, but in either case a contrast is missing. This failure is due primarily to Bacon's omission of a reference given in *Ds* 13 to Aristotle's *On the Soul*. Basically, what Bacon says clearly in the *De signis* (13-15) and should say here is this. Only signs by inference and configuration are natural in the sense this term has in *On the Soul* (2. 1. 412a12-14) where nature is contrasted with soul or any kind of intentionally given act. But signs given by a soul like a dog's bark are also called natural in the broader sense this term has in the *Physics* (possibly 2. 1. 192b8-23) where any acts that are not the products of free, deliberative, purposeful choice are called natural. In consequence signs by inference and configuration are natural in both senses while signs like a dog's bark are natural only in the sense of *Physics* 2. Given the confusion in the text, it is still clear that his semiotics draws on the distinction in *On the Soul* 2 for its initial division of signs but it is equally clear that Bacon is willing to introduce the distinction of *Physics* 2. The confusion could have been avoided by speaking of signs like a dog's bark simply as "given by a soul with instinctive intent." Why he felt compelled to superimpose the latter distinction (found also in *On Interpretation* 2 and the *summulae*) is never explained.

109. The question is whether or not the intent of an artist to produce something which faithfully represents something else constitutes a free or a configurative sign relation between the artifact and what it signifies. Bacon's response is that two relations are involved, but that neither is a sign relation at pleasure: the first is a causal one and it is constituted by the free, deliberative intent of the artist to produce the artifact; the second is a configurative relation that arises only upon the termination of the causal one in the finished product, and it arises not by intent but simply because the artifact (by its essence or nature) looks like something else. This theory is clearly stated in *Ds* 15 where Bacon also notes that signification by configuration would occur even if the artist intended something else or had no knowledge of the person or thing the artifact actually resembles. (Bacon

does not discuss the case where an artifact looks like nothing previously known. Presumably he would say that it would not be a sign by configuration.) The point is simply that it is within one's power to create an artifact but, if the artifact is known to resemble something else, configurative signification has occurred whether intended or not. Finally, Rashdall suggests (*Cst*, p. 7) that "*arti*" be read to mean "by art" and not "to art". I find no justification for this, and his observations seem to confuse the response here with that of the objection that follows.

110. This objection presents various problems for interpretation. First, it probably does not focus on the freedom of an artist to select any saints for which he or she will create an image, since the implications of that for signification were raised in the previous objection. Rather the objector seems to have in mind the case where, e.g., a sculptor creates various human figures on a portal of a cathedral and calls one of them Christ and the others by the names of various apostles and saints, or sculpts a form to represent allegorically one of the virtues. Second, the response can be read in more than one way depending on whether the supplied expression "*sed signum*" is to be translated "[but *the* sign]" or "[but *a* sign]," and each presents problems of its own. (Unfortunately, there is no parallel text in the *De signis*.) In the first reading Bacon would be saying that the image in question signifies in both modes, implying that it is related to the saint by two distinct sign relations, the one configurative and the other at pleasure. But this is clearly impossible. The former requires that sign and significate be related independently of rational intent where the latter is constituted precisely by such intent. Hence the two are mutually exclusive. The second reading, however, is also problematic. If the text is taken as translated, the generic reference to "a sign," providing no explicit response to the objection, trusts the reader to apply the semiotic rules previously given and to arrive at a proper conclusion. Thus I suggest that one interprets Bacon's response accurately if one inserts two clarifying clauses whereby the text would read:

> I concede that then there is a sign, but a sign is distinguished in one mode as natural, configured by its essence to another thing [as was the case in the previous example, and] in another mode at pleasure and through imposition, [as is the case here].

This reading introduces no new theory of signification, but it does assume two things: that the image in question is not strictly representational and that Bacon intends a response containing this contrast.

111. Here Bacon resumes his discussion of signs given by a soul that signify naturally, where 'naturally' means by nonrational, nondeliberative intent. This use, we have been told, has the sanction of *Physics* 2, and I have noted that it is found in the *summulae* and *On Interpretation* 2.

112. Bacon probably has in mind the distinction Aristotle makes in the *Nicomachean Ethics* (5. 7. 1134b18-24) between natural and legal justice where the former is a characteristic of an act irrespective of our wishes and the latter the result of an act being in conformity with a law freely enacted. This is clearly the same type of distinction he found in *Physics* 2. I think the text requires the insertion of 'nondeliberative' for without it this passage would have Bacon saying that an act is natural if it arises from the nature of an individual. This sounds like a restatement of the principle that entities operate in conformity with their natures. But his reference to *Nichomachean*

Ethics 5 indicates that he is aware that he needs a sense of 'natural' that will apply to all signs except those given deliberatively at pleasure. Without the more restricted meaning Bacon could be understood to say that even signs at pleasure are natural in the sense that they proceed from a (free and rational) nature and are common to all and only those individuals sharing that nature.

113. Two paragraphs below Bacon will return to these signs and speak of cries of joy, happiness, grief, hope, and fear that we utter instinctively without deliberation. In *Ds* 8 he says they are caused by one's rational soul "at the instance of the sensitive soul (*ad motum animae sensitivae*)." This statement must be understood in the light of his theory of resumption (*resumptio*) as presented in his *Questiones supra libros prime philosophie Aristotelis* (*Opera*, 10, ed. Steele with Delorme, p. 261.21-26), written probably in or shortly after 1245. In virtue of this theory a person is a unity composed of many forms where the highest, being a completion of the lower, exercises the lower functions of vegetative and sensitive life. Thus the intellectual soul has activities that are proper to humans alone but also some in common with other animals. In *Ds* 12 he calls the intellect acting in this latter way the practical intellect (*intellectus practicus*) and describes some of the things it does other than utter the cries in question: "For it seeks to be in its body naturally, rejoices, experiences, rules, governs, and has many other feelings (*affectiones*) without any deliberation and choice, [rational] purpose, and exercise of reason." For further analysis of Bacon's theory of resumption see Crowley, *Roger Bacon*, pp. 136-141.

114. See *De doctrina christiana* 2. 1. 2 and 2. 2. 3, ed. Joseph Martin, *Corpus Christianorum, Series Latina* 32, p. 33.20-24 and .9-18; transl. D. Robertson, Jr., *St. Augustine: On Christian Doctrine* (New York: The Liberal Arts Press, 1958), p. 35.

115. As early as about 1250 Bacon wrote in his *Sumule dialectices* (p. 233.22-27) that animals are able to communicate with one another of the same species and he appealed to the same evidence. Because of his clear conviction then and my suspicion that he embarked on this new classification of signs in part to give a better understanding of the proper role these signs play in signification, I have translated "*ex intentione fiant*" as "they would come from intent" rather than in the weaker form of "they may come from intent." Unfortunately, there is no parallel text in the *De signis*.

   Since this is the last time Bacon will refer to "animal talk" one might also note that in the *Sumule dialectices* (pp. 233.31-234.8), Bacon points out that, while a magpie can be taught to utter cries understandable by humans, they do not signify the same thing to other magpies because they do not proceed from intent. Similarly, he says, a cock's crow may tell us the time of day, but this is not because the cock intends it. In the *De signis* (4) he specifies that the latter is a sign to us by necessary inference, though, no mention is made of the magpie.

116. Violating his proposal to proceed "in an orderly way from first to last" (see above, #19), Bacon here and in the following two paragraphs pauses to show how what he has been discussing—nondeliberative, nonrational acts of a rational soul—is relevant to theological matters.

   The delay he mentions possibly refers to the practice (still observed) in the Catholic Church of delaying a child's first Confession until he or she has reached the age of discrimination, i.e., until rational and volitional faculties are sufficiently developed' to enable him or her to make correct moral judgments between right and wrong. Until such time the child is considered to be incapable of commiting serious personal sin.

117. The Master here is Peter Lombard. (See his *Libri IV Sententiarum*, vol. 1, 2nd. ed., ed. Fathers of the College of St. Bonaventure [Ad Claras Aquas near Florence: Bonaventure College Press, 1916], book 2, distinction 33, chapter 4.) When Bacon says that he wishes "to argue a point, [but] not render a judgment" he means, as will be seen, that he intends to pose certain problems for a theory that attempts to explain how original sin is passed on to us from Adam and Eve, but not offer any solution. (There is no parallel text in the *De signis*.) One should keep in mind that Bacon was a Master in the faculty of Arts, not a Doctor of Theology; and while he attended lectures on theology at Paris (*Opus minus*, ed. Brewer, p. 354.6-13) and possibly at Oxford (*Opus tertium*, ed. Brewer, p. 186.12-16 and .32-35) and even uses the phrase "we theologians" (*Opus minus*, ed. Brewer, p. 350.2), it is debated whether he ever seriously pursued a bachelor's degree in that field. Crowley thinks he did; Easton disagrees. (See Crowly, *Roger Bacon*, pp. 25-28, and Easton, *Roger Bacon*, pp. 19-20 and 29-34.)

118. In the text "*esset macula ... non suae voluntatis*" could mean that the will has no stain on it, reading '*voluntatis*' as an objective genitive. However, I think this would be wrong for two reasons. First, the will is a faculty of the substance of the soul, and I know of no theory that could explain how the will could be unaffected if that of which it is a faculty is stained. Second, the central issue in this incursion into theology is not whether the will is in some way affected by original sin—presumably Bacon would grant this—but rather, whether the will is the cause of the presence of this sin in a soul. This is why he points out that all sin is voluntary. The translation, then, assumes that '*voluntatis*' is to be taken as a subjective genitive. Given this reading and assuming several unstated premises, Bacon is arguing that, since the union of polluted flesh with a soul is an involuntary act, and all sin is the result of a voluntary act, then this union of itself cannot be the cause of the transmission of original sin. The argument, however, is theologically unsophisticated. In using 'sin' univocally, as his argument requires, he has placed himself in a dilemma. Either he must deny that original sin is sin, which would be heresy, or he must acknowledge a distinction between original sin and personal sin (mortal or venial), which would ruin his argument.

119. The previous rejoinder left open the possibility that original sin in our souls could be explained by the fact that the corruption which human flesh has is itself sinful. Here Bacon attempts to show that even this account of the "contact theory" has problems. His argument in a somewhat more complete form runs like this, with unstated or previously stated premises in parentheses: (since original sin is sin); and (all sin involves an act of a will); and (flesh has no will of itself); then flesh is not subject to sin, i.e., flesh is not sinful, i.e., cannot cause sin. Bacon is arguing that the basic assumption of this version of the "contact theory" is faulty in that it contends that the corruption which flesh has is sinful. Hence sinful flesh cannot be invoked as the cause of the transmission of original sin.

120. Given the reading here of '*voluntatis*' as an objective genitive and the addition in the text, Bacon should be understood here simply to be restating his bill of particulars: the stain of original sin is not caused by the corruption

flesh has; it is not caused by an act of the will; yet the soul does have original sin. This is similar to the case of the apple: its meat was spoiled, not by its skin and not by some act of its own, but by dirt.

121. Bacon suggests (and attacks) here a third version of the "contact theory": if neither involuntary contact with polluted flesh nor a sinfulness in flesh can be adduced as the cause of original sin in us, then it must be the result of a natural (nondeliberative, involuntary) inclination in our souls that occurs when they are joined to flesh. Here we can see an even closer link with the matters discussed immediately prior to this incursion into theology. 'Natural' is used as before in the sense of *Physics* 2 and *Nicomachean Ethics* 5. There an intellect acting without deliberation was given (in a parallel text in the *De signis*) a new name, "practical intellect"; here the will operating in the same instinctive way is called "pure will." But while the theory he challenges is stated clearly, his response is somewhat confusing because of the use of 'mortal' and 'mortal sin' in reference to natural inclinations. In the technical sense, current in his day and most assuredly known by him, a mortal sin is a freely chosen, premeditated act of vice of such magnitude that, if unrepented, would merit damnation. I am inclined to think that this is not the sense Bacon intends here for two reasons. First, it would have him repeat what in essence has already been argued in the first rejoinder, namely, that no involuntary act can be sinful because every sin is voluntary. He would only be reminding here that this includes mortal sin. Second, Bacon would surely know in 1292 that no orthodox theologian would accept his statement that mortal sin and original sin are the same kind of sin. Just eighteen years earlier the Church in the Second General Council of Lyons had implied a distinction when pronouncing dogmatically on their consequences: "Moreover, the souls of those who die in mortal sin or with only original sin soon descend into hell (*infernum*) to be punished, but with different kinds of penalties (*poenis tamen disparibus*)." (See *Encheridion Symbolorum Deffinitionum Et Declarationum de Rebus Fidei Et Morum*, Heinrich Denzinger and Adolf Schonmetzer, eds., 33rd. ed. [New York: Herder, 1965], pp. 276-277.) There was still debate over the nature of the penalties incurred by those who die with only original sin on their souls, but the issue whether they suffered the penalties of the damned had been magisterially resolved. And if he simply meant to say that Peter Lombard and others erred in the past, then he is beating a dead horse. However, 'mortal' can also have a meaning that is less technical and more closely tied to its etymological root. It can mean death-inducing where 'death' can be taken in both a physical and spiritual sense. Any of his contemporaries would certainly accept the statement that original sin is mortal in this sense. If this is what he intends, then he has indeed introduced a rejoinder to the "contact theory" not previously mentioned. He would be saying here that any attempt to explain original sin in us by contending that it is caused by a natural (nondeliberative), involuntary tendency of our wills that occurs when our souls are united to flesh would imply that a natural tendency does not incline to the benefit of an individual but rather to his or her very destruction. (And if one such works to our disadvantage, he adds, there is no good reason for not saying that all do.) Left unstated in the argument is some statement like "Given two alternatives, nature always inclines to the better," and Bacon's contemporaries would have recognized such as a reasonably accurate rendering of Aristotle's remark in *On Generation and*

Corruption: "For in all things, as we affirm, Nature always strives after 'the better'. Now 'being' ... is better than 'not-being' ..." (See 2. 10 336b27-30, transl. Harold H. Joachim, *The Basic Works of Aristotle*, Richard McKeon, ed. [New York: Random House, 1941], p. 527.)

122. While Bacon has raised three objections to the "contact theory" of original sin, he has granted throughout that original sin is sin (though fails to indicate how the former differs from personal sin); that we are all born with original sin on our souls; and that the flesh we inherit in direct descent from Adam and Eve is a polluted or corrupt flesh.

123. The reference is to a third Part that is still missing. (See above, p. 9 and n. 39; see also below, #83 and n. 183.)

124. See Aristotle *On Interpretation* 2. 16a19-29 and 3. 16b6-12. For a second time Bacon introduces the second class of signs given by a soul. They differ from all other signs in that they are in no way natural. While they arise by intent (*ex intentione*), as does a dog's bark, he specifies that the intent here is rational: they signify for a purpose (*ex proposito*). Bacon will be speaking of this class of signs whenever he refers to signs at pleasure (*ad placitum*), signs for a purpose (*ex proposito*), or signs with deliberation (*cum deliberatione*). They are signs that arise only by imposition.

125. Bacon's treatment of the signification of interjections is highly sketchy here. However, some help in understanding these remarks can be found in three of his earlier works. In his *Summa grammatica* he states (*Opera*, 15, ed. Steele, 18.13-21) and endorses (p. 19.21-34) a theory that claims that there is a kind of proportion between the clarity with which we conceive something and the clarity with which we express it: "If there is no perfection in the concept, there is none in the vocal sound (*in voce*); and if it is present [in the concept], it will be there [in the vocal sound]" (p. 18.20-21). In his *Communia naturalium* (*Opera*, 2, ed. Steele, p. 110.17-111.7) he seems to draw on this theory and goes on to point out that the same feeling, e.g., pain, can be signified in three different ways: naturally, by an instinctive groan; at pleasure, by the term 'pain'; and finally by an interjection (e.g., 'agh!'). The differences, he says, stem respectively from a complete absence, presence, or partial (*imperfecta*) presence of deliberation and conception prior to utterance. Interjections, he argues, are the result of an impeded psychological process. One experiences, e.g., pain, and begins to form a concept of it, but the process is cut short by the intensity of the pain. The result is an ill-formed utterance that is the mark of incomplete conceptualization and deliberation. The essential features of this explanation are found in the *De signis* (9-11) with only a shift in accent: in the *Communia naturalium* and here he says interjections signify in the way of a feeling and not in the way of a concept (*per modum affectus, non per modum conceptus*); in the *De signis* he accents the partial conceptualization by describing them as signifying by way of imperfect concepts (*per modum conceptus, licet imperfecti*). Interjections, then, are significative utterances (*voces*) that stand midway between signs given by a soul naturally and those at pleasure. This is why in the *De signis* (10) he refers to them as intermediary utterances (*voces mediae*). For a broader reflection on the nature of interjections in medieval literature see Jan Pinborg, "Interjectionen und Naturlaute" in *Classica et Mediaevalia* 22 (1961) 117-138.

126. This completes Bacon's presentation of a general theory and classification of signs. While his initial division is claimed to have Augustine's authority,

in point of fact, I have argued, it is original. (See above, Introduction, pp. 22-24). Representing a break with the traditional way of dividing signs found in the *summulae* of his times, it seeks its foundation in *On the Soul* 2, employing the earlier tradition only to characterize a subclass of signs about which Augustine was indecisive. Signs arise, he says, either by nature of by intent of a soul. The former relate to what they signify either by our (necessary or probable) inference or by the mere fact that they look like it; the latter are constituted signs by either instinctive or rational intent. Given this kind of semiotics, he is now in a position to address what he will call his "principal intent," namely, an analysis of the many modes in which linguistic utterances signify.

127. Bacon alters the sequence of *questions* somewhat in the ensuing discussion. Between the first and second he inserts another: "Does [an unimposed vocal sound] signify in any other way before imposition?" The third and fourth are then recast into a single *question*: "After a vocal sound has been imposed for some thing outside a mind, what does it principally signify by force of the imposition?" The subject of this chapter is the signification of vocal sounds (*voces*), but it is clear from the context throughout as well as the parallel texts in the *De signis* (16-18, 27-35, and 162-169, especially 30) that the vocal sounds in question are not the instinctive articulated cries of animals and humans. Rather, they are freely articulated human utterances. The consequence of this is that whenever Bacon speaks of natural signification in this chapter he will intend it in the sense of the distinction in *On the Soul* 2, i.e., as signification without rational or nonrational intent.

128. For the quotation see above, #23.

129. As a first step in understanding the signification of vocal sounds Bacon asks the reader to consider the signification of those to which no one has yet attached any meaning. (In the *De signis* [16] he asks one to consider an imposed vocal sound as if it had not been imposed.) He is speaking of nonsense utterances and his remarks assume a theory that maintains that one cannot speak without having in one's imagination a mental model of the vocal sounds to be uttered. This model is what he calls the species of a vocal sound and he appeals in the *De signis* (17) to Aristotle's *On the Soul* 2 and Boethius' commentary on Aristotle's *On Interpretation* for support for the theory. (See respectively 2. 8. 420b33-35 and *Commentarium* [*maius*] *in librum Aristotelis Peri herméneias* 1, ed. Karl Meiser [Leipzig: B.G. Teubner, 1880], p. 4.28-29, where, however, it is far more probable that both are talking about the imagery associated with our knowledge of things about which we speak than mental models of speech itself.) Given Bacon's interpretation and the general theory, one knows that whenever there is an articulate sound there must also be its species, and hence a spoken vocal sound (*vox prolata*) is a natural sign of its own species in the first mode of a natural sign. (In the *De signis* [18] he further specifies that it is a natural sign by necessary inference.) In virtue of the theory of species presented in his *De multiplicatione specierum* the species mentioned would be either one generated by some previous speaker, received and retained in the memory of the present speaker, and now used as a model for the present utterance, or a new creation, elaborated in the present speaker's imagination and composed of several sound-species previously received. (See above, #20, n. 71.) Bacon's analysis indicates that he is considering only the case where the speaker does not accidentally utter an unintended vocal sound. In this case the vocal

sound would have no mental mode. Nevertheless, it would still be a natural sign by necessary inference that its source is nearby. (Cf. *Ds* 17.)

130. Since the vocal sound is an articulated likeness of a mental structure or model, it signifies the latter by configuration. Again, the analysis does not consider the case of an unintended utterance. But since Bacon treats vocal sounds as artifacts, he would presumably apply to them the same principles said in the *De signis* (15) to govern the configurative signification of all artifacts. Thus if it resembled some other mental model known to another, and that person was brought to an awareness of that other because of the resemblance, it would be a configurative sign of the latter even though the speaker did not intend it. If it resembled nothing known to any hearer, it would not be a configurative sign at all. (See above, #33, n. 109.)

131. Since this objection and response is essentially the same as that presented in regard to all artifacts, see above, #30.

132. Since the reference to imposition in the *question* rules out signification at pleasure and given Bacon's semiotics, the issue is whether they can signify by instinctive intent, i.e., naturally, where 'naturally' is taken in the sense of *Physics* 2 and *Nicomachean Ethics* 5. (See above, #32 and #35, respectively.) Such signification is explicitly excluded in *Ds* 30 and the statements there and here are probably rooted in the theory that instinctively given articulate sounds require no mental models.

133. The grammatical form of this objection has been changed in the translation from the conditional mood ("If it be cautiously objected ...") to the imperative to simplify its syntactical relation to the next objection and the response that follows both. (For a parallel text see *Ds* 33.)

   Any logician in Bacon's time would grant that the subject and predicate in an expression (*oratio*) are signs at pleasure; that an expression taken as a whole is also a sign at pleasure; and that "A man is a man" is an expression (*oratio perfecta*). (See Bacon's *Sumule dialectices*, p. 240.14-29.) Second, they would also grant that such tautologous expressions must necessarily be true when stated as propositions, since they assert an identity between the classes named by the subject and predicate. What happens then when one substitutes 'buba', a vocal sound with no meaning whatsoever, for 'a man' in the expression above? The objection raises the question whether a meaningless utterance can gain meaning by this kind of use. It argues that since expressions (in the indicative mood) having a subject and predicate can be true; since tautologous expressions are necessarily true; since the subject and predicate of such expressions are signs at pleasure; and since "Buba is buba" is a tautologous expression, 'buba' can be a sign at pleasure without prior imposition.

134. To grasp the intent of this objection one must read "Buba is a vocal sound" in such a way that avoids allowing 'buba' to have any meaning of itself. It is not taken here as the name of itself as a vocal sound, for this would require that it already had this meaning prior to use in this "expression," and the whole point of the objection is to show that an utterance with no prior meaning can acquire one through use alone. The previous objection attempted to show that this can be done by appeal to the principle of identity; this one, using 'buba' in a complete disjunction, attempts to draw on the principle of the excluded middle to force one of two "expressions" in response: "Buba is a vocal sound that signifies [at pleasure]" or its denial. Since both would be expressions, claims the objector, and subject terms in

such are signs at pleasure, whether one affirms or denies one must grant an unimposed vocal sound has become a sign at pleasure through use in an expression.

135. This response, while ostensibly referring to the second objection, serves equally well for the previous one, for in both it has been assumed that the utterances in question can legitimately be called expressions. Bacon correctly points out that such instances of use do not result in expressions for the simple reason than an expression is by definition an utterance each of whose principal parts is a sign at pleasure independently of any signification when taken together. 'Buba' does not meet this test in any of the examples given.

Medievals were confronted with the problem of what to call compound articulated sounds one or all of which lack imposition. They are not a vocal sound (*vox*) in the usual sense since they are made up of more than one *vox*; they are neither a statement (*sermo*) nor an expression (*oratio*) because of the lack of signification at pleasure. (See "Introduction," p. 29.) Today we would speak of them as "expressions," using quotation marks to indicate that 'expressions' is to be taken in an altered sense. (The translation, as here, will supply quotation marks when appropriate in Bacon's responses but not in the objections since there the proper meaning is intended.) Bacon variously designates an "expression" of the type in question by all three of the terms mentioned above. (See here and immediately below for all three and, e.g., below, #123, where they are repeated.)

136. Bacon's illustration is the following. Take the "sentence" "__ is a word" and place, e.g., an apple in the blank. What does the "sentence" mean? Nothing, because written or spoken expressions require that all principal components have some meaning of themselves when they are used, i.e., that they already be signs by imposition. This is not a denial that one could devise a code wherein rocks, a piece of wood, and fruit could convey meaning, but among the requirements of such would be that each have a meaning acquired by imposition prior to an effective use of the code. However even then the result could be called an expression only equivocally, since the components would be neither written nor vocal sounds.

137. For a comment on the use of 'vocal sound' to name such "expressions" as "Buba is" see above, #52, n. 135.

138. The third question turns from nonsense utterances to reflexive ones where a speaker chooses to talk about a certain vocal sound by using the sound itself. (For parallel texts see *Ds* 27-35.) In the language of supposition theory these terms are said by Bacon to have simple supposition when used in an expression. (See his *Sumule dialectices*, p. 269.3-7.) Thus 'Man' in "Man is a vocal sound" stands for a particular vocal sound and not human beings in general. In the *De signis* Bacon acknowledges that there is some question in his time about the signification of these reflexive utterances, some contending that they are natural signs of themselves. (See *Ds* 28.) He does not indicate who held this theory, but may imply by what he says in *Ds* 30 that it is a particular instance of the more general claim that everything is a natural sign of itself. It is conceivable that someone would want to argue that, since sign and significates are, in a fundamental sense, the same, signification by necessary inference or configuration is involved. It would then have to be decided whether a reflexive utterance signifies itself only by nature or also at pleasure. It has already been argued that Bacon's

semiotics rejects such dual signification (see above, #34, n. 110), and in the *De signis* (30-31) he clearly states that these utterances signify themselves at pleasure and not naturally. Hence his present remark that they can signify at pleasure should be understood more broadly to mean not only that they do signify in this way but also that this is the only way they can signify themselves.

139. One is free to select any vocal sound to name something in an utterance; one could choose 'zerd' to be the name of the vocal sound 'buba'. But if one chooses the same vocal sound to name itself as a vocal sound, then one has created a reflexive utterance. Bacon avoids the paradoxes of self-reference by never claiming that reflexive names are names of names. They are names of unimposed vocal sounds or names of names considered without reference to the latter's imposition.

140. A vocal sound is a thing; it can become the name of anything, including itself, by imposition. On Aristotle's authority 'white thing' is just such a vocal sound. In "A snowflake is a white thing" it is used as the name of a white thing; but in " 'white thing' is a vocal sound" it is used as the name of a certain vocal sound, i.e., its own. For the reference to Aristotle see *On Sophistical Refutations* 14. 174a9, though Bacon may also have in mind Aristotle's more general statement about the difference between names and things having names in 1. 165a5-11. For a parallel text see *Ds* 27.

141. See Augustine *De dialectica* 10, ed. Jan Pinborg; transl. B. Darrell Jackson, *Augustine: De Dialectica, Synthese Historical Library* 16 (Dordrecht; Boston: D. Reidel, 1975), p. 112; ed. Crecilius, p. 17.4-5 and 9. 'Tullius' is the name by which medievals often referred to Mark Tully Cicero, Roman orator-statesman. The name appears in the translation in its Latin form since the context requires a name having three syllables with an accent on the first. "Tullius is a dactyl foot" can be true or false depending on the meaning of 'Tullius'. It will be false if the subject is taken as the name of the orator-statesman, for he is not a metric foot. It will be true, however, if it is taken as the name of the dactyl vocal sound 'Tullius'. While 'Tullius' would be a sign at pleasure in either reading, it is the fact that it can be used in the second sense that shows that it can be imposed for itself and thereby signify itself at pleasure. There is no parallel text in the *De signis*, though Augustine's example is mentioned in *Ds* 88 to illustrate a case of equivocation.

142. The grammatical form of this objection has been changed in the translation from the conditional mood ("If it be objected ...") to the imperative to simplify its syntactical relation to the next objection and the response that follows both. (There is no parallel text in the *De signis*.)

The prominence of the term 'the other (*aliud*)' in this definition suggests that Bacon probably has in mind Augustine's second definition in *On Christian Doctrine* (see above, #24, n. 91), and he uses the term to focus attention on an issue especially relevant to reflexive utterances: if signification involves a sign and significate, must not the sign be one thing and what it signifies something other? If so, argues the objector, then a vocal sound could not be said to be a sign of itself at pleasure. Note that Bacon's own definition of a sign simply speaks of that which designates *something*. (See above, #24, n. 91.)

143. This is an interesting use of commercial advertisement to illustrate a point of semantic importance. (In the *De signis* [27] Bacon says the difference

[*alietas*] in question is relevant to a discussion of relational entities [*relativa*] in general.) The objection draws on Aristotle's distinction between substance and accident where 'substance' refers to the nature of an entity by which it is, e.g., bread and not cheese and 'accident' refers to an attribute such as size, weight, color, etc. Being-for-sale is just such an attribute; it is something bread of itself does not have but bread for sale does. The objection implies that this ontological difference is sufficient to meet the requirement of all signification that sign and significate be in some sense different. Since the objection focuses on this particular difference, it would seem that a case is intended where the bread in the window is not itself for sale. The objector, acknowledging the difference here, is not convinced that an analogous difference is preserved in the case of reflexive utterances.

144. The two objections claim that some degree of otherness must obtain between a sign and its significate. Bacon grants this and agrees that a difference is preserved in the case of bread used as an advertisement, but then merely asserts that an (analogous) difference obtains in the case of reflexive utterances. He does not say what the differentiating attribute (mode and condition) is. However in a parallel text in the *De signis* (27) he points to the difference between a vocal sound taken simply and one having the attribute of being the target of an act of imposition: "The substance of a vocal sound is the sign, but that same thing as capable of being subject [to imposition] and capable of being talked about [*prout est subiectibilis et praedicabilis*] is signified." The difference here is not one in substance but in attribute.

   A summary, then, of Bacon's position on the signification of nonsense utterances would read something like this. Of itself a vocal sound like 'buba' is simply a vocal sound. But because we know that it is the articulated sound of a human being, and that such are uttered in conformity with a speaker's mental model (species), and assuming he or she speaks without mishap, it is a natural sign by necessary inference that the speaker has a model in his or her mind and that the speaker is audibly near. It is also a natural sign by configuration of that model. It is not a sign given by a soul with instinctive intent both because it does not signify a feeling and because it is not a spontaneous utterance. As a nonsense utterance it cannot be used in an expression, since all components of such are signs by imposition. However, because it is an utterable thing and the intellect is free to select whatever it is aware of and can properly utter for the purpose of speech, it can become a part of speech by imposition, name itself, and be properly used in an expression like " 'Buba' is a vocal sound." Such reflexive utterances meet the fundamental requirement of all signification, namely, that sign and significate differ in some way, since the same vocal sound as sign has the attribute of being-imposed and as significate that of being-imposed-for.

145. Given the fact that we can name only things we know about, and given the Aristotelian theory that we know things outside a mind only by way of their mental representations, does an imposed vocal sound principally signify the thing named or the representation by which the thing is known? This was a celebrated *question* in Bacon's time as one can see by reading the summaries of the debate in the opening pages of the commentaries of Scotus, Burleigh, and Ockham on Aristotle's *On Interpretation* (For Aristotle's text see above, #24, n. 91). Between 1269 and 1272, a few years before Bacon wrote the

parallel sections in the *De signis* on this issue (162-169), Aquinas gave his opinion on Aristotle's intent, and his commentary can be used as a backdrop for understanding Bacon's position in the debate. (See Aquinas, *Sententia super Peri hermenias*, lib. 1, lect. 2, nn. 4-5; transl. Jean T. Oesterle, *Aristotle: On Interpretation: Commentary by St. Thomas and Cajetan* [Milwaukee, Wisconsin: Marquette University Press, 1962], p. 25.) First, the sign in question is a vocal sound imposed for a thing outside a mind and hence a sign at pleasure. Second, while Aristotle was most probably speaking only of sensory images as the significate of these sounds (see above, #24, n. 91), Aquinas, following the tradition of Boethius, understands Aristotle's *pathêma* (*passiones*, affections) to be concepts in the intellect (*intellectus conceptio*). (For Boethius see his *Commentarium* [*maius*] *in librium Peri hermêneias* 1, ed. Karl Meiser [Leipzig: B.G. Teubner, 1880], p. 7.12-16.) On these two points both sides are in agreement. But they part company over the relation of the first to the second, the side embraced by Aquinas contending that imposed vocal sounds are signs at pleasure directly (*immediate*) of the concepts by which things are known and indirectly (*mediate*) of the things themselves. Bacon addresses this third point in terms of principal and, assuming that the terminology later used in regard to connotation can be applied here, secondary signification (see below, #75), and I shall argue that the way he addresses this issue warrants the different terminology. (See below, #60, n. 147.)

146. In signification at pleasure sign and significate must not be related on their own (by their essence) but only in virtue of a free, deliberative, purposeful choice of the sign-giver. It is the result of a well-focused intent to relate a vocal sound to a designated object whereby the latter is named. Applying this notion with rigorous precision, Bacon concludes that the significate of a name as a name is exclusively the object named because it alone, in virtue of the act and intent of imposition, is targeted, and we have just seen that he contends that a vocal sound can become a name only by such a well-focused intent. It is important to note that his claim is not a denial that, when naming occurs, some other mode of signification may also arise. He simply argues that nothing other than the intended object is, strictly speaking, the significate of the vocal sound taken as a sign at pleasure.

147. This text presents Bacon's most complete position in the controversy and several things should be noted. First, he is responding directly to Aristotle's claim that spoken sounds are signs first of affections in the soul, and he implies that his opponents have misunderstood Aristotle's intent. (For Aristotle's text see above, #24, n. 91.) Second, it is clear that the species he mentions is not the model in accord with which a speaker articulates a name, nor any other datum in the (sensitive) faculties of memory and imagination, nor even a concept taken as an object of direct, reflexive knowledge (*medium quod*). Rather, it is the likeness described in his *De multiplicatione specierum* as generated by an object and received in the intellect via the senses; it is a concept by which actual things are known (*medium quo*). (For his theory of species see above, #20, n. 71.) Given this, he claims, the name of a thing cannot be first a name of the species for two reasons. (1) A vocal sound acquires the character of being a name (sign at pleasure) only by imposition. But imposition is a free act directed with great precision in accord with a namer's intent, and here the intent is to name a thing, not its mental representation. This point is exemplified in the *De signis* (164) where

Bacon argues that, when one says "Socrates runs," one does not intend to say that the species of Socrates is running. The result is a freely constituted relation between a vocal sound and the thing, the former being a sign of the latter at pleasure. While he does not call this direct signification, it is clear that any problem he has with the language of direct-indirect signification is not based on some notion that names do not signify something at pleasure directly. (2) If one knows from repeated experience that one cannot name anything without previously being aware of the object, then one also knows that if naming has occurred, the species of the things named must be present in the intellect of the namer. Since this is the basis for natural signification by inference, Bacon concludes that imposed vocal sounds are (also) natural signs of the species of things that as names they signify at pleasure. (In a parallel text in the De signis [165] he further specifies that this signification is by necessary inference.) To explicate these two modes of signification he does here implicitly what he explicitly did earlier in the case of reflexive utterances (see above, #58), namely, draw on the Aristotelian distinction between substance and accident: a name is a vocal sound (substance) having the attribute of imposition (accident). The knowledge it conveys in virtue of its attribute is not what it conveys in virtue of its substance. Bacon's position in this debate is one that speaks of names as names signifying at pleasure the things of which they are names and names as vocal sounds signifying naturally the species of these things, and the justification for this approach derives from his theory that that which is a name, being an entity composed of substance (vocal sound) and attribute (imposition), conveys knowledge in different ways reflective of the different relations each part has to what a name conveys.

Given this theory, is the language of direct-indirect signification suitable, i.e., could Bacon have said that names as names signify at pleasure directly the things of which they are names and indirectly the species of these things? The first part presents no problem, but the second does: they are signs at pleasure *only* of that intended by the namer; they are in no sense names of species. Bacon's theory needs language that draws on values implicit in his semiotics and reflects his analysis that vocal sounds as names signify the thing for which they are imposed more importantly (given the purpose of language), in the highest mode of signification (freely), and in virtue of their distinguishing attribute (imposition), and that they signify as vocal sounds the mental representations of these things less importantly, in a less noble mode (naturally), and not in virtue of their distinguishing character. A distinction between principal and secondary signification seems quite appropriate. If these are the considerations that led him to cast the problem in this terminology rather than in that of direct and indirect signification, then he must also be reading Aristotle's remark that spoken sounds are first signs of mental affections in a different light than, e.g., Aquinas. Since names signify species in virtue of their substance, Bacon could "meet" the implied objection by the claim that 'first' reflects the priority of substance over accident, not the notion of directness. Finally, were one to object that Aristotle does not even mention natural signs in this passage, Bacon could point to Aristotle's claim that mental affections of things are the same for all people and argue that this is indication that Aristotle also had in mind natural signs in this passage. And this is exactly what Bacon does in a section of the De signis (166) omitted here. Aristotle, of

course, says only that they are likenesses of things, but one should recall
that Bacon broadened his definition of a sign precisely to include these
likenesses as signs, thinking that in so doing he was correctly interpreting
Aristotle's intent. (See above, #24, n. 91.)

148. Bacon is clearly misrepresenting Boethius. The latter does indeed say that
(imposed) vocal sounds signify concepts (*intellectus, conceptiones animi, passiones*) of the things they name, but he expressly states that they do this principally. Things outside the mind are said to be signified by these vocal
sounds secondarily and by way of their concepts. (Boethius *Commentarium*
[*maius*] *in librum Aristotelis Peri herméneias* 1. 1, ed. Karl Meiser [Leipzig:
B.G. Teubner, 1880], p. 33.24-33.) He also takes it to be Aristotle's view
that (imposed) vocal sounds are not natural signs of concepts. (Ibid., p.
37.20-27.)

149. Later Bacon correctly attributes this quotation to Priscian. (See below,
#63.) When one says that an imposed vocal sound signifies a *conceptum mentis*, the ambiguity in the Latin allows two meanings. If '*conceptum*' is taken
as the accusative of '*conceptus*', then one is speaking of a concept of a mind;
but if it is taken as a neuter substantive adjective in the accusative, then one
is referring to a conceived thing (*res concepta*). Bacon argues that the quotation was intended to be read in the second sense. However, the full text of
Priscian's remark suggests that he intended the first reading. He says: ''For
what other is it [to be] a part of speech but a vocal sound indicating a concept of a mind, that is, thought (*Quid enim est aliud pars orationis nisi vox indicans mentis conceptum, id est cogitationem*)?'' See Priscian *Institutiones grammaticae* 11. 2. 7, ed. Martin Hertz, *Grammatici Latini* 2, ed. Heinrich Keil
(Leipzig: B.G. Teubner, 1859; reprinted Hildesheim: Georg Olms, 1961),
pp. 551.1-2.

150. See *Metaphysics* 7. 7. 1032b12-14. Before a builder constructs anything he or
she conceives the essence of the object to be something of this kind rather
than that. In this sense a concept of a house is a cause of an actual house.
One is free, however, to impose the vocal sound 'house' for an actual house
or its concept, but, since imposition is a well-focused act, the intent of the
namer will fall on one or the other but not both at the same time. Having
made the choice, one is free to reimpose the same name for the other and
the result will be that one name has two meanings. This, Bacon points out,
is a case of equivocation: the name of one thing has been transferred to
something whose definition is in some way different. The objection, Bacon
implies, serves only to underscore a case of equivocal usage, not to impugn
his theory of signification. For a parallel text in the *De signis* see Ds 162.

151. This is clearly the most difficult text in this whole work to interpret. Actually Augustine acknowledges uncertainty about the significate of '*nihil*' and
only suggests an affection of a soul as a possibility. (See his *De magistro* 2. 3.
4. and 7. 19. 2, ed. Guenther Weigel, *Corpus Scriptorum Ecclesiasticorum
Latinorum* 77 [Vienna: Hoelder-Pichler-Tempsky, 1961], pp. 6.21-7.9 and
26.25-27.8; transl. George G. Leckie, *Concerning the Teacher And On the Immortality of the Soul* [New York: Appleton-Century-Crofts, 1938], pp. 7 and
27.) Bacon and Augustine are in agreement that nothing is something intelligible; it can be named and talked about, just as we are doing now. It has
an ''essence'' in the sense that it can be defined, but its ''existence'' is obviously different from that of, e.g., a house. The question here concerns its
precise ontological status: is it simply an entity such as a concept, as

Augustine is said to claim, or is it an entity in some sense outside a mind, granted it is not something outside a mind in the same sense as an existing house? In point of fact it would in no way pose a problem for Bacon's theory of imposition for him to grant that nothing is merely a concept, for he has already acknowledged that such mental entities can be named. All one need do is become aware of it reflexively and name it. So Bacon's purpose in referring to what he takes as Augustine's position must simply be to present his own theory that the names of nonentities are not instances where concepts are in fact named.

His theory is determined by what he takes the process of privation to be, and unfortunately he spells this out neither here nor in the parallel text in the *De signis* (105). Given what he does say, and drawing on his final remarks in this chapter, I suggest the following as reasonably close to his intent, without claiming total accuracy. (See also *Ds* 19-20.) We come to a knowledge of nothing by first becoming aware of some actually existing thing. The thing generates a species which passes through the senses and is received into the intellect. (This is knowledge by species [*medium quo*].) But then this process ceases and a different intellectual process begins, privation. We focus our attention on the nature of the thing and its attributes but think of it as not existing, the result being that we are left with an awareness of something intelligible as nonexistent. It is not a concept as Augustine is said to claim, because it is not there as a means of knowing some existing thing—nonentities cannot generate species—but as an object of knowledge known by way of privation of the species of an existing entity. In virtue of its privative, intentional relation to an existing entity (via the latter's species) there is a sense in which it is outside a mind (though the claim that it "is sufficiently in a real place outside a mind" is a needlessly extreme way of making the point) and it is only because of this relation that it can be named. (See *Ds* 105.) In short, then, a nonentity is something intelligible, existing outside a mind in the sense that it is related by privation to an actually existing entity, not known by way of its own species, but known indirectly through the privative awareness of the species of an actual entity. Since we can name whatever we know, and we are aware of a nonentity, we can name it 'nothing' and speak of it as a nonentity.

152. See above, #61, no. 149.

153. The objection assumes that the only things in an intellect are the means (species) by which intellectual knowledge occurs. Bacon points out that more than just the means of knowing is there or knowledge would never take place. The object known is in some sense (*quodam modo*) there. Intellectual awareness is the result of an intentional union of a knower and some object known, a union mediated by the species (likeness, concept, cognitive habit) of the object whereby it becomes intentionally present within the knower. The object as known is not an attribute of an intellect, though its species is. Given these two possible ways of being in an intellect, Bacon claims that nonentities, being intelligible entities, are there as intentionally present objects, not means, of knowledge.

154. In the preceding chapter Bacon pointed out various things that are signified naturally by a name. Here he directs attention to another group which, while they relate to a name in a way different from those, are still signified naturally. He discusses these thoroughly in the *De signis* (100-133) but never refers to them as "things connoted" or "co-understood"; they are called

secondary significates or are simply said to be that which names signify naturally.

One should note that connotations (*connotata*) are not consignificates (*consignificata*). In *Ds* 104 these are distinguished on the basis that the latter have no essential relation (*essentialem respectum*) to the principal significate of a name where the former do. Consignificates arise in virtue of the grammatical qualities of a term such as number, gender, case, and mood.

Although no mention of it is made in this chapter Bacon speaks of the double signification of connotative terms in the *De signis* as a special kind of analogical signification. (See below, #67, n. 158.) He also notes with Avicenna (980-1037) and Algazel (+ 1111) that words signify a more or less infinite number of things in this way and, captured by the aesthetical import, remarks: "And to consider this is [something] of wonderous usefulness and beauty" (*Ds* 103).

155. The relation between a name and that for which it is imposed is a relation at pleasure. But what happens when one is aware that this significate is itself necessarily related to other things? Given his semiotics, one might expect Bacon to say that the principal significate of a name is a natural sign by necessary inference (of that which it is known to accompany always or for the most part), and that therefore one becomes aware of the additional significates by *sequential* acts of signification, the first at pleasure and the second natural. This is precisely the analysis of what is called the spitirual sense of scripture, and Bacon alludes to it at the end of this chapter. (See below, #83 and n. 182.) However this is not what he understands connotation to be. Here and throughout he will focus on a double signification of the *name*, not a sequential signification by two different things. When introducing connotation in the *De signis* (102) Bacon links the double signification with something he says will follow and the editors correctly refer to the sections (165-169) where he presents his theory that the names of things imposed for something outside a mind signify it at pleasure and the concepts of these naturally. This is the distinction between a name as a name and a name considered simply as a vocal sound, and it clearly lies behind Bacon's contention that a connotative name (as a sign at pleasure) signifies principally the thing named and secondarily (as a natural sign) whatever else is known to be necessarily related to its principal significate (see, e.g., below, #75 and #82). In *Ds* 132 the distinction is expressly applied to connotation. (For a correction in that text see below, #83, second paragraph of n. 183.) Thus when someone utters the vocal sound 'creature', another may well be brought to think of a creator, and (a creating) God. Bacon takes a first step in explaining how a name can accomplish this by pointing out that the latter two accompany the name by necessary consequence, i.e., by an inference made by an interpreter based on his or her awareness of the existence of the implied relationships between the additional significates and the principal significate of the name. For parallel texts see *Ds* 103, 106, and 107.

156. A person could, e.g., at one time have red hair and later grey without ceasing to be the same person, but in the view of the medievals one would not be a human being were one to lack the ability to laugh. These examples serve to indicate the Aristotelian and medieval view that some attributes are so inexorably tied to the essence of something that, wherever one finds the one, one also finds the other. This is what many called a property and what

Bacon refers to as a proper attribute, i.e., that which, while not part of an essence, is found in all individuals of a given species. One should note, however, that Bacon's language here is not so precise as it should be. From the opening words of this chapter is it clear that connotation is a function of names in a certain set of circumstances, not of their principal significates. Yet here he says that a proper accident connotes its subject. Similarly in the *De signis* he can be seen to say in one and the same section that the *name* of an attribute gives one to understand a substance and follow this with the statement that *substance* necessarily gives one to understand accident. (See *Ds* 108.) Since connotation presupposes imposition, the latter should be viewed as a less precise way of expressing this type of double signification.

157. In the *De signis* Bacon points out that the reason why these names can signify secondary significates is because imposition falls on them necessarily in some sense ("... *quia impositio cadit super ea necessario aliquo modo* ..."), not freely as is the case with primary significates. (See *Ds* 130.) Then he adds that nothing prevents such double signification since natural signification can occur without imposition and, in the case of connotation, imposition falls on one thing and the natural signification on another. (See *Ds* 131.) Thus, e.g., the universal term 'man' names man in general and connotes the indeterminate particular "some man." 'Some man' and 'Mary', the name of a determinate particular, both connote the species "man," where 'man' also connotes the genus "animal." (In *Ds* 110-120 Bacon argues that, if no individuals exist, then neither can universals.) 'Father' connotes son and 'son' connotes father. (See *Ds* 122 where Bacon distinguishes two types of *per se* correlatives from those *per accidens*.) And the name of any substance connotes its essential principles of matter and form. (See also *Ds* 108.) A person who already knows about those relations can be brought to a renewed awareness of both terms of the relations by hearing the name of the first. While Bacon never expressly makes the point, given what he says here and coupled with his statement in *Ds* 108 that there is no (created) substance, simple or composed, that does not have some relation (*propria passio*), it would seem that all names can be connotative terms with the sole exception of 'God'. (For this exception see *Ds* 106.) Bacon even finds reason in the *De signis* (109) to call attention to the fact that, when Aristotle says that substance is prior to attribute, he is not speaking of temporal priority, the implication being that were substance to exist at any time without attributes, 'substance' would not connote attributes. (Bacon refers there to *Metaphysics* 10, but see 7. 1. 1028a29-33.)

158. See above, #26. The objection assumes that connotation is an instance of signification at pleasure and in consequence must represent either univocation or equivocation. Bacon escapes the dilemma by noting that connotation is natural signification to which his peers would readily grant these notions do not apply. However in the *De signis* he introduces his analysis of connotation by comparing it with these two forms of signification at pleasure. (For what follows see *Ds* 100-102 and 129.) In univocation, he says, there is one name, one imposition, one significate, and one definition of the thing named; in equivocation there is one name, but more than one imposition, and the definitions differ. Pure equivocation occurs when the significates are as different as an entity and a nonentity, as in the case where 'Caesar' is said of the Roman Emperor when alive and when dead. All other cases of equivocation are also called analogy. Since connotation

involves only one act of imposition for one thing, it can be neither pure equivocation nor the kind of equivocation that is also analogy; since more than one thing is signified, it cannot be univocation. But because in connotation there is one name and the things signified are related in some way, Bacon concludes that it is a special type of analogy. As he says in *Ds* 36: "For it is one thing for a vocal sound to be imposed and another to signify." Thus connotative terms are names (univocal, purely equivocal, or analogical) of that for which they are imposed but natural signs of anything they call to mind in relation to their principal significates. Secondary significates become known not by name but by inference, and this can occur with or without the intent of the speaker, though Bacon never makes the latter point.

159. The conclusion of the objection must be read with the insertion of 'at pleasure' as provided in the translation for two reasons. First, the whole point of connotation is that these secondary significates are indeed signified in some way by the name of the principal significate. Second, the response indicates that Bacon agrees with the "objection" that running is properly predicated only of the whole composite and not of one of its integral parts.

160. While Bacon denies that the names of composites are also names of their integral parts, he reminds that these parts can have names of their own simply by being submitted to imposition. Then they would be brought to mind by name and not by inference or connotation. For parallel texts see *Ds* 123, 124, and 133.

161. See Aristotle *Metaphysics* 8. 3. 1043a29-1043b4. The person referred to here as "the Commentator" is Ibn Rush (1126-1198), known to the Latin West as Averroes. In the parallel text in the *De signis* (126) those who hold the view here attributed to Averroes are referred to simply as "some very foolish ones (*aliqui stulti nimis*)." Later he speaks of their insanity. (See *Ds* 128.)

162. Bacon is certainly referring to *Metaphysics* 8. 3. 1043a29-38, where Aristotle concludes: " 'Animal' might even be applied to both [a soul in a body and a soul], not as something definable by one formula, but as related to a single thing." (*The Basic Works of Aristotle*, ed. Richard McKeon, transl. W.D. Ross, [New York: Random House, 1941], pp. 814-815.) Cf. *Ds* 121 where Avicenna and Algazel are mentioned in support of the proposition that one essential part (of a whole) signifies another.

163. While Bacon will be seen to insist on this point, he grants in the *De signis* (127) that were one considering the case where the same name has been imposed through two (equivocal) impositions for a composite and its form, the form would have greater title to it than the composite—"*magis et prius respicit formam quam aggregatum*"—because the composite can only be understood and named in virtue of its form. (Cf. also *Sumule dialectices*, p. 208.10-16 and .22-26.) However he quickly adds that, where only one imposition is involved (as in the case of connotation), the name names only that for which it is imposed and that the significate, whether the composite or the form, becomes thereby its principal significate.

164. See Averroes *Metaphysica* 8. 4, ed. Iuntina, 8 (Venice: 1562; reprinted Frankfort on the Main: Minerva, 1962), f. 215vK-L. Interestingly, when Bacon addressed this problem in the *De signis* (127) he indicated that both Aristotle and the Commentator support his own position.

165. I find no such reference to Averroes in the preceding pages, but see above, #10, n. 40.

166. One shows this inductively by looking at a sufficient sample of expressions having subjects and predicates and recognizing that in each case a sign at pleasure represents something being talked about (subject) and something being said (predicated) of it. This would hold also for two place propositions such as "He runs," for medieval logicians, following Aristotle, sometimes also speak of verbs as names since they are signs at pleasure of something. (See Aristotle, *On Interpretation* 10, 19b20.) This is brought out in Ackrill's translation but not in Edghill's. See respectively J.L. Ackrill, *Aristotle's Categories and De Interpretatione* (Oxford: Clarendon Press, 1963; reprinted with corrections, 1979), p. 54 and Richard McKeon, ed., *The Basic Works of Aristotle* (New York: Random House, 1941), p. 49.

167. The translation of the quotation is a loose version of the adage "*Unumquodque propter quod illud magis.*" Bacon also refers to it in *Ds* 80 where the context suggests a base from which to infer it. See also Aristotle's *Posterior Analytics* 1.2. 72a28.

168. See above, #71, n. 164.

169. For a parallel text see *Ds* 127.

170. This is a clear and concise statement of the two types of signification that Bacon contends occur when something is named that is known to be related necessarily to something else. The distinction between principal and secondary signification is not one between what a speaker intends first by a name and what secondly, for in connotation, as described by Bacon, the things connoted are not signified by any kind of intent, direct or indirect. The fact that a speaker would deliberately choose a connotative term in order to convey an additional significate would (presumably) be judged by the same principles with which he responded to the case of the artist who freely chooses to paint a portrait of someone. The result was said to be a natural sign of the person depicted, not a sign at pleasure. The speaker is simply choosing a natural mode of signification. (See above, #33, n. 109). Thus Bacon correctly avoids speaking of direct and indirect signification here as he did in the previous chapter when addressing the issue of how imposed vocal sounds signify both the things they name and the concepts by which one knows those things. While one might want to argue that, since an interpreter must first be aware of the principal significate before he or she could think of its relation to something else, the distinction between principal and secondary refers to a time differential in the interpreter's awareness, one should note that Bacon pays little attention in this work or in the *De signis* to the interpreter's role in signification. His focus is primarily on the giving of signs. Thus I have argued that these terms were adopted by him to reflect ontological and axiological differences between signification by rational intent and that which arises by necessity. (See above, #60, n. 147.) While I take these differences to be implicit in his semiotics, the present text seems to give voice to them when Bacon says that names imposed for composites signify them "in the principal mode of signification of vocal sounds and names ..."

171. Bacon says that it is *dignius* for a name of a composite to have its own name because a composite has the *dignitas* of its form and its matter. Unfortunately, I have not been able to think of one English word that can do duty in both situations.

172. See *Metaphysics* 2. 1. 993b30.

173. Medievals in the Aristotelian tradition considered all entities in this world to be composed on several different levels. They are composed of attributes and substance or essence, the latter being a further composition of matter and form where 'matter' designates the metaphysical principle by which they are capable of change and 'form' the principle by which they are the kinds of things they here and now are. But since some things exist and others do not, an additional principle must be inferred to account for this difference. This they called the being (*esse*) of a thing or its act of existing (*actus essendi*). Bacon, in contradistinction to many others, holds the view that in an actually existing entity each of the constitutent principles has being in its own right and contributes this to the being of the composite. A little later he will state his reason: to deny that (metaphysical) mater has its own act of existence is to contend that it is nothing, i.e., that it is not something real. (See below, #80.) Others, considering matter to be a passive principle in relation to form, resolve the issue by arguing that being is brought into (*adduci*) the whole composite in virtue of the latter's active principle, its form. Thus Bacon's theory contends that the being of a composite is itself a composed principle where the other position, granting that the entity is a composite, argues that its act of existence is uncomposed. Note, however, that neither of these theories contends that the principles of a composite have existence prior to their union in a composite. The theories represent inferences that attempt to give an account of composites that already exist.

174. While I do not find this notion in the *Prior Analytics*, Aristotle does speak in the *Physics* (1. 1. 184a16-20) of a mental process that proceeds from what is more knowable to us to what is more knowable intrinsically, though more obscure to us. Earlier Bacon rephrased this notion to speak of a process that proceeds "from easier things to the more difficult." (See above, #18.) Here he seems to draw on the same text but chooses the term '*confusum*' to express the first stage in the process. He is trading on the fact that the term can be taken to refer both to a mental state, which links it in part with Aristotle's remark, and in its etymological meaning to something made up of (distinct) parts, which links it to the notion of a composite.

175. By 'general differences' Bacon is referring to the principle within a substance or nature by which two things of the same genus differ in species. Ordinarily this is called a specific difference and things differ in species in virtue of their different substantial forms. This being the case, his reference to *Meteorology* 4 is a generalization based on 4. 12. 390a10-23, where Aristotle, drawing on the principle that one determines the nature of a thing by observing its functions, points out that because the functions of the most elementary parts of a thing are not easily detected by physical examination, one cannot easily determine (by inference) what forms are present. Since Aristotle is speaking there only of formal differences, Bacon forgoes the opportunity to remind his readers that in his own opinion composed things differ substantially from one another also in virtue of their material differences. For the theory that genus is differentiated by the addition of both a new form and new matter see his *Communia naturalium*, *Opera*, 2, ed. Steele, pp. 52.29-64.29, esp. 59.9-16.

176. See above, #71, n. 164.

177. In his *Sumule dialectices* (p. 205.14-27) Bacon mentions three types of denominative terms, the third representing, e.g., the case where one takes the abstract term 'humanity' and derives the concrete term 'humans' from it. Since 'humanity' signifies the substantial form by which humans differ from other types of entities, human beings are said to be denominated by the name 'humans'. In this way many composites have denominative names which are derived from the abstract names of the forms to which they bear a relation. The fact that in the text under consideration Bacon distinguishes between the denomination of a composite and the name of its form suggests that he has in mind something like the following objection: in the case where a composite has a denominative name, since the name is taken from the name of a form, the name of the composite must signify principally that form in the composite and only secondarily the composite itself. Bacon indicates how he would reply to this when he asks his readers in the *De signis* (128) to distinguish between that *from* which a name is imposed and that *for* which it is imposed. He grants that the denominative name is taken from the name of a form, or, as he says, imposed from a form, but says that it is imposed to signify a composite having that form. In other words it is one thing to derive a name and another to impose it, once derived. Since one is free to choose any vocal sound with which to name something, the choice of a denominative name does not preclude imposing it solely for a composite, granted it will then connote in the composite the form from whose name the name of the composite is derived.

178. For Bacon's theory of the relation of matter, form, and being see above, #76, n. 173.

179. See above, #71, n. 164.

180. The Latin text of this paragraph reads "when, moreover, Averroes argues ... it must be said ...".

181. See above, #71, n. 164.

182. The literal sense of a term is that which is signified (in Bacon's language) principally by it. Thus the literal sense of "David was King of Israel" is the historical fact of David's kingship. However, medieval exegetes also argued that some of the things and events signified by the literal sense of Scripture were themselves to be taken as signs of something else. Thus David's relation to his people was understood to be a sign prefiguring Christ's relation to His Church. They called this sequential type of signification the spiritual sense of Scripture, divided its significates into things to be believed, things under moral command to be done, and things to be hoped for, and spoke respectively of the allegorical, tropological, and anagogical senses of Scripture. Thus the spiritual sense is the significate of the literal significate of certain expressions in Scripture and it distinguishes itself in two ways from connotation: it does not depend on a name that also functions as a natural sign and it does require that the principal significate of a name be taken as a sign. For further analysis of the notions of a literal and spiritual sense and for a suggestion of how the latter's three divisions can be seen to correlate with the triple division of the Trivium see Anthony Nemetz, "Literalness and the *Sensus Spiritualis*," *Speculum* 34 (1959) 76-89.

183. Given this last paragraph and his division of signs, the temptation to speculate about what may be found in Part Three of this work and the missing parallel sections of the *De signis* is irresistible. Looking into the Scriptures Bacon could take, for example, the divine promises, King David, and

the rainbow, all three the significates of words as signs at pleasure (literal sense), and note that each is a further sign of something else. Assuming the Scriptures to be in some sense the word of God, and assuming divine veracity, the divine promises could be claimed to be signs by necessary inference that what they promise will come true; David's relation to his people could be explained as a sign by configuration of Christ's to his Church; and the rainbow could be said to function as a sign at pleasure that the world would never again be destroyed by flood. Thus the literal sense would signify the spiritual sense in all three modes open to it. And given the medieval fondness for seeing Old Testament personages and events as types or figures of things to come, it is not surprising to hear Bacon say that signs by configuration are especially operative in the Scriptures. Whether or not these three modes also play a part in the correlations Nemetz has worked out between the triple division of the spiritual sense and the respective branches of the Trivium needs further research. I suspect they do. (Cf. Nemetz, *art. cit.*, pp. 81-87.

Returning to the issue of connotation and given Bacon's full presentation of his theory, one is in a position to address a text in the *De signis* that, if corrected, gives further clarification to one of his initial remarks in this chapter, namely, that names do not otherwise necessarily accompany what they connote. (See above, #66.) In *Ds* 132 Bacon writes:

> Likewise there is no problem with the fact that (*Nec similiter impedit quod*) a vocal sound itself in virtue of its substance (*secundum substantiam suam*) does not infer a secondary significate, nor also does the fact that it is actually signifying (*est actu significativa*) infer it of itself, because, since an actually signifying vocal sound, and accepted as such, infers (*infert*) the first significate and the first infers the second, the vocal sound itself, as actually signifying, sufficiently infers the second significate, and hence it is called a natural sign of the second significate because of that inference.

This is the only text I know of where Bacon says "an actually signifying vocal sound ... infers the first significate ..." (See midway in the quotation.) Whether 'actually signifying vocal sound' refers to a name as a name or (as more probably here) to a name considered only as a vocal sound, it cannot be said to be related to its principal significate by *inference* without contradicting all Bacon has said about the way vocal sounds relate to the things for which they are imposed. He would be presenting the theory that an interpreter, otherwise ignorant of what a speaker chose to intend by an utterance, could infer it on the basis of the vocal sound alone. I suspect, then, that Bacon has simply misspoken himself and that 'infers (*infert*)' should be something like 'is related to (*refertur ad*)'. Then he would be pointing out that names or their substances are not related of themselves to secondary significates but only in virtue of their being imposed for something which in turn is related to other things.

184. In this chapter Bacon continues his explorations of univocal signification and enters one of the major controversies of his time. The issue is whether, e.g., 'man' said of a living and dead person is to be taken as a univocal or an equivocal term. Bacon's position on this topic has received more attention from scholars than any of his other theories. In brief he rejects any attempt to circumvent what he takes to be a psychological fact with semantic consequence, namely, that when one names one intends to name only ac-

tually existing things and not some kind of essence or being (*esse*) common to entities and nonentities. Nonentities, he argues, receive their names and are spoken of only in virtue of a second imposition, one which results in an equivocal name. Thus to say "man" and mean (dead) Caesar is to equivocate on the term 'man'. For parallel sections in the *De signis* see *Ds* 134-142; for a description of the theories against which Bacon is contending see Introduction, pp. 13-16 and 17-19. The second of the two "principles mentioned in the rubric will be the subject of the next chapter.

185. While medievals spoke of terms being univocal, equivocal, and analogical, they were also accustomed to speaking of the significates of these as univocals, equivocals, and analogicals. Thus two things that are identical in nature are univocals and can be named by one univocal term where two things that have absolutely nothing in common but their name are equivocals. Note that Bacon acknowledges here and immediately below that the position he takes is a minority one.

186. The reference to Christ in the tomb should be taken in conjunction with the earlier mention of heresies to be detested. If 'man' signifies an entity having a body and rational soul, then to call Christ a man during the three days, Bacon implies, would be to deny that he died, i.e., that his soul separated from his body.

'Ampliation' and 'restriction' are the names of theories that attempt to account for the fact that in discourse common terms sometimes are to be taken in different senses. Thus 'man' can mean man in general, present, past, or future man, the concept "man," the picture of a man, or the term 'man', but in a given context it will signify only one of these. In "The man who was is" its reference is restricted to someone in the past who is still living; in "Man is wont to be" it is ampliated to refer to present and future people. In the *De signis* (89-99) Bacon treats of these notions and rejects the common explanation that they are functions that occur by the very nature of qualifying expressions, certain verbs, or the tenses of verbs, and contends that such simply offer an occasion for the intellect to transpose or reimpose these terms for significates other than those for which they were originally imposed. (See *Ds* 97.) According to Bacon, then, the efficient cause of ampliation and restriction is the speaker's intellect, and the result is equivocation. Given this explanation, Bacon has no hesitation in saying that " 'Man' is a vocal sound," "Man is [a concept] in the soul," and "Man is a picture" are all instances of ampliation. He grants that others do not speak of them in this way, but gives assurance that it is not only permissible to do so but that reason teaches it (see *Ds* 91). (For his earlier and different treatment of ampliation and restriction see his *Sumule dialectices*, 280.16-281.14.) Ampliation and restriction, in spite of his claim in the present text, are not treated *ex professo* in the rest of this work as we have it.

187. See above, Part One, Chapter Two.

188. Richard of Cornwall, also known as Richard the Red (*Rufus*), was an Englishman who entered the Franciscan Order in 1238 and died at Oxford around 1260. Philosopher and theologian, he wrote two commentaries on the *Sentences* of Peter Lombard and probably a lengthy one on Aristotle's *Metaphysics*. Immediately below and a little later (see below, #128) Bacon will imply that Richard was the first to hold the theory that 'man' said of Christ during the three days in the tomb is predicated univocally, but Landgraf's study has shown that this is not the case. (See Introduction,

p. 14, n. 66.) For sections of one of Richard's commentaries on the *Sentences* relevant to his theory of univocal signification and habitual being see references in Introduction, pp. 13-14.

189. Steward Easton offers the following comments on Bacon's relation to Richard. (See his *Roger Bacon*, pp. 94-97.) First, Adam Marsh and Thomas of Eccleston were both in a position to know about Richard and both thought very highly of him, neither giving any hint he was reproved while teaching at Paris. Second, pursuing a suggestion by A.G. Little, Easton presents the following hypothesis as a possible explanation for Bacon's undying hatred for Richard: if Bacon was somehow involved in Richard's sudden decision to move from Oxford to Paris around 1252 or 1253—perhaps by an abrasive public challenge to Richard's position on the "three days"—then Richard may have later used the prestige of his office as Regent Master of Franciscan theologians at Oxford, a post he held by 1256, to prevent Bacon from receiving the acclaim the latter thought he deserved. In attempting to assess the plausibility of this hypothesis, however, one should also take into account three other facts not mentioned by Easton. (a) Bacon addressed the issue of whether a name could univocally signify an entity and a nonentity in his *De signis* of 1267 and he did so without invective and without even mentioning Richard, just as he had done in his *Sumule dialectices* of 1252. (See respectively 134-142 and pp. 277.17-288.36.) (b) It has already been seen in regard to Averroes that Bacon was quite capable of lashing out even at those with whom he had no personal contact whatsoever. (See above, #72.) And (c) as Alain de Libera has suggested, Bacon was obviously very deeply concerned about the "new theories" being taught at Oxford at midcentury, and Richard may well have played too prominent a role in Bacon's judgment in giving access to them. (See Introduction, p. 19.)

190. Bacon is probably thinking of *Metaphysics* 3. 3. 999a6-8. However it should be noted that Aristotle is not speaking there of temporal priority. For a parallel text see *Ds* 135.

191. See *Physics* 4. 8. 214b12-216b20 where Aristotle contrasts the nature of the void with that of place and moving bodies and concludes that there is no separate void. There is no parallel text in the *De signis*.

192. The medievals understood Aristotle's *Categories* to provide a list of the ways in which things exist: whatever exists is either a substance or one of nine types of attributes. Bacon's point is that, e.g., while a horse and the color black have it in common that they are both (though analogically) said to be entities, an entity and a nonentity have absolutely nothing in common.

193. For a parallel text see *Ds* 137.

194. This text, when taken with the one that follows, presents a good illustration of the way in which medievals thought of the notion of predication. Here Bacon says a name is predicated; next he will say that the significate of a name is predicated. There is no parallel text in the *De signis*.

195. See Boethius *In Categorias Aristotelis libri quatuor*, ed. Migne, *PL* 64. 184A, and Ps.-Augustine *Anonymi paraphrasis themistiana*, ed. L. Minio-Paluello, *Aristoteles Latinus* 1. 5, ed. L. Minio-Palluello (Leiden: E.J. Brill, 1961), pp. 145.24-149.2.

196. The objection implies a distinction between the essence of something and its being (*esse*). If all things other than God and nonentities are composed of the two principles essence and being, does one intend to name the essence,

the being, or both when one names a created thing? The objection contends that imposition prescinds from the being, whether past, present, or future. If this is the case, then 'Caesar', imposed for the Roman emperor while alive, would still name his essence univocally even given a change from present to past existence. For a parallel text see *Ds* 140.

197. Bacon intends here to provide support for his central claim that names are originally imposed for existing entities, and in this regard three things should be noted. (1) While the support is expressly derived only from cases of proper naming it is clear from the context of this chapter and the *De signis* (110 and 115) that he intends the theory to cover also the case of common terms, the latter being originally imposed for the common essences of existing entities. Thus in *Ds* 110 he says that "Man is" gives one to understand either a vague particular as in "Some man is" or a designated particular (by disjunction) as in "Socrates is or Plato is, etc." (2) The claim requires that Bacon would have been in a position to know what original impositors intended when they coined words. To build a theory on this kind of a prerequisite is especially curious for one who, as we have seen, repeatedly also insists that that and only that is named which the impositor freely intends. However, (3) he is on more substantial grounds when he acknowledges that names do not consignify present time, that a temporal dimension accrues to the significate in virtue of its own present being and not as a quality of the name. Bacon would be comfortable with the statement that a name signifies something temporal but that it does not do this temporally. (See below, #105, n. 211.)

198. Something is in potency when it is not yet what it will or at least can become. Thus essences in the past or future have it in common with an entity in potency that they are not something in the same sense that they would be were they actually existing. Bacon implies that one commits a fallacy when one argues, e.g., "A corpse is a dead man; therefore a man is a corpse" since 'man' in the premiss refers to a man only in a certain sense (*secundum quid*) where it refers in the ordinary way (*simpliciter*) in the conclusion. (See his *Sumule dialectices*, p. 351.18-19.) For the relation of this fallacy to the sophism "This is a dead man; therefore this is a man" see Introduction, pp. 15-16.

199. The reference is to two paragraphs above.

200. If the distinction Bacon draws here between actual being one with essence (*esse actuale idem quod essentia*) and the same as the proper passion of essence (*propria passio essentiae*) is a reference to the debate whether essence is really or only conceptually distinct from being (*esse*), then Bacon's argument is essentially this: since essence cannot exist unless it is accompanied by actual and present being—it will not remain in existence without it—whether one holds that essence and being are or are not really distinct, the being of essence must be actual and present. There is no parallel text in the *De signis*.

201. A thing is the kind of thing it is in virtue of its (substantial) form. Thus in living things form is the vital principal and hence is also called a soul. Since Bacon believes in the immortality of the human soul, he speaks of its separation at death where in all other cases the complete (substantial) destruction of the thing is called a corruption of the thing or its form. Thus the verb 'corrupt' and its cognates here and elsewhere in the chapter refer to a total destruction, not simply a change in attributes.

202. For the reference see above, #90-91.

203. Neither the argument nor the metaphor of restriction is particularly clear of itself. But if Bacon's reference is to what was said above in #90-91, then he probably has this in mind. In virtue of the principle of the excluded middle a thing is what it is and nothing else. If it is a thing of the past, it is a thing neither of the future nor the present. However, since it is said to be, i.e., to have habitual being, the only way it can be is to have actual being. Thus the nature of existence constricts the possible ways things can be (past, present, future) to one only, namely, to actual being. Yet this being is not common to entities and nonentities. There is no parallel text in the *De signis*.

204. Bacon is probably referring to *On the soul* 2. 1. 412a19-29 where the difference between having knowledge and using it is given as the basis for distinguishing between first and second grades of actuality. If the proponents of the theory of habitual being are also drawing on this distinction—Bacon does not say they are—then they would be arguing that just as one can have knowledge (first act) without exercising it (second act), so one can have habitual being without actual being, and the former is sufficient for something in the past or future to be named. Bacon argues that even if there were such a thing as habitual being, it would ultimately be related to form, and when something loses its form in corruption, it would also have to lose this habitual being.

205. The theory notes that participles, like verbs, consignify time in virtue of their grammatical tenses. (For the notion of consignification see above, #65, n. 154.) Thus, e.g., 'having died (*mortuus*)' refers to an act that took place at a point in the past that was then in present time. Bacon would grant this. He would also concede that names that are nouns, pronouns, and adjectives do not consignify time, but he insists that they are first imposed only for something in present time.

206. The theory Bacon opposes contends that the significates of nouns and participles are different because of the way the significates relate to being (*esse*). Bacon argues that what these parts of speech signify is the same, though the way they do it is different, i.e., that their signification is the same but their consignification is different. Thus when one says "John is a being" and "John, being here, was happy," 'being' functions respectively as a name and as a participle, but it refers to the same entity, namely, John. '*Amans*' was left in Latin in the translation because the English version, "lover" and "loving", being paronymns, would not reveal exactly the same case presented by Bacon. For other examples see *Ds* 43 and 117; for the reference to Priscian see his *Institutiones grammaticae* 11. 1. 5, ed. Martin Hertz, *Grammatici Latini* 2, ed. Heinrich Keil (Leipzig: B.G. Teubner, 1859; reprinted Hildesheim: Georg Olms, 1961) p. 550.

207. The reference to potential and aptitudinal being (*esse in potentia* and *esse in aptitudine*) suggests a theory something like the following, though its relevance would seem to be limited to participles in the future tense. 'About to love (*amaturus*)' signifies the quality of loving-in-the-future and (hence) the aptitude for loving, and, since such potential or aptitudinal being is "midway" between being and not-being, it can serve as the prerequisite communality for univocal naming.

208. From the way Bacon uses the terms 'potential being' and 'aptitudinal being' it would seem that they are synonyms. The Aristotelian theory of privation holds that when a thing is lacking something that nature intended, the thing is in a state of privation; and the term 'blind', e.g., refers to

such a condition. (See Aristotle's *Topics* 6. 6. 143b34-35 and *On the Soul* 2. 1. 412b18-22.) The theory presumes that something is preventing nature from achieving its end. Bacon's point is that, until the cause of blindness is removed, the man has sight only potentially, i.e., he has the aptitude for sight but is not seeing.

209. Earlier (#101) Bacon spoke of habitual being (*esse habituale*); here he says there is more to be said about *esse habitudinis*. The translation assumes that these notions are the same. The reference is to a section of this work (and a parallel part of the *De signis*) still missing. At the end of his treatment of connotation in the *De signis* (120) Bacon gives a hint about what one can expect to find in the missing section and it bears on the present issue:

> Many other things can be objected, but they touch on propositions more than terms since they endeavor to show that this is true, "Man is animal," when no man exists, and that Caesar would be a man when he does not exist, and the like. Such will be sufficiently touched on later in their proper place.

See also *Ds* 142 and below, #111, n. 227.

210. The division between the first and second part of the problem is possibly a reference to Bacon's stated intent to prove what is true and to present the opposite. (See above, #85.)

211. A previous objection contended that while names (in contrast to participles) do not consignify time, they do signify "with some kind of communality in act with an entity and a nonentity." (See above, #102.) Here the second part of the claim is omitted and the objection focuses on one of the essential (and accepted) parts of the definition of a name. (See Aristotle *On Interpretation* 2. 16a19-20 and Bacon's *Sumule dialectices*, p. 234.15-16.) In his *Sumule dialectices* (p. 234.20-23) Bacon explains that while a name like 'day' can signify a time "it does not consignify time or it does not signify with time, i.e., time does not accrue to its principal significate (*principali suo significato non accidit tempus*)." Since Bacon insists also in that work that names of themselves (*de se*) only concern things in present time (see. p. 280.29-32), the last part of the quotation must be understood to mean that time does not accrue to a name's principal significate in virtue of a formal quality of the name, but only from the material fact that its significate is in time.

212. Examples of an impossible and an infinite would be, respectively, a square circle and nonman (or not-man). Boethius says that Aristotle invented the terms 'infinite name' and 'infinite verb' because one who hears such understands an infinite number of things that are disjoined from a name by the prefix 'non'. (See his *In librum Aristotelis Peri herméneias commentarium*, 1st ed., ed. Karl Meiser [Leipzig: B.G. Teubner, 1880], pp. 52.19-23, 59.25-26, and 60.22-26.) Thus 'infinite' does not refer to an unlimited entity such as God, but to the complement of some finite entity. Bacon chooses these particular examples because one cannot ascribe any particular time to them, and hence it would be impossible for their names to consignify a temporal frame.

213. Bacon's example broadens the types of significates in question from those which can never have existence in a particular time to include those that do, in this case, Caesar. Implied is the principle stated earlier that "names are imposed for infants and all things under present being." (See above, #99.) Since things like impossibles, infinites, and anything that once existed or will exist but is not now existing does not have actual being, their names

cannot reflect the same intent one has when one names a present and actual thing. Thus 'Caesar', first imposed for a living person and later imposed to name him as a thing in the past, refers equivocally to an entity and a non-entity.

214. A privative term is one that names an existing thing which for one reason or another lacks something it ought to have, and 'unjust' is an example. 'Not-just' (or 'nonjust') is an infinite term naming the class of all things, entities and nonentities, that are not just. A negative term like 'not to be just' or 'is not just' as in "he is not just" is one that denies some predicate of an entity or a nonentity but does so without naming any other classes. For this and what followes see Aristotle *On Interpretation* 2. 16a30-33, 3. 16b13-15, and 10. 19b24-39, *passim*. See also his *Prior Analytics* 1. 46. 51b36-52a17 and Bacon's *Sumule dialectices*, pp. 285.1-286.16 and *Ds* 141.

215. Bacon would agree that the first inference is correctly said to be valid and the second correctly said to be invalid, so long as one assumes that the man discussed in the first instance is living—a dead man cannot correctly be said to be unjust—and the one in the second dead—it could correctly be said of a living man who is not just that he is unjust or not-just. The objection implies that, on Aristotle's authority, 'man' can be said univocally of a living man (entity) and a dead man (nonentity).

216. This is the second (and final) instance in this work where Bacon mentions a chronology by which his *Sumule dialectices* can be dated. (See *Sd*, pp. 283.20-287.10 and above, #86.)

217. This can be seen by taking the inference in question "A man is not just; therefore he is unjust" under the conditions already established, namely, that the subject discussed in the premiss is a dead man and the one in the predicate a living man. The premiss is a denial, i.e., being just is denied of the dead man, and since the negative refuses any positive information about him at all, no evidence is supplied whereon to base a positive inference that he is unjust. But "He is unjust" is not a denial but an affirmation, granted what is affirmed of the living man is a privation, one that he shares with all existing things that are not just or are not-just. Hence while a privative and an infinite term have it in common with a negative one that they signify something lacking or absent (see *Ds* 141), when they are predicated in an affirmation employing the copula 'is', the affirmation conveys some information, namely, that the subject exists and that it belongs to the class designated by the predicate. Hence the conclusion of the inference requires more data than is warranted by the premiss, and the cause of this is the fact that one is arguing from a denial with a nonentity for a subject to an affirmation with an entity as its subject. This is the fallacy of "something said in a certain sense and simply."

218. 'Sortes' is to be taken as the name of a person, and in medieval texts it is often, though not always, used as an abbreviated form of 'Socrates'. (Bacon uses the term 'expression [*oratio*]' loosely when he refers to 'Sortes' as "an ambiguous expression." See Introduction, p. 29.) Note that none of the examples employs a privative or infinite predicate in an affirmation whose subject stands for a nonentity. This bears out what is said in the *De signis* (141) and was noted immediately above.

219. Subalternate propositions are those derived from universal (affirmative and negative) propositions and speak of at least one but not all members of a class having more than one member, as in "Some man is handsome."

While the examples that follow are not expressly stated in *On Interpretation* in the way indicated here, Aristotle discusses at length the kinds of opposition that arise among categorical propositions in *Prior Analytics* (see 2. 15. 63b-23-30) and employs these notions throughout *On Interpretation*.

220. Bacon has already discussed the relevance of the distinction between potential and actual being (*esse*). Here he introduces talk of another kind of being, namely becoming. It is the being proper to a state of transition from not yet being something to being that something, i.e., proper to the transition from potency to act. The major point here is Aristotle's endorsement of the proposition that that which comes to be is not (yet) what it will be.

221. For two propositions to be subcontraries they must both (among other things) have the same subject. Bacon could challenge the objection by asking whether 'something' in "Something is" and "Something is not" signifies the same thing. Clearly it designates the not-yet-built-house in the negative proposition, but what does it signify in the affirmative one? Given his theory of naming, Bacon's response will attack the problem of the subjects of the propositions by focusing on the negative proposition.

222. To take a term "simply (*simpliciter*)" means to take it in accord with the meaning it has in virtue of its original imposition, and this stands in contrast with taking a term "in a certain sense (*secundum quid*)," i.e., in accord with some other meaning it may have acquired by a subsequent act of imposition.

223. Bacon's response assumes his theory that names are originally imposed for existing entities and that the subject terms of subcontrary propositions must signify the same thing. "Something is not" and "Something is coming to be" must be judged, he says, to be false since the former would in effect be saying that an existing thing does not exist and the latter that an existing thing is (only) in the state of coming to be an existing thing. For them to be true, he implies, 'something' in each must be taken to signify, respectively, a nonentity and a potential entity, not an existing one. But then "Something is" and "Something is not" could not be subcontrary propositions since the subject terms would be equivocal, the former referring to an existing entity, the latter a nonexistent one. The point of Bacon's response is to argue that 'something' said of anything but an actually existing entity is the product of a second imposition, a word that equivocates with the same term as originally imposed for an existing entity.

224. See *Metaphysics* 9. 6. 1048a34-35. The implication of the objection is that, if 'knowledgeable (*sciens*)' can signify one who knows a science as well as one who is only learning it, then an example has been given of a term that signifies univocally an entity (one who knows the science) and a nonentity (one who has not yet mastered it). Recall that 'nonentity' (or 'not-entity'). being an infinite term, refers to every thing that is not the entity in question. In the present case it refers to a boy who, while he exists, does not exist as an entity having full knowledge of a particular science.

225. Medievals in the Aristotelian tradition considered motion to be a process of transition from a state of potentiality to actuality. Its being (*esse*), though real, is sui generis, i.e., it is neither potential being nor actual being, but the being of something passing from the former to the latter. Aristotle mentions four types of motion, the third, generation, being at issue here. (See Aristotle, *Physics* 3. 1. 201a10-14.) Medievals also considered time to be intimately linked, though not strictly identifiable, with motion: it is the

numbering of a before and after in regard to any definite point in a certain motion. (See ibid., 4. 11. 219b1-2.) Now Bacon has just made the claim that 'something' can never be used univocally in a proposition unless it signifies something having actual being. The objection seeks to show that this would lead to the conclusion that motion and time could not be named by the term 'something' univocally since they involve not actual being but coming to be. In defense of his theory Bacon points out that there are two ways of coming to be. One is proper to things in a process of becoming something other than what they are now. The other is proper to motion and time where each by its very nature is something fluid, something not headed toward becoming anything other than it already is and where each has the most complete type of being it can have. At no point in time will another type of being complete (or as Bacon says "remove") the being it presently has. Bacon's response, then, seems to imply that things in a state of coming to be in the second sense are sufficiently close to present actual entitites to enable them to be univocally named by 'something' where those in a state of coming to be in the first sense are not. Too far removed from the notion of present and actual entities the latter can only be named by this term equivocally. And since he has only been talking up to this point about things coming to be in the first sense, the objection does not, he implies, invalidate his claim that names originally imposed for things having present and actual being cannot signify univocally anything whose being is not proper to it, i.e., anything in a process of becoming something other than it now is.

226. Bacon does not return to this issue in the known sections of this work.

227. The form under which the principal issue in this chapter was debated was also addressed in Bacon's time in discussions on the sophism "Man is animal when no man exists (*Homo est animal nullo existente homine*), but the formulation seems to have had little appeal to Bacon. He simply alludes to it here and in the *De signis* treats of the issue by arguing that universals cannot exist without particulars. (See *Ds* 26, 110, 115, 120, and 142.) In *Ds* 110 the context is connotation and there he says that a universal gives one to understand (connotes) a vague particular or by disjunction a determinate particular, i.e., that 'man' signifies at pleasure universal human nature but connotes (signifies naturally) some person or either Socrates or Plato, etc. The theory seems to be that the rejection of Platonism requires one to accept a necessary relation between the being (*esse*) of a universal nature and that of the individuals that participate in it (see *Ds* 110 and 115), the necessary relation providing the foundation for the inference that enables connotation to be a case of natural signification.

228. The reference is possibly to sections included in the missing third Part. The case is the same with the parallel texts in the *De signis*. (See *Ds* 120 and 142.)

229. Obviously not all terms in current usage refer to existing entities. Having argued in behalf of the theory that names are (first) imposed only for such, Bacon must now explain how it is that we can say, e.g., 'man' and mean a dead person or someone who does not yet exist. Various theories were appealed to in his time (see Introduction, pp. 13-16 and 17-19, esp. pp. 15-16), but his solution, at least given the present stage of research, seems to be unique. It is expressed in three claims: (1) words fall away from their signification, i.e., they no longer function as signs at pleasure when that for which they were originally imposed ceases to exist; (2) if they are to become

names again they must be reimposed; and (3) this reimposition results in the name becoming an equivocal term. The defense of this theory requires him to make an interesting distinction between vocally expressed and tacit imposition (*impositio vocaliter expressa et apud intellectum*), the latter being introduced to account for the fact that more often than not these subsequent equivocal impositions go unnoticed by both the speaker and the listener. If then people use terms equivocally without giving notice, how does the listener know what was intended? Bacon's response is tendered with no elaboration or defense but may employ a variant on the theory that the context of such utterances supplies the clue: the listener, he says, receives the utterance in the same sense as the speaker understands it. Parallel discussion of the issues in this chapter are found in *Ds* 143-161.

230. See Boethius *Liber de divisione*, ed. Migne, *PL* 64. 889D, where the author says: "... if no subject (*subiecta*) be a thing which it signifies." Others interpreted this text differently. For example William of Arnaud, commenting between 1235 and 1244 on the *Tractatus* of Peter of Spain, argues that Boethius' statement refers to (nonsense) utterances like 'buf' and to cases where no referent exists either in reality or in the mind. See his *Lectura Tractatuum*, lectio 1, ed. L.M. de Rijk, "On the Genuine text of Peter of Spain's *Summule logicales*," *Vivarium* 7 (1969) 143-144. For the parallel text see *Ds* 145.

231. In the parallel text in the *De signis* (146) Bacon specifies this analogy with a little more detail: just as the substance of the father remains, though he loses the attribute of fatherhood, so the substance of a vocal sound remains, but without the attribute of being a sign of that for which it was imposed.

232. The Latin text can be read to mean that *every* vocal sound existed at one time without the attribute of imposition, or, that it is the nature of a vocal sound that it can exist as a complete entity without the attribute of imposition, recalling the case of nonsense utterances that subsequently become names by being imposed for themselves (or something else). (See above, #50-52.) The translation follows the latter interpretation because it is easily understood in the light of Bacon's treatment of nonsense utterances, because it supports the theory that signification (at pleasure) is not part of the nature or essence of a vocal sound, and because the first reading would involve the needlessly extravagant claim that all names were first nonsense utterances, one that finds no other support in this work or in the *De signis*. There is no parallel text in the *De signis*.

233. While I have not found the reference to '*faxo*' in Priscian's *Institutiones grammatici*, Donatus mentions it as a verb that cannot be properly (*rite*) declined. (See his *De arte grammatica libri* 2. 12, ed. Keil, *Grammatici Latini* 4 [Leipzig: B.G. Teubner, 1864; reprinted Hildesheim: Georg Olms, 1961], p. 383.16.) Clearly Virgil uses it with the sense of "I shall make." (See his *Aeneis* 12. 316-317, ed. and transl. H. Rushton Fairclough, *Virgil* 2, Loeb Classical Library [Cambridge, Mass.: Harvard University Press; London: William Heinemann, 1918; revised 1934], pp. 320 and 321.) For the parallel text see *Ds* 144.

234. Later Bacon proposes the case where one misinterprets the circle for a sign that wine is actually present when in fact there is no wine. See below, #127. For the parallel text see *Ds* 147.

235. For the notions of an infinite and an infinite name see above, #106, n. 214.

236. For the notion of understanding a nonentity through the privation of an entity see above, #63, n. 151.

237. The translation substitutes "Suppose that of Augustine ... be objected" for "If that of Augustine ... be objected" in order to simplify the syntax of what in the Latin text is a lengthy conditional sentence expressing both objection and response. The change in no way alters Bacon's intent. The objection is not a direct quote, but it is an accurate paraphrase of *De dialectica* 10. (See ed. Jan Pinborg; transl. B. Darrell Jackson, *De dialectica*, Synthese Historical Library 16 [Dordrecht; Boston: D. Reidel, 1975], p. 114; ed. Crecilius 18.4-5, 10.)

238. The issue here is the sense in which it can be true to say of someone who is dead that he *is* anything. Bacon has consistently employed the principle that affirmations with finite predicates can only be made univocally of existing entities. His solution, mostly unstated, draws on his notion of ampliation as a case of equivocal imposition (see above, #85, n. 186) and implies that, when Augustine made the utterance 'Tullius is an orator,'' he freely reimposed the terms 'Tullius' and 'orator' for new significates, dead Cicero and an orator of the past, respectively, with the result that the subject and predicate terms in the expression were then uttered equivocally with regard to their original significates, living Cicero and a living orator. While Bacon's solution at first seems to accept one of the options in the dilemma proposed by the objection, namely, that 'Tullius' stands for a dead person, it does so only in part. Since the objection claims that it would be false to say that a dead man is an orator, it is clear that 'orator' is being taken to refer to a living orator. Bacon would agree that such an expression is false. This is why his solution requires that 'orator' also be taken to stand (equivocally) for a past orator. Since the significates of the subject and predicate terms are then both nonentities, the present tense copula is appropriate, for dead Cicero is now and forever will be an orator of the past.

239. In the Latin text this objection is stated in the antecedent of a conditional sentence whose consequent was intended to be either unexpressed or the response to the next objection. To avoid this anomaly the translation substitutes "Suppose it be said" for "If it be said" in the text without detriment to Bacon's intent.

The same type of argument was previously used to argue that "Buba is buba" is a legitimate expression, each of whose principal parts must therefore signify at pleasure. (See above, #50.) The present objection draws on principles accepted by Bacon, namely, that complete expressions in the indicative mood must be either true or false; that tautologous expressions are necessarily true; that the expressions in question are tautologies; and that any expression is a vocal sound that signifies at pleasure, each of whose principal parts signify something at pleasure. (See *Sd*, pp. 240.14-30 and 241.8-11.) The objection then translates the element of necessity to mean that what at one time can be uttered as necessarily true will at any subsequent time (always) be true, so long as the expression retains the same terms, 'Caesar' and 'man' continuing to be univocal names.

240. For the reference see above, #52. Given Bacon's theory that names fall away from their signification when those things for which they were originally imposed cease to exist, 'Caesar' holds the same status as any nonsense utterance, and as such does not meet the fundamental requirement of becoming a part of a legitimate expression, namely, that it have a

significate at pleasure. As Bacon will state a little below, 'Caesar' needs to be reimposed, this time for a man of the past, and the result will be a new tautology whose terms equivocate with the original spoken during Caesar's lifetime.

241. Imposition by chance occurs, e.g., whenever two different people just happen to be given the same name. It does not refer to the case where a person misspeaks himself or herself. See Boethius *In Categorias Aristotelis libri quatuor*, ed. Migne, *PL* 64. 166B.

242. For a comment on the use of 'statement', 'vocal sound', and 'expression' to name utterances with unimposed terms see above, #52, n. 135.

243. While it is not immediately clear which of the points discussed Bacon considers the first point, perhaps it is that the (principal) parts of an expression, once imposed, do not continue to signify after their significates cease to exist.

244. The translation substitutes "And thus suppose [the following] be objected" for "And thus if it be objected" in order to simplify the syntax of Bacon's objection and response. The objection recalls the second attempt above to argue that 'buba' can gain reference without imposition. (See above, #51, n. 134.) Here the use of a complete disjunction purports to show that 'Caesar', once imposed, cannot lose its signification because one must use the term in an expression to deny its significative force, the subject and predicate terms in expressions being vocal sounds that signify at pleasure.

245. The reference is to the second *question* in Part Two, Chapter Two. (See above, #52.)

246. Since imposition is a free human act, the statement "it is necessarily renewed" must be read to mean that it is necessary to conclude that the name is (freely) renewed. (See also immediately below in the text.)

Bacon treats of the two types of imposition in the *De signis* (154-161) and in defense of the distinction says:

> That, moreover, this be possible is clear because imposition (*positio*) is at pleasure; therefore in as much as it pleases a man he can mentally (*in mente sua*) give a vocal sound to a thing or express the imposition vocally (154).

Then by way of example he continues:

> Likewise, he who first saw a white monk, [i.e., a monk in white clothing], did not first say that such a monk should be called [by the name] 'white monk' under the vocally expressed form of imposition, but he transferred [the name]. ... And every day we create (*facimus*) and renew significates of words (*dictionum*) in this way without the vocally expressed form of imposing as [happens in the latter case when] a name is given to infants (155).

While tacit imposition (*apud intellectum solum*) occurs more frequently than vocal, nevertheless Bacon calls the latter the "first and principal and customary" form of imposition, presumably because it is more explicit, was the form used by Adam, and because of its role in the construction of new languages. (See *Ds* 158 and 156.) In this last regard Bacon describes (see *Ds* 156) how such languages are to be devised, noting that Latin was not constructed by art while others, like those of the ancient Saxons and Angles (*"ut antiqui Saxonicum et Anglicum"*) were.

Finally, one can note that, were Bacon interested in explicating the role of an interpreter in this work and the *De signis*, his treatment of tacit imposition would offer an especially appropriate occasion for doing so.

247. This statement touches the question debated in the thirteenth century whether imposition occurs before, during, or after use in an expression (see above, Introduction, pp. 17-18) and Bacon's earlier remarks in the *De signis* (160) are not without some ambiguity. Speaking of tacit imposition he seems to formulate his position in three ways: (1) ordinarily these (equivocal) impositions do not occur unless at the same time use is made of the terms ("*... non fiunt multum istae impositiones, nisi simul fiant enuntiationes de illis terminis*"); (2) there is no detectable time lag between imposition and use, not even the slightest ("*... non est tempus sensibile nec minimum inter impositionem et enuntiationem*"); and (3) the vocal sounds are not uttered or formed except when they are used in speech. The force of 'ordinarily' in (1) suggests that some instances of tacit (equivocal) imposition are ones where imposition precedes use, but no such exceptions are implied in (3). How significant is the term 'detectable' in (2)? Does Bacon mean that there is no time lag, not even the least, or that, while there is a slight time lag, it is so small that it escapes notice? The first reading squares nicely with (3) and results in the claim that in (equivocal) tacit impositions the imposition ordinarily occurs during use. But the second reading acknowledges that imposition precedes use, granted the temporal factor is imperceptable, this fact being sufficient to ground the contrast with vocally expressed imposition. My suspicion is that Bacon wants to claim in the *De signis* that imposition in these cases ordinarily occurs during use. But if this is correct then it should be noted that the *Cst* reveals a change in his theory, for we here see him saying that 'John' must be reimposed *before* the speaker says "John is dead," and the example is surely not to be counted as one of the exceptions provided for in formulation (1) in the *De signis*. In short, then, the earlier Bacon presumably held that in cases of tacit (equivocal) imposition the imposition occurs during use (allowing for exceptions) and that the later Bacon contends that tacit (equivocal) imposition precedes use. In both works, however, vocally expressed imposition seems to be a case where imposition precedes use, though this is never stated. While this narrows the contrast between the two kinds of imposition in the *Cst*, the important difference is still preserved, namely, the fact that one is noticeable and the other is not.

248. The phrase '*oratio plena*' is difficult to translate, and to render it by "highly charged expression" is, at best, a valiant attempt. In the *De signis* (161) Bacon speaks both of *oratio plena* and *sensus orationis impletus* and associates these notions with the communication of strongly felt emotions (*affectus*).

The clause "since [this type of imposition] happens to everyone" should be taken in conjunction with another (unstated) premiss like "Things that happen to everyone (and frequently) are things which are not perceived clearly."

249. The point of the last three sentences is clear: a person moved by grief to exclaim, "John is dead," pays so much attention to what he or she intends to communicate that no attention is given to what, on analysis, can be inferred as an instance of a new (and equivocal) imposition. In the *De signis* Bacon lists four reasons to account for the fact that these impositions go unnoticed, the fourth being the one just given in this work: (a) a person does

not pay close enough attention (158); (b) vocal imposition is more clear (*manifestum*) (159); (c) imposition occurs during use (160); and (d) because of preoccupation with the content of an expression when emotion is involved (161).

250. Without detriment to Bacon's intent the translation substitutes "Suppose the following also be objected" for "If it also be objected that" in order to simplify the syntax of what follows.

251. A traveller, desiring wine, comes upon a scene where he sees a building with a circle out front and enters it in order to buy wine. In point of fact, however, there is no wine in the building. The question is what moved him to enter this particular building. The objector points to the circle as the motivating factor and claims that it has remained a sign. Bacon rejects this explanation because it assumes the theory that signs at pleasure are imposed without reference to the existence or nonexistence of their significates and offers the counter-claim that the traveller reimposes the circle for what he only imagines to be wine. Bacon's explanation is an appeal to equivocal signification since the significates of the original imposition and the traveller's are radically different, i.e., real and imagined wine. Perhaps one finds here a Baconian principle not explicitly stated, namely, that all cases of mistaken interpretation are instances of equivocal imposition on the part of the one in error. In the *De signis* (147) Bacon adds the further note that the new imposition is an act of imagination: "... *apud imaginationem suam constituunt circulum esse signum vini aestimati ab eis et imaginati, et sic fit circulus signum novum.*" I suggest, however, that this notion is more the result of careless expression than deliberate choice for two reasons. First, Bacon has consistently described imposition as an act of intellect and/or will. Second, if Bacon intends to posit the existence of this kind of imposition, since imagination is a faculty of the sensitive soul (or the intellectual soul resuming lower functions [see above, #35, n. 113]), there would be at least an a priori reason for ascribing such impositions to brutes. Yet Bacon comes no way near such ascriptions elsewhere.

252. The reference is to Richard of Cornwall. (See above, #86.)

253. Earlier Bacon attributes this statement to St. John Chrysostom. (See above, #10.) Note also that he has just ascribed all three of the causes of human error mentioned in Part One to his opponents here. (See above, #7.)

254. The reference is to Part One, Chapter Two, which discusses the general causes of error.

255. In this chapter Bacon takes a close look at things named by the same name but which represent varying degrees of differences and classifies them in six modes or degrees of equivocation, all but the first also being modes of analogy. (For the notions of equivocation and analogy as Bacon understands them see above, #67, n. 158.) In his *Communia naturalium* (*Opera*, 2, ed. Steele, p. 51.4-15) he mentions that he has already written abundantly on *five* modes of equivocation in his *Metaphysica* and then describes them again. (No mention of these is found in the fragments of the *Metaphysica* edited by Steele, *Opera*, 1 [Oxford: Clarendon Press, (n.d.)].) The first mode focuses on things with nothing in common and the fifth on those having the least difference. Hence the basic movement is from pure equivocation toward univocation. In the *De signis* (38-99) Bacon offers a much more thorough analysis of equivocation, distinguishes five modes, but reverses their order in the middle sections of his treatment. Thus his presentation (38-45)

follows the progression of the *Communia naturalium*, though modes three, four, and five are called "one mode," "another mode," and "a third mode" (41, 42, and 43-45 respectively). Then in 46 the progression is reversed, first mode equivocation being closest to univocation. This has no consequences for his further remarks on the third mode (47-52) since it maintains its numerical position in both sequences, but his reflections from 53 to 80 should be understood to refer to second mode equivocation in the original enumeration even though, e.g., in 53 and 70 he says he is speaking of the fourth mode. In 81 all the modes are mentioned and the same reverse order is maintained, but from 82-88 he returns to the original sequence where things having the most difference are classified in a first mode. The remaining sections on equivocation (89-99) treat of ampliation and restriction but no reference is made to modes. Turning to the *Cst* one finds that Bacon has preserved the original sequence but has added a sixth mode in which he classifies some of the examples given in the fifth mode (original order) in *Ds* 43. (These are not mentioned in the *Communia naturalium*.) Finally, one other contrast can be noted: the *De signis* discusses equivocation before it addresses the issue whether a term signifying an entity and a nonentity is univocal or equivocal.

256. The quotation is not direct but is probably meant to express what is found in *Topics* 1. 18. 108a38-108b5.

257. For the reference see above, Part Two, Chapter Four, esp. #88-95.

258. In the *De signis* (38) Bacon says that this is the purest form of equivocation because "there is a complete difference and distance between something and nothing, since [it is] infinite, and neither is there an absolute agreement, as is clear, nor a relational [agreement], because there neither is order nor [is there] relation of something to nothing." By implication, then, all the instances of equivocation mentioned in Part Two, Chapters Four and Five, are cases of pure equivocation, not of analogical signification.

259. Given Bacon's desire to distinguish various grades of equivocation in this chapter, and having begun with significates that are in no way similar, he now must classify in the second mode of equivocation those which, given a minimum degree of similarity, have the maximum difference possible. Thus Bacon chooses as his first example two things which have only this in common: one is dependent on the other for existence and the relation is not reciprocal. Given such a difference, one can only predicate equivocally (analogically), for example, 'substance' of God, a being who is in no way dependent on anything else for His existence, and any creature, each of which is totally dependent on God for its existence. Since 'substance' was originally imposed for created substance, the nature of the entity signified by 'creator' in "The Creator is a substance" requires that the meaning of the predicate term be transferred (reimposed) to signify something that is only relationally similar. For the reason why some of the terms mentioned in the text have been left in Latin see the following paragraph in the text.

260. Among *created* thing the greatest difference and least similarity obtains between substance and any of the nine classes of attributes. Given that the definition of attribute includes the notion of substance, the relation of attribute to substance would be an intrinsic one. However, since the converse is not true, Bacon's statement that they "do have an order among themselves" should be read to imply that substance is extrinsically related

to attribute. Thus 'entity' in "A Substance is an entity" and in "Red is an entity" is predicated equivocally (analogically) and the degree of equivocation is less than that in the first mode. For the parallel text see *Ds* 40.

261. If one excludes 'thing' and 'creature' in the preceding sentence all the terms at issue can be taken grammatically as adjectives or neuter substantives and this difference is reflected in what they signify. Taken adjectivally '*unum*', e.g., would be translated by 'one' as in 'one body (*unum corpus*)' and would signify a form or quality of unity. This is what Bacon calls the first significate of '*unum*'. Now since unity can be predicated of anything that exists and the form remains the same in all such cases, the first significate of '*unum*' (and all adjectives) is predicated univocally. But '*unum*' can also be taken substantively as a neuter substantive, be translated by 'unit' or 'a one' as in "The body is a unit," and in this case would signify a *thing* having the form or quality of unity. This is its second significate. And since things are distinguished according to the rules that govern classification as substance or attribute, i.e., on the basis of whether they have being of themselves or in virtue of something that has it of itself, '*unum*' in its second sense would be predicated equivocally of a substance and a quality. The color "black" is the same wherever it appears, but a black automobile is not the same kind of entity as the color "black." Given the ambiguity in the grammatical forms of the terms in question (except, again, 'thing' and 'creature') Bacon must indicate in which sense they are to be taken and he does this by referring to their second significates. Possibly, however, he also considers 'thing' and 'creature' to be derivative terms, in which case they too would have this double signification. If not, their status as substantives sufficiently indicates that any use of them as said of a substance and an attribute would be equivocal.

One should note that the distinction here between first and second significates is not the same as that seen earlier between principal and secondary significates, the latter serving to distinguish between what a namer directly intends and whatever else may be necessarily related to it. (See above, #75 and n. 170.) The principal significates of the terms in question are their second significates, whatever else they may signify or connote. While Bacon does not indicate the basis for a ranking of "first" and "second" I suspect that it is linked with the notions that forms are the causes of things, that causes are of a higher order than their effects, and that derivative names are taken from the names of the forms they signify as denominative terms.

While the long list of terms is not mentioned when Bacon first discusses this mode of equivocation in the *De signis* (41) he discusses them at length later, invoking the authority of Avicenna against Averroes. (See *Ds* 53-80.)

262. In the *Sumule dialectices* (p. 209.27-210.7) Bacon, treating of denominatives, points to the issue of whether these terms can be predicated in the same way as names. He is inclined to think that they cannot but concludes by saying, "... but the certification of this is inquired about elsewhere" (ibid., p. 210.7). However he does not return to this issue in that work. In the *De signis*, after presenting the second mode of equivocation (40), he goes into great detail about the equivocation of denominative terms (53-80) and refers to "a noteworthy difficulty," namely, how to explicate the equivocation in "Oneness is one" and "Man is one" (72-73). He also argues, against others, that not only terms like 'one', 'true', and 'good' are

predicated of themselves (e.g., "Oneness is one") but also all adjectives (74-80). Presumably, then, it is issues like these to which Bacon refers here and says are treated in ensuing chapters, ones still missing from this work.

263. In the proper sense of the term only living things can be said to be healthy, i.e., to have the accidental form called "health." However other things are said to be healthy, not because health is one of their accidental forms, but because they are related in various ways to health in a living thing. Thus the color of urine is a sign of the state of one's health, medicine a cause, and proper diet something that preserves health. Since each of these relations represents a different notion, and all three are related to the proper notion, 'healthy' can only be an equivocal (analogical) term when said of any two. For the parallel text see *Ds* 40.

264. The form called "heat" is in a person, not the spices; but to eat them causes one to acquire the form. Hence to say "Pepper is hot" is to signify, not the presence of the form "heat" in a pepper, but a particular causal relation.

265. In *Categories* 8. 8b25-10a25 Aristotle refers to four subclasses of the category "Quality": (1) habit and disposition, i.e., the condition of something that is either permanent or changing, where heat is mentioned as a disposition; (2) an inborn capacity like hardness and softness; (3) affective qualities, i.e., those like heat and cold that are able to produce an affect in their subjects which is then able to be perceived; and (4) figure and shape.

266. See above, #133, n. 262.

267. Possibly Bacon has in mind *Physics* 2. 2. 194a11. He makes no reference to a "special example" of something said of matter and form when discussing this mode of equivocation in the *De signis* (40); the issue is simply mentioned when he discusses the next mode in *Ds* 41.

268. In the *Physics* (2. 2. 194b8) Aristotle says that 'matter' is a relative term since each form has a corresponding special matter. Commenting on Book Two of that work Bacon acknowledges in his *Questiones supra libros quatuor Physicorum Aristotelis* that matter and form have a mutual relation (*mutuus respectus*) and adds that each in its own way is a principle of motion and rest and that each is an inner power (*vis insita*) making a nature or substance an integral whole. (See *Opera*, 8, ed. Delorme with Steele, p. 60.4.-15.) In the later *Communia naturalium* (*Opera*, 2, ed. Steele, p. 51.22-25) they are said to be essentially different but related since matter is the subject of form and form the perfection of matter. Thus their agreement is not absolute but relational and the degree of difference in the two notions is such that anything said of both would equivocate in this mode.

269. The question whether angels are entities composed of matter and form or are simply forms was fiercely debated in Bacon's time. Those like Bacon who understood the notion of matter in the sense of pure potentiality saw no good reason for not ascribing it to all entities other than God. Those who understood it to be extrinsically linked to physical attributes denied it of God and angels, speaking of the latter as pure forms or intellectual substances. While the reference to "one of the so-called authors" could be to any one of several of Bacon's opponents, it may well be to Thomas Aquinas. See the latter's *Summa contra gentiles*, Book Two, Chapter 50, transl. James F. Anderson (Notre Dame, Indiana: University of Notre Dame Press, 1975), pp. 149-151. Bacon does not return to this issue in any of the known parts of this work.

270. 'Substance' in "Matter is substance" and "Form is substance" is an equivocal term in the second mode of equivocation (first mode of analogy) because matter and form have nothing in common but a mutual relation. Up to this point there has been more difference than similarity between significates of the same term. Now Bacon turns to those things that reflect the opposite. His focus in this third mode of equivocation (second of analogy) is the difference and similarity that obtain between a whole and its parts. He mentions this mode in his *Communia naturalium* (*Opera*, 2, ed. Steele, p. 51.9-10, .15-23) and gives extensive examples and analysis in the *De signis* (41 and 47-52).

271. See below, #137, where genus and species are discussed in regard to the fourth mode of equivocation. Since it is clear from the preceding that significates in this mode do have something in common, some of Bacon's statements here and immediately below need to be qualified to indicate that what is denied of the significates in question is the kind of communality that could serve as a basis for univocal predication. Thus the translation inserts '[univocally]' to indicate this.

272. If 'substance' is taken to mean that which is composed of parts that are intrinsically uncomposed, then it would be false to say that matter or form is a substance. However, if it is defined in contradistinction to attribute as that which has being (*esse*) of itself, then it could be predicated of a composite and one or the other of a composite's essential parts. Bacon will immediately add that such predication can only be equivocal and the implied reason is that the notion of a whole and that of one of its parts is clearly different: each shares being in a different way, though the difference is not so great as that between the way substance and attribute share being.

273. The point in the last six sentences is this. The relation between a whole and one of its parts or between a genus and one of its species is such that anything said of them equivocates in this mode. For example, since there are many kinds of relations, and opposition is one of them, relation stands to opposition as genus to species. And since there are many kinds of opposition, and one of them is contradiction, opposition is related to contradiction as genus to species. The notion, then, of the most determinate species of relation and that of the most general genus "Relation" reflect a difference, granted there is greater similarity than that between matter and form and substance and attribute. Given this difference, whatever is said of 'relation' in its most general and specific senses can only be equivocal. For something to be able to be predicated univocally of both would require that it include both in its notion. But this would make it a higher genus than "Relation" itself which would then contradict what was originally assumed, namely, that "Relation" is one of the ten ultimate genera.

274. In the *De signis* Bacon mentions other examples of terms that equivocate in this mode: 'indiction (*indictio*)', meaning either a period of fifteen years or one of those years (41); nouns and adjectives (or compounds) used as proper names like 'Rose', 'Clement' (48), 'Bonaventure', and 'Goodman' (49), and all modes of supposition (48-52) because, as he says, "a word (*dictio*) does not supposit for something in an expression unless it signify it and unless it be imposed for it ..." (50). He also adds that all the errors about the proposition "Only one is (*tantum unum est*)" can be resolved simply by recognizing that it involves a case of third mode equivocation: it is true if

'one' is taken to signify a universal but false if taken to signify a designated particular. (See *Ds* 47 and 52.)

275. See Aristotle *Physics* 7. 4. 249a22-24 and also *Metaphysics* 10. 7. 1057b35-1058a9. For an analysis of equivocal signification in this mode see below, #137, n. 277.

276. In the *De signis* (42) Bacon says that the essence of genus in any of its species is differentiated (*diversificata*) before it receives any additional specific difference.

277. The claim here is that two species of the same genus (or two individuals of different species of the same genus), taken concretely and not abstractly, differ not simply in virtue of their specific differences but even more fundamentally because of the generic element in each. A horse is an animal in a way that a donkey is not. In the parallel text in the *De signis* (42) Bacon indicates that he takes the relation between genus and species to be analogous to that of natural matter to form and thereby prompts one to look into his *Communia naturalium* for help in understanding his theory of genus. There (*Opera*, 2, ed. Steele, pp. 52.29-60.15, esp. pp. 57.11-58.17) he contends that matter is not the same in all composites. In support of this he argues that if one considers composites and descends from the most general to the most determinate there is a parallel addition of differences in the order of matter as well as that of form. No composite could be considered to be new, he argues, if it differs from that from which it came only formally. And since matter and form are substantial parts of a composite, the being (*esse*) appropriate to each at any stage in the descent is essential and not accidental. (See ibid., p. 58.14-17.) Matter at any given stage in the process of generation is not in potency to just any form; only matter made suitable (*materia apta*) can be united with a determinate form, and this notion finds expression in the *De signis* (42) when Bacon writes:

> ... but the accruing difference (*differentia adveniens*) accrues to the essence of a genus changed, made suitable, and apportioned (*appropriatam*) to one species and one difference of a species, just as matter must be apportioned to form so that, apportioned to each other, they may constitute a proper composite. And likewise it happens the same way when the essence of genus is moved to the second species.

Were matter not already differentiated before it was apportioned to the formal difference of a horse and a donkey, argues Bacon, it would not be suitable matter for the different kinds of forms. The same is the case with genus in regard to its various species. So while genus is one root in all of its species, it is a root that already has various kinds of being (*esse*) before (or as) it is moved in the process of generation into different species of the same genus or different individuals of different species of the same genus. 'Animal', then, said of a horse and a donkey is an equivocal term, and, since two species of the same genus have more in common than a whole and one of its parts or a universal and one of its particulars, the equivocation here must be classified in a mode closer to univocation than the preceding. For additional analysis of Bacon's position on the lack of numerical material unity in things created see Crowley, *Roger Bacon*, pp. 91-100.

278. Earlier it was pointed out (see above, #67, n. 158) that Bacon distinguishes univocation from equivocation not on the basis of whether more than one significate is involved but on whether more than one imposition occurs. It is only in virtue of this precision that he is now (and in the next mode) able to

speak of cases involving one term and one significate as being instances of equivocation. He discusses this mode in *Ds* 43 but also includes reference to significates classified in the *Cst* in the sixth mode of equivocation.

279. The three utterances mean "lover of him," "loving him," and "I love." They are left in Latin because Bacon will next make reference to a single vocal sound that can signify either as a name or a participle. The addition of '*amo*' confuses things somewhat. In the *De signis* (43) '*amor*' is used as an example of one term signifying one thing as a name ("love") and as a verb ("I am loved"). Either he intends in the present text to admit paronyms to this mode of equivocation or '*amo*' should be corrected to read '*amor*,' an example independent of '*amans*'. For the reference to Priscian see above, #102, n. 206.

280. Latin vocal sounds are composites of a stem (substance) and a case-ending (attribute), and the latter serves to indicate how the sound is to function in an expression: '*homo*', '*hominis*', '*homini*' mean "a man," "of a man" and "to a man," respectively. However some case endings are identical, with the result that when one of these endings is affixed to a stem it is not immediately clear which case is intended. (In the *De signis* [43] Bacon gives the example of '*cornu*' which, he says, remains the same in all its cases.) To show how equivocation can occur when such vocal sounds are used in two different cases Bacon offers a "syllogism" and in his *Sumule dialectices* (p. 332.5-7) points out that in order for the major and minor to be true '*episcopi*' must be taken in the nominative plural in the major and genitive singular in the minor, which however introduces four terms in the argument and prevents the formation of a well constructed syllogism. (William of Sherwood and Peter of Spain understand the equivocal term to be the same as Bacon, so Rashdall errs in pointing to '*asini*' as the culprit. (See respectively Martin Grabmann, "Die *Introductiones in logicam* des Wilhelm von Shyreswood," *Sitzungsberichte der Bayerischen Akademie der Wissenschaften, Philosophisch-historische Abteilung*, Jahrgung 1937, Heft 10 [Munich: Verlag der Bayerischen Akademie der Wissenschaften, 1937], p. 88.12-15; Peter of Spain, *Tractatus*, ed. L.M. de Rijk [Assen: Van Gorcum, 1972], p. 108.19-20; and *Cst*, p. 19.) Bacon's point is that whenever a vocal sound having the same suffix in more than one case is imposed on more than one occasion to signify the same object under different conditions which correlate with the case distinctions, the term will be equivocal because of the different ways the suffix (accident) of the term signifies these different conditions.

281. The difference between one part of speech and another is greater than that between one part of speech in a particular grammatical case (or tense) and the same in another. This point does not serve as a basis for distinguishing correspondingly different modes of signification in the *Communia naturalium* and *De signis*; both present only five modes of equivocation. (Cf. respectively *Opera*, 2, ed. Steele, 51.13-15 and *Ds* 43.) However in the *Cst* Bacon does make this distinction and speaks of the former as signifying essentially and the latter accidentally.

282. See Virgil *Georgica* 1, ed. and transl. H. Rushton Fairclough, *Virgil: Eclogues, Georgics, Aeneid I-V*, 1, Loeb Classical Library (Cambridge, Mass.: Harvard University Press; London: William Heinemann, 1950), pp. 80 and 81.

283. Bacon will next point out what has been assumed throughout this chapter, namely, that analogy is based on a similarity of proportion. Every term has its own proper notion. For example, the proper notion of 'substance' is "that which has existence of itself." The term becomes analogical when one takes it to mean "that which has existence" and in this broader sense accidents are said to be substances. The justification for doing this is the way attributes relate to substance, just as the reason for calling medicine healthy is because of the relation of medicine to health in that of which 'health' is predicated according to its proper notion. Thus while 'substance' and 'healthy' are each said of only one thing according to their proper notions they are said of anything that is related to that one thing according to their common or extended notions. Analogical terms, then, supposit for that which they signify according to this latter meaning, and they can do this because of the similarity of proportion by which the analogates are related to one thing. And when they are taken in this way they can be said to signify properly, even though they do this less properly than when they are taken to signify according to their proper notions.

But imposition is at the free disposition of a speaker and vocal sounds are also used in another way, i.e., to supposit or stand for things which they signify according to neither their proper nor common notions. People smile and are joyful, but to smile and to be joyful are not predicated in the examples Bacon gives because of some relation they have to causing these effects in people. That is, the basis for transferring these terms to meadows and crops is not a similarity of proportion that would render them analogical terms. Rather, it is what medievals called a similarity of proportionality: since humans smile and are joyful when confronted with goodness, fecundity, and beauty, so meadows and crops *are said* to smile and be joyful when possessing these qualities. To speak this way is to speak figuratively or metaphorically and since the class of all things properly or commonly signified by 'smile' and 'joyous' would not include meadows and crops, it is easily seen that terms used figuratively are different from those used analogically: they do not supposit for what they signify, and one uses them only to reflect a similarity of proportionality. Because of this Bacon says that figurative speech can be said to be the kind of equivocation that is also analogy only in an improper sense. And since he says in *Ds* 50 that terms in speech supposit only for what they signify, one can also add that their supposition is also improper.

284. For the reference to Tully see Cicero, *Timaeus* 13, ed. Johann Wrobel, M. *Tulli Ciceronis Scripta Quae Manserunt* 47, *Bibliotheca Scriptorum Graecorum Et Romanorum Teubneriana* (Leipzig: B.G. Teubner, 1975), pp. 186.26-188.1; for the notion that there is no comparison between significates in the first mode of equivocation see above, #131. While Bacon prided himself on his knowledge of Greek and did indeed write a Greek grammar (see above, Introduction, p.   ) it is not at all clear that he was proficient in it, certainly not to the same degree as someone like Robert Grosseteste (1175-1253).

285. The interpretation of this text requires one to understand how '*ens*' and '*unum*' taken as signifying the qualities of being in a subject (*esse in subiecto*) (see *Ds* 56) and unity (their respective first significates) can be predicated of a substance and an attribute in a way that (1) is not equivocal (or analogical) in any of the six modes just described, (2) does acknowledge the priority of substance over attribute, (3) can be reconciled with the earlier

statement (see above, #133) that these terms signify a substance and an attribute univocally when taken according to their first significates, and (4) merits the name "analogically" in some sense. While considerable conjecture is required, I would suggest the following as plausible.

Bacon has already indicated that the first significates of '*ens*' and '*unum*' are not substances having being and unity respectively but attributes. (See above, #133, and *Ds* 56.) So he is talking about accidental forms. In the same text above these were said to be predicated univocally of a substance and an attribute in that when I say, e.g., "Substance is one" and "Attribute is one" I am using 'one' in the same sense on both occasions. However it should be noted that, while in such expressions what is predicated is the same, the subjects of predication are different. There is a "first and second" (*per prius et posterius*) relation between substance and accident because of the way each relates to being: substance has being of itself while attributes only in virtue of inherence in some substances. Because of this Bacon is led to say in *Ds* 62—and I am indebted to Jan Pinborg for calling my attention to it—that the being and unity of an attribute is derived from the being and unity of substance. Hence while attributes are predicated univocally they are in a certain sense related necessarily to different grades of entities when predicated of substance and attributes. Difference enters the picture not in virtue of the attributes but by reason of the subjects of which they are predicated. This possibly is behind what Bacon intends by his statement that '*ens*' and '*unum*' agree more (*per prius*) with substance than attribute when taken according to their first significates. Such terms are not equivocal (or analogical) in any of the six modes because the diversity pertains to the subjects of predication and not to what is predicated.

At this point it seems to me that Bacon's earlier remarks offer some clue in meeting conditions (1) to (3) prescribed above for a clarification of his intent. But in what sense can these univocal predications also be termed analogical? Two things suggest appeal to his notion of connotation: an extrapolation from another earlier remark, namely, that every proper attribute connotes its subject (see above, #66 and the claim in the *De signis* (102) that connotation—granted the term is not used in that work—is analogical signification in a special sense. (For this notion see also above, #67 and n. 158.)

Applying these to the present case Bacon would be taken to imply that, while the principal significates of '*ens*' and '*unum*', understood according to their first significates are respectively the qualities existence and unity, they connote (signify naturally) a subject in which to inhere since attributes are necessarily related to substance. Because they signify one thing at pleasure (an attribute) and another naturally (substance) they are analogical terms in the special sense of 'analogy', and this kind of analogical signification, recall, was said not to be incompatible with univocal signification. (See above, #67 and n. 158.) When looked at, then, from Bacon's theory of connotation these terms, taken according to their first significates, seem to represent cases of "analogy where there is not equivocation."

To the degree that the above presents a plausible explication of the remarks in question, there still remains the mystery why, having proposed his special theory of analogy in the *De signis*, he chooses only this rather cryptic way of reintroducing it into the *Cst.* I suspect that the discovery of "the following chapters" will help little to dispel the mystery.

286. In *Metaphysics* 10. 7. 1058a4-8 Aristotle acknowledges that a horse and a man are different sorts of animals, but I have not found where he says the latter is more an animal than the former.

287. The work ends with a note written in a later hand "*Quaere residuum* (Look for the rest) p. 221." Rashadall says that "p. 221" refers to f. 113 of R. and adds: "The treatise referred to is the version of the *Communia naturalium* (?) beginning '*Ostensum est*'" (see Appendix" (*Cst*, p. 69, n. 2). For his reference to (A.G. Little's) appendix see ibid., p. 100.

BIBLIOGRAPHY

What follows is a list of titles that pertain primarily to the study of Bacon as a semanticist. For works that cover Bacon's career more broadly see especially the entries under Alessio (1), Crowley (1), Easton, and Hackett and Maloney.

A. Works by Bacon

Brewer, J.S., ed. *Fr. Rogeri Bacon Opera quaedam hactenus inedita.* "Rolls Series." London, 1859; reprinted Nendelin: Kraus Reprint, 1965.
Compendium studii philosophiae pp. 393-519.
Opus minus, pp. 313-389.
Opus tertium, pp. 3-310.
Bridges, John Henry, ed. *The 'Opus maius' of Roger Bacon.* 3 vols. Oxford, 1879-1900; reprinted Fankfort on the Main: Minerva, 1964. Vol. 3 contains a revised text of vol. 1, Parts 1-3, along with corrections and additional notes for vols. 1-2.
Burke, Robert Belle, transl. *The Opus Maius of Roger Bacon.* 2 vols. Philadelphia: University of Pennsylvania Press; London: Humphrey Milford; Oxford: University Press, 1928.
Duhem, Pierre, ed. *Un fragment inédit de l'opus tertium de Roger Bacon précédé d'une étude sur ce fragment.* Quaracchi: St. Bonaventure College Press, 1909.
Fredborg, Karin Margarita, Lauge Nielsen, and Jan Pinborg, eds. "An Unedited Part of Roger Bacon's '*Opus maius: De signis*'." *Traditio* 34 (1978) 75-136.
Gasquet, Francis Aidan. "An Unpublished Fragment of a Work by Roger Bacon." *English Historical Review* 12 (1897) 494-517.
Lindberg, David C. *Roger Bacon's Philosophy of Nature: A Critical Edition, with English Translation, Introduction, and Notes of De multiplicatione specierum and De speculis comburentibus.* Oxford: Clarendon Press, 1983.
Little, A.G., ed. *Part of the Opus tertium of Roger Bacon Including a Fragment Now Printed for the First Time.* Aberdeen: University Press, 1912; reprinted Farnborough: Gregg Press, 1966.
Massa, Eugenio, ed. *Rogeri Baconis Moralis Philosophia.* Zurich: Thesaurus Mundi, [1953].
Nolan, Edmond, and S.A. Hirsch, eds. *The Greek Grammar of Roger Bacon And a Fragment of His Hebrew Grammar.* Cambridge: University Press, 1902.
Rashdall, Hastings, ed. *Fratris Rogeri Bacon Compendium studii theologiae.* Aberdeen: University Press, 1911; reprinted Farnborough: Gregg Press, 1966.
Steele, Robert, ed. *Opera hactenus inedita Rogeri Bacon.* 16 fasc. Oxford: Clarendon Press, 1905?-1941.
   Fasc. 1. *Metaphysica Fratris Rogeri Ordinis Fratrum Minorum de viciis contractis in studio theologie,* 1905?
   Fasc. 2. *Liber primus communium naturalium Fratris Rogeri,* 1905? (Parts 1-2.)
   Fasc. 3. *Liber primus communium naturalium Fratris Rogeri,* 1911. (Parts 3-4.)
   Fasc. 4. *Liber secundus communium naturalium Fratris Rogeri de celestibus,* 1913. (Parts 1-5.)
   Fasc. 5. *Secretum secretorum cum glossis et notulis: tractatus brevis et utilis ad declarandum quedam obscure dicta Fratris Rogeri,* 1920.
   Fasc. 8. *Questiones supra libros quatuor Physicorum Aristotelis,* ed. Ferdinand Delorme with Steele, 1928.
   Fasc. 10. *Questiones supra libros prime philosophie Aristotelis,* with Delorme, 1930.
   Fasc. 13. *Questiones supra libros octo Physicorum Aristotelis,* ed. Ferdinand Delorme, with Steele, 1935.

Fasc. 14. *Liber de sensu et sensato* [*et*] *Summa de sophismatibus et distinctionibus*, 1937.
Fasc. 15. *Summa grammatica magistri Rogeri Bacon necnon Sumule dialectices magistri Rogeri Bacon*, 1940.

B. Other Works

Ackrill, J.L., transl. *Aristotle's Categories And De Interpretatione.* Oxford: Clarendon Press, 1963; reprinted with corrections, 1966.
Alessio, F. "Un secolo di studi su Ruggero Bacone." *Rivista critica di storia della filosofia* 14 (1959) 81-102.
(Alessio, F.). See also Lambert of Auxerre.
Anderson, James F. See Thomas Aquinas (2).
Angelelli, Ignacio. "The Techniques of Disputation in the History of Logic." *The Journal of Philosophy* 67 (1970) 800-815.
Aristotle. *Aristoteles Latinus.* Edited by L. Minio-Paluello. Brussels; Paris: Desclée de Brouwer, 1939-; Leiden: E.J. Brill, 1972-.
(Aristotle). *The Basic Works of Aristotle.* Edited by Richard McKeon, New York: Random House, 1941.
Ashworth, E.J. *The Tradition of Medieval Logic And Speculative Grammar from Anselm to the End of the Seventeenth Century: A Bibliography from 1836 Onward.* Subsidia Mediaevalia. Toronto: Pontifical Institute of Mediaeval Studies, 1978.
Augustine. *Concerning the Teacher.* Translated by G. Leckie. *Concerning the Teacher And On the Immortality of the Soul.* New York: Appleton-Century-Crofts, 1938.
(Augustine). *De dialectica.* Edited by Jan Pinborg; translated by B. Darrell Jackson. *Augustine: De dialectica.* Synthese Historical Library. Vol. 16. Dordrecht; Boston: D. Reidel, 1975.
(Augustine). *De doctrina christiana.* Edited by Joseph Martin. *Corpus Christianorum, Series Latina.* Vol. 32. Tournai: Brepols, 1962.
(Augustine). *De magistro.* Edited by Guenther Weigel. *Corpus Christianorum Ecclesiasticorum Latinorum.* Vol. 77. Vienna: Hoelder-Pichler-Tempsky, 1961.
(Augustine). *On Christian Doctrine.* Translated by D. Robertson, Jr. *St. Augustine: On Christian Doctrine.* New York: The Liberal Arts Press, 1958.
Averroes. *Metaphysica.* Ed. Iuntina. *Opera.* Vol. 8. Venice, 1562; reprinted Frankfort on the Main: Minerva, 1962.
Avicenna. *Metaphysica.* Ed. Iuntina. *Opera Philosophica.* Venice, 1508; reprinted Frankfort on the Main: Minerva, 1961.
Basore, John W. See Seneca (1) and (2).
Bickford-Smith, R.A.H. See Publilius Syrus (1).
Bird, Otto. "The Tradition of the Logical Topics: Aristotle to Ockham." *Journal of the History of Ideas* 23 (1962) 307-323.
Bochenski, I.M. "De consequentiis scholasticarum earumque origine." *Angelicum* 15 (1938) 92-109.
Boehner, Philotheus. "Ockham's Theory of Signification." *Franciscan Studies* 6 (1946) 143-170.
Boethius. *Commentarium* [*maius*] *in librum Peri hermêneias.* Edited by Karl Meiser. Leipzig: B.G. Teubner, 1880.
(Boethius). *Contra Eutychen et Nestorium.* Edited and translated by H.F. Stewart, E.K. Rand, and S.J. Tester. *Boethius: The Theological Tractates.* Loeb Classical Library. London: William Heinemann; New York: G.P. Putnam's Sons, 1918.
(Boethius). *De hypotheticis syllogismis.* Ed. and transl. (Italian) by Luca Obertello. *A. M. Severino Boezio De hypotheticis syllogismis.* Testi Classici di Logica 1. Ed. by Domenico Pesce. Brescia: Paideia, 1969.
(Boethius). *De topicis differentiis.* Translated by Eleonore Stump. *Boethius' De topicis differentiis.* Ithaca: Cornell University, 1978.
(Boethius). *In Categorias Aristotelis libri quatuor.* Ed. Migne. *PL* 64. 159-294.

(Boethius). *In librum Aristotelis Peri hermêneias commentarium*. 1st. ed. Edited by Karl Meiser. Leipzig: B.G Teubner, 1880.

(Boethius). *Liber Aristotelis de decem praedicamentis*. Edited by L. Minio-Paluello. *Aristoteles Latinus* 1. 1. Edited by L. Minio-Paluello. Leiden: E.J. Brill, 1961.

(Boethius). *Liber de divisione*. Ed. Migne. *PL* 64. 875-892.

Bottin, F. *Le antinomie semantiche nella logica medievale*. Padua: Editrice Antenore, 1976.

Braakhuis, H.A.G. "The Views of William of Sherwood on Some Semantical Topics and Their Relation to Those of Roger Bacon." *Vivarium* 15 (1977) 111-142.

(Braakhuis, H.A.G.). See also de Libera (1).

Bregola, Giacomo. "Il valore delle lingue e delle scienze nell' apologetica di Ruggero Bacone." *La Scuola Cattolica* 65 (1937) 372-391.

Brind'Amour, Lucie. See de Libera (2).

Callus, D.A. "Introduction of Aristotelian Learning into Oxford in the Thirteenth Century." *Proceedings of the British Academy* 29 (1943) 229-281.

The Cambridge History of Later Medieval Philosophy: From the Rediscovery of Aristotle to the Disintegration of Scholasticism 1100-1600. Edited by Norman Kretzmann, Anthony Kenny, and Jan Pinborg; associate editor, Eleonore Stump. Cambridge, London, New York, New Rochelle, Melbourne, Sydney: Cambridge University Press, 1982.

Catholic University of America. See Weisheipl (3).

"Chronicle of the Twenty-four Generals." *Analecta Franciscana* 3 (1897).

Cicero. *Academica*. Edited and translated by H. Rackham. *Cicero: De natura deorum, De academica*. Loeb Classical Library. Cambridge, Mass.: Harvard University Press; London: William Heinemann, 1933; revised 1951, 1956.

(Cicero). *Tusculanae disputationes*. Edited and translated by J.E. King. *Cicero: Tusculan Disputations*. Loeb Classical Library. Camridge, Mass.: Harvard University Press; London: William Heinemann, 1927; revised 1945.

(Cicero). *Timaeus.* Edited by John Wrobel. *M. Tulli Ciceronis Scripta Quae Manserunt*. Vol. 47. *Bibliotheca Scriptorum Graecorum Et Romanorum Teubneriana*. Leipzig: B.G. Teubner, 1975.

(Cicero). *Topica*. Edited and translated by H.M. Hubbell. *Cicero: De inventione, De optimo oratorum, Topica*. Loeb Classical Library. Cambridge, Mass.: Harvard University Press; London: William Heinemann, 1949.

Coleman, Timothy. "Modistic Grammar." Unpublished Ph.D. dissertation. Toronto: University of Toronto, 1977.

Congar, M.-J. *A History of Theology*. Garden City, New York: Doubleday, 1968.

Corcoran, John. See Kretzman (1).

Crombie, A.C. *Robert Grosseteste And the Origins of Experimental Science 1100-1700*. Oxford: Clarendon Press, 1953, pp. 139-162.

Cross, F. See Engels (1).

Crowley, Theodore. *Roger Bacon: The Problem of the Soul in His Philosophical Commentaries*. Louvain: l'Institut Supérieur de Philosophie; Dublin: James Duffy, 1950.

(Crowley, Theodore). "Roger Bacon: The Problem of Universals in His Philosophical Commentaries." *Bulletin of the John Rylands Library* 34 (1951-1952) 264-275.

Denifle, H. and A. Chatelain. *Chartularium Universitatis Parisiensis*, 1. Paris, 1889.

Denzinger, Heinrich. See *Encheridion Symbolorum*.

Dod, Bernard C. "*Aristoteles Latinus*". In *The Cambridge History of Later Medieval Philosophy: From the Rediscovery of Aristotle to the Disintegration of Scholasticism, 1100-1600*. Edited by Norman Kretzmann, Anthony Kenny, and Jan Pinborg; associate editor Eleonore Stump. Cambridge; London; New York; New Rochelle; Melbourne; Sydney: Cambridge University Press, 1982, pp. 45-79.

Donatus. *De arte grammatica libri*. Edited by Heinrich Keil. *Grammatici Latini*. Vol. 4. Edited by Heinrich Keil. Leipzig, 1864; reprinted Hildesheim: Georg Olms, 1961.

Easton, Stewart C. *Roger Bacon And His Search for a Universal Science: A Reconsideration of the Life And Work of Roger Bacon in the Light of His Own Stated Purposes*. London, 1952; reprinted New York: Russell and Russell, 1971.

Ebbesen, Sten. "Anonymus Aurelianensis I: Commentarium in Sophisticos Elenchos." *Cahiers de l'Institut Du Moyen-Âge grec et latin.* Vol. 34. Copenhagen: University of Copenhagen, 1979.

(Ebbesen, Sten). "Can Equivocation Be Eliminated?" *Studia Mediewistyczne* 18 (1977) 103-124.

(Ebbesen, Sten). "The Dead Man Is Alive." *Synthese* 40. Dordrecht; Boston: D. Reidel, 1979, pp. 43-70.

(Ebbesen, Sten). "Jacobus Veneticus on the *Posterior Analytics* And Some Early 13th Century Oxford Masters on the Elenchi." *Cahiers de l'Institut du Moyen-Âge grec et latin.*

(Ebbesen, Sten). "Roger Bacon And the Fools of His Times." *Cahiers de l'Institut du Moyen-Âge grec et latin.* Vol. 3. Copenhagen: University of Copenhagen, 1970, pp. 40-44.

(Ebbesen, Sten) and Jan Pinborg. "Studies in the Logical Writings Attributed to Boethius de Dacia." *Cahiers de l'Institut du Moyen-Âge grec et latin.* Vol. 3. Copenhagen: University of Copenhagen, 1970.

Edwards, Paul. See Kretzmann (2) and Wolter.

Encheridion Symbolorum Deffinitionum Et Declarationum de Rebus Fidei Et Morum. 33rd. ed. Edited by Heinrich Denzinger and Adolf Schönmetzer. New York: Herder, 1965.

Engels, J. "La doctrine du signe chez saint Augustine." *Studia Patristica* 6, ed. F. Cross. *Texte und Untersuchungen* 81. Berlin: Akademie-Verlag, 1962, pp. 366-373.

(Engels, J.) "Origine, sens et survie du terme boécien *'secundum placitum'*." *Vivarium* 1 (1963) 87-114.

Eschbach, Achim. See Ebbesen (5).

Fairclough, H. Rushton. See Horace and Virgil (1) and (2).

Fathers of the College of St. Bonaventure. See Peter Lombard.

Fredborg, Karin Margarita. "Roger Bacon on *'Impositio Vocis ad Significandum'*." In *English Logic And Semantics: From the End of the Twelfth Century to the Time of Ockham and Burleigh.* Acts of the 4th European Symposium on Mediaeval Logic and Semantics, Leiden-Nijmegen, 23-27 April 1979. Edited by H.A.G. Braakhuis, C.H. Kneepkens, L.M. de Rijk. Nijmegen: Ingenium, 1981, pp. 167-191.

Gasquet, Francis Aidan. "Roger Bacon And The Latin Vulgate." In *Roger Bacon Essays.* Edited by A.G. Little, q.v., pp. 89-99.

Gauthier, Renatus, ed. See Aristotle (1), *Ethica Nicomachea,* vol. 26, fasc. 2-4, 1972.

Glunz, Hans H. *History of the Vulgate in England from Alcuin to Roger Bacon, Being an Inquiry into the Text of Some English Manuscripts of the Vulgate Gospels.* Cambridge: University Press, 1933.

Grabmann, Martin. See William of Sherwood (1).

Gummere, Richard M. See Seneca (3).

Hackett, Jeremiah M.G. "The Attitude of Roger Bacon to the *Scientia* of Albertus Magnus." *Albertus Magnus And The Sciences: Commemorative Essays, 1980.* Edited by James A. Weisheipl. Toronto: Pontifical Institute of Mediaeval Studies, 1980, pp. 53-72.

(Hackett, Jeremiah M.G.) and Thomas S. Maloney. "A Roger Bacon Bibliography (1957-1985)." *New Scholasticism,* forthcoming, 1987.

Henry, D.P. *The De grammatico of St Anselm: The Theory of Paronomy.* Notre Dame, Indiana: University of Notre Dame Press, 1964.

Hertz, Martin. See Priscian.

Hirsch, S.A. "Roger Bacon And Philology." *Roger Bacon Essays.* Edited by A.G. Little, q.v., pp. 101-151.

Hissette, Roland. *Enquête sur les 219 articles condamnés à Paris le 7 mars 1277.* Philosophes médiévaux 22. Louvain: Publications Universitaires; Paris: Vander-Oyez, 1977.

Hoffmans, Hadelin. "La genèse des sensations d'après Roger Bacon." *Revue Néoscolastique de Philosophie* 15 (1908) 474-498.

Horace. *Ars poetica.* Edition and translation by H. Rushton Fairclough. *Horace: Satires, Epistles, And Ars poetica.* Loeb Classical Library. Cambridge, Mass.: Harvard University Press; London: William Heinemann, 1947.

Hubbell, H.M. See Cicero (4).

Hutton, Edward. *The Franciscans in England*. London: Constable and Co., 1926.

Jackson, B. Darrell. "The Theory of Signs in St. Augustine's *De Doctrina Christiana*." In *Augustine: A Collection of Critical Essays*. Edited by R.A. Marcus. Garden City, New York: Doubleday, 1972.

(Jackson, B. Darrell). See also Augustine (2).

John Chrysostom. *Commentarius in S. Matthaeum evangelistam*. Ed. Migne. *PG* 58. 471-794.

Josephus. *Jewish Antiquities*. Edited and translated by H.St.J. Thackeray. *Josephus*. Vol. 8. Loeb Classical Library. London: William Heinemann; New York: G.P. Putnam's Sons, 1930.

Keil, Heinrich. See Donatus and Priscian.

Kenny, Anthony. See *The Cambridge History of Later Medieval Philosophy*.

King, J.E. See Cicero (2).

Kirwan, Christopher. "Aristotle And the So-Called Fallacy of Equivocation." *The Philosophical Quarterly* 29 (1979) 35-46.

Kneale, William, and Mary Kneale. *The Development of Logic*. Oxford: Clarendon Press, 1962.

Kneepkens, C.H. "Roger Bacon's Theory of the Double *Intellectus*: A Note on the Development of the Theory of *Congruitas* and *Perfectio* in the First Half of the Thirteenth Century." In *The Rise of British Logic*. Acts of the Sixth European Symposium on Medieval Logic And Semantics, Balliol College, Oxford, 19-24 June 1983, pp. 115-143. Edited by P. Osmund Lewry, q.v. Toronto: Pontifical Institute of Mediaeval Studies, [1985].

(Kneepkens, C.H.) See de Libera (1).

Kretzmann, Norman. "Aristotle on Spoken Sound Significant by Convention." In *Ancient Logic And Its Modern Interpretations*. Edited by John Corcoran. *Synthese*. Vol. 9. Dordrecht; Boston: D. Reidel, 1974, pp. 3-21.

(Kretzmann, Norman.) "Semantics, History of." In *Encyclopedia of Philosophy*. Vol. 7. Edited by Paul Edwards. New York: Macmillan and the Free Press; London: Collier Macmillan, 1967, pp. 358-406.

(Kretzmann, Norman.) See also *The Cambridge History of Later Medieval Philosophy* and William of Sherwood (3) and (4).

Kupfer, Joseph. "The Father of Empiricism: Roger not Francis." *Vivarium* 12 (1974) 52-62.

Lambert of Auxerre. *Logica. Lamberto d'Auxerre: Logica (Summa Lamberti)*. Edited by F. Alessio. Florence: La Nuova Editrice, 1971.

Lampen, W. "De Fr. Richardo Rufo Cornubiensi, O.F.M." *Archivum Franciscanum Historicum* 21 (1928) 403-406.

Landgraf, Artur M. "Das Problem *Utrum christus fuerit homo in triduo mortis* in der Frühscholastik." *Mélanges Auguste Pelzer*. Louvain, 1947, pp. 109-158.

Larkin, Miriam. *Language in the Philosophy of Aristotle*. Paris: Mouton, 1971.

Layman, D. See Publilius Syrus (2).

Leckie, G. See Augustine (1).

Lewry, P. Osmund, ed. *The Rise of British Logic*. Acts of the Sixth European Symposium on Medieval Logic And Semantics, Balliol College, Oxford, 19-24 June 1983. Toronto: Pontifical Institute of Mediaeval Studies, [1985].

Libera, Alain de. "Roger Bacon et le problème de l'*appellatio univoca*." In *English Logic And Semantics: From the End of the Twelfth Century to the Time of Ockham and Burleigh*. Acts of the 4th European Symposium on Mediaeval Logic and Semantics, Leiden-Nijmegen, 23-27 April 1979. Edited by H.A.G. Braakhuis, C.J. Kneepkens, L.M. de Rijk. Nijmegen: Ingenium, 1981, pp. 193-234.

(Libera, Alain de.) "Textualite logique et forme summuliste." In *Archéologie du signe*. Edited by Lucie Brind'Amour and Eugène Vance. Cahier d'études médiévales/ Papers in Mediaeval Studies 3. Toronto: Pontifical Institute of Mediaeval Studies, 1983, pp. 213-234.

Little, A.G. "The Franciscan School at Oxford in the Thirteenth Century." *Archivum Franciscanum Historicum* 19 (1926) 803-874.

(Little, A.G.) *The Grey Friars in Oxford*. Oxford: Clarendon Press, 1892.

(Little, A.G.) "On Roger Bacon's Life And Works." In *Roger Bacon. Essays*, edited by A.G. Little, q.v., pp. 1-31.

(Little, A.G.), and Franz Pelster. *Oxford Theology And Theologians*. Oxford: Clarendon Press, 1934.

(Little, A.G.), ed. *Roger Bacon: Essays Contributed by Various Writers on the Occasion of the Commemoration of the Seventh Centenary of His Birth*. Oxford, 1914; reprinted New York: Russell and Russell, 1972.

(Little, A.G.) See also Thomas de Eccleston.

Longpre, E. "La Summa Dialectica de Roger Bacon." *Archivum Franciscanum Historicum* 13 (1938) 204-205.

Loose, Patrice Koelsch. "Roger Bacon on Perception: A Reconstruction And Critical Analysis of the Theory of Visual Perception Expounded in the *Opus Maius*." Ph.D. dissertation, Ohio State University, 1979. Ann Arbor, Michigan; London: University Microfilms International, 1979.

Maierù, A. *Terminologia logica della tarda scolastica*. Rome: Edizioni dell' Anteneo, 1972.

Malcolm, J. "On Grabmann's Text of Sherwood." *Vivarium* 9 (1971) 108-118.

Maloney, Thomas S. "The Extreme Realism of Roger Bacon." *Review of Metaphysics* 38 (1985) 807-837.

(Maloney, Thomas S.) "Roger Bacon on Equivocation." *Vivarium* 22 (1984) 85-112.

(Maloney, Thomas S.) "Roger Bacon on the *Significatum* of Words." In *Archéologie du signe*. Edited by Lucie Brind'Amour and Eugène Vance. Cahier d'études médiévales/Papers in Mediaeval Studies 3. Toronto: Pontifical Institute of Mediaeval Studies, 1983, pp. 187-211.

(Maloney, Thomas S.) "The Semiotics of Roger Bacon." *Mediaeval Studies* 45 (1983) 120-154.

(Maloney, Thomas S.) "The *Sumule dialectices* of Roger Bacon And the Summulist Form." In *Archéologie du signe*. Edited by Lucie Brind'Amour and Eugène Vance. Cahier d'études médiévales/Papers in Mediaeval Studies 3. Toronto: Pontifical Institute of Mediaeval Studies, 1983, pp. 235-249.

(Maloney, Thomas S.) See also Hackett (2).

Marcus, R.A. See Jackson (1).

Martin, Joseph. See Augustine (3).

Maurer, Armand. "St. Thomas And the Analogy of Genus." *The New Scholasticism* 29 (1955) 127-144.

McKeon, Richard. See Aristotle (2).

Meiser, Karl. See Boethius (1) and (6).

Minio-Palluello, L. See Boethius (7) and Ps.-Augustine.

Mozley, J.H. See Statius.

Mullally, J.P. See Peter of Spain (1) and (3).

Nemetz, Anthony. "Literalness And the *Sensus Spiritualis*." *Speculum* 34 (1959) 76-89.

Newbold, William. *The Cipher of Roger Bacon*. London: Oxford University Press, 1928.

Nuchelmans, G. *Theories of the Proposition: Ancient and Medieval Conceptions of the Bearers of Truth and Falsity*. Amsterdam: North-Holland Publishing Co., 1973.

O'Donnell, J.R. See William of Sherwood (2).

Oesterle, Jean T. See Thomas Aquinas (1).

Palladius. *Opus agriculturae*. Edited by Robert Rodgers. Bibliotheca Scriptorum Graecorum et Romanorum Teubneriana. Leipzig: B.G. Teubner, 1975.

Pelster, Franz. "Der Oxforder Theologe Richardus Rufus O.F.M. über die Frage: 'Utrum christus in triduo mortis fuerit homo'." *Recherces de Theologie Ancienne Médiévale*, 16 (1949) 259-280.

(Pelster, Franz). "Roger Bacons 'Compendium studii theologiae' und der Sentenzen-kommentar des Richardus Rufus." *Scholastik* 4 (1929) 410-416.

(Pelster, Franz). See also Little (4).

Perreiah, Alan R. "Approaches to Supposition-Theory." *New Scholasticism* 45 (1971) 381-408.

Peter Lombard. *Libri IV Sententiarum*. Vol. 1. 2nd. ed. Edited by Fathers of the College of St. Bonaventure. Ad Claras Aquas: Bonaventure College Press, 1916.

Peter of Spain. *Summulae logicales*. Edited and translated by J.P. Mullally. *The Summulae logicales of Peter of Spain*. Notre Dame, Indiana: University of Notre Dame Press, 1945.

(Peter of Spain). *Tractatus*. Edited by L.M. de Rijk. *Peter of Spain: Tractatus, Called Afterwards Summule logicales*. Assen: Van Gorcum, 1972.

(Peter of Spain.) *Tractatus Syncategorematum And Selected Anonymous Treatises*. Translated by J.P. Mullally. Milwaukee: Marquette University, 1964.

Picavet, Francois. "La place de Roger Bacon parmi les philosophes du xiiie siècle." *Roger Bacon Essays*. Ed. A.G. Little, q.v., pp. 55-88.

Pinborg, Jan. "The English Contribution to Logic before Ockham." *Synthese* Vol. 40. Dordrecht; Boston: D. Reidel, 1979, pp. 19-42.

(Pinborg, Jan.) *Die Entwicklung der Sprachtheorie im Mittelalter*. Münster i. Westfalen: Aschendorfsche Verlagsbuchhandlung, 1967.

(Pinborg, Jan.) "Interjektionen und Naturlaute." *Classica et Mediaevalia* 22 (1961) 117-138.

(Pinborg, Jan.) *Logik und Semantik im Mittelalter: Ein Überblick*. Stuttgart-Bad Constatt: Frommann-Holzboog, 1972.

(Pinborg, Jan.) "Roger Bacon on Signs: A Newly Recovered Part of the *Opus Maius*." *Miscellanea Medievalia*. Vol. 13. Berlin; New York: Walter de Gruyter, 1981, pp. 403-412.

(Pinborg, Jan.) See also Augustine (2), *The Cambridge History of Later Medieval Philosophy*, and Ebbesen (8).

Plato. *Timaeus*. Edited by J.H. Waszink. *Timaeus a Calcidio translatus commentarioque instructus*. 2nd. ed. Corpus Philosophicum Medii Aevii: Plato Latinus, vol. 4. Edited by Raymond Klibanski. London: The Warburg Institute; Leiden: E.J. Brill, 1975.

Pliny. *Naturalis historia*. Edited and translated by H. Rackham. *Pliny: Natural History*. Vol. 1. Loeb Classical Library. Cambridge, Mass.: Harvard University Press; London: William Heinemann, 1938; revised 1949.

Priscian, *Institutiones grammaticae*. 2 Vols. Edited by Martin Hertz. *Grammatici Latini*. Vols. 2-3. Edited by Heinrich Keil. Leipzig, 1855 and 1859; reprinted Hildesheim: George Olms, 1961.

Ps.-Augustine. *Anonymi paraphrasis themistiana*. Edited by L. Minio-Paluello. *Aristoteles Latinus* 1. 5. Edited by L. Minio-Paluello. Leiden: E.J. Brill, 1961.

Ps.-Boethius. *De disciplina scholarium*. Ed. Migne. *PL* 64. 1223-1238.

Publilius Syrus. *Sententiae*. Edited by R.A.H. Bickford-Smith. London: C.J. Clay and Sons, 1895. Translated by D. Lyman, Jr. *The Moral Sayings of Publius Syrus, A Roman Slave*. New York: Andrew J. Graham, 1862.

Rackham, H. See Cicero (1) and Pliny.

Rand, E.K. See Boethius (2).

Rijk, Lambert Marie de. "The Development of Suppositio Naturalis in Mediaeval Logic." *Vivarium* 9 (1971) 71-107 and 11 (1973) 43-79.

(Rijk, Lambert Marie de). *Logica Modernorum: A Contribution to the History of Early Terminist Logic*. 2 Vols. Assen: Van Gorcum, 1962 and 1967.

(Rijk, Lambert Marie de). "On Ancient And Mediaeval Semantics And Metaphysics." *Vivarium* 15 (1977) 81-110; 16 (1978) 81-107; 18 (1980) 1-62; 19 (1981) 1-46 and 81-125. (To be continued.)

(Rijk, Lambert Marie de). "Significatio y suppositio en Pedro Hispano." *Pensiamento* 25 (1969) 225-234.

(Rijk, Lambert Marie de). See also Libera (1) and William of Arnaud.

Robertson, Jr., D. See Augustine (4).

Rodgers, Robert. See Palladius.

Rolfe, J.C. See Sallust.

Rose, Valentine. See *Vita Aristotelis*.

Sallust, *Iugurtha*. Edited and translated by J.C. Rolfe. *Sallust*. Loeb Classical Library. Cambridge, Mass.: Harvard University Press; London: William Heinemann, 1921; revised 1931.

Schönmetzer, Adolf. See *Encheridion Symbolorum*.

Seneca. *De beneficiis*. Edited and translated by John W. Basore. *Seneca: Moral Essays*. Vol. 3. Loeb Classical Library. Cambridge, Mass.: Harvard University Press; London: William Heinemann, 1935.

(Seneca.) *De vita beata*. Edited and translated by John W. Basore. *Seneca: Moral Essays*. Vol. 2. Loeb Classical Library. Cambridge, Mass.: Harvard University Press, London: William Heinemann, 1932; revised 1935 and 1951.

(Seneca.) *Epistulae*. Edited and translated by Richard M. Gummere. *Seneca: Ad Lucilium epistulae morales*. Vols. 1 and 2. Loeb Classical Library. Cambridge, Mass.: Harvard University Press; London: William Heinemann, 1917 and 1925, respectively.

Sharpe, Dorothea Elizabeth. *Franciscan Philosophy at Oxford in the Thirteenth Century*. Oxford, 1930; reprinted New York: Russell & Russell, 1964.

Sinkler, Georgette. "Roger Bacon on the Compounded And Divided Senses." In *The Rise of British Logic*. Acts of the Sixth European Symposium on Medieval Logic And Semantics, Balliol College, Oxford, 19-24 June 1983, pp. 145-171. Edited by P. Osmund Lewry, q.v. Toronto: Pontifical Institute of Mediaeval Studies, [1985].

Slattery, Michael. "Genus And Difference." *Thomist* 21 (1958) 343-364.

Spade, Paul Vincent. "Recent Research on Medieval Logic." *Synthese*. Vol. 40. Dordrecht; Boston: D. Reidel, 1979, pp. 3-18.

Statius. *Thebais*. Edited and translated by J.H. Mozley. *Statius*. Vol. 1. Loeb Classical Library. London: William Heinemann; New York: G.P. Putnam's Sons, 1928.

Steele, Robert. "Roger Bacon As Professor: A Student's Notes (Reprobationes R.B.)." *Isis* 19 (1933) 58-71.

Steenberghen, Fernand van. *La philosophie au Xii^e siècle*. Philosophes médiévaux 9. Paris: Béatrice-Nauwelaerts, 1966.

Stewart, H.F. See Boethius (2).

Stump, Eleonore. See Boethius (4) and *The Cambridge History of Later Medieval Philosophy*.

Tester, S.J. See Boethius (2).

Thackeray, H. St. J. See Josephus.

Thomas Aquinas. *Sententia super Peri hermenias*. Translated by Jean T. Oesterle. *Aristotle: On Interpretation: Commentary by St. Thomas And Cajetan*. Milwaukee: Marquette University Press, 1962.

(Thomas Aquinas.) *Summa contra gentiles*. Translated by James F. Anderson. *Summa Contra Gentiles: Book Two: Creation*. Notre Dame, Ind.: University of Notre Dame Press, 1975.

Thomas de Eccleston. *Tractatus de adventu Fratrum Minorum in Angliam*. Edited by Andrew George Little. Quaracchi, 1885; reprinted Manchester: University Press, 1951.

Thorndike, Lynn. "The True Roger Bacon." *American Historical Review* 21 (1916) 237-257 and 468-480.

(Thorndike, Lynn), ed. *University Records And Life in the Middle Ages*. New York: Columbia University Press, 1944.

Trabant, Jürgen. See Ebbesen (5).

Vance, Eugène. See Libera (2).

Vanderwalle, C.B. *Roger Bacon dans l'histoire de la philologie*. Paris, 1929. (Reprinted from *France Franciscaine*, 1928.)

Virgil. *Aeneid*. Edited and translated by H. Rushton Fairclough. *Virgil*. Vol. 2. Loeb Classical Library. Cambridge, Mass.: Harvard University Press; London: William Heinemann, 1916; revised 1935.

(Virgil.) *Georgica*. Edited and translated by H. Rushton Fairclough. *Virgil*. Vol. 1. Loeb Classical Library. Cambridge, Mass.: Harvard University Press; London: William Heinemann, 1916; revised 1935.

Vita Aristotelis. Edited by Valentine Rose. *Aristotelis Qui Ferebantur Librorum Fragmenta*. 1886; reprinted Stuttgart: B.G. Teubner, 1966.

Vogl, Sebastian. "Roger Bacons Lehre von der Sinnlichen Spezies und vom Sehvorgange." *Roger Bacon Essays*. Edited by A.G. Little, q.v., pp. 205-227.

Weigel, Guenther. See Augustine (4).

Weijers, Olga, ed. *Pseudo-Boèce: De disciplina scholarium. Studien und Texte zur Geistesgeschichte des Mittelalters*, vol. 12. Leiden; Cologne: E.J. Brill, 1976.

Weisheipl, James A. "Bacon, Roger." *New Catholic Encyclopedia*. Edited by Catholic University of America. New York; St. Louis, San Francisco; Toronto; London; Sydney: McGraw-Hill, 1967, pp. 552-553.

(Weisheipl, James A.) "Curriculum of the Faculty of Arts at Oxford in the early Fourteenth Century." *Mediaeval Studies* 26 (1964) 143-185.

(Weisheipl, James A.) "The Parisian Faculty of Arts in Mid-thirteenth century: 1240-1270." *American Benedictine Review* 25 (1974) 200-217.

(Weisheipl, James A.) See also Hackett.

Welborn, Mary Catherine. "The Errors of the Doctors according to Friar Roger Bacon of the Minor Order." *Isis* 18 (1932) 26-62.

William of Arnaud. *Lectura tractatuum*. Edited by L.M. de Rijk. "On the Genuine Text of Peter of Spain's *Summule logicales*." *Vivarium* 7 (1969) 120-162.

William of Sherwood. *Introductiones in logicam. Die Introductiones in logicam des Wilhelm von Shyreswood*. Edited by Martin Grabmann. Sitzungberichte der Bayerischen Akademie der Wissenschaften. Phil.-hist. Abt., Jq. 1937, Heft. 10. Munich: Verlag der Bayerischen Akademie der Wissenschaften, 1937.

(William of Sherwood.) *Syncategoremata*. "The *Syncategoremata* of William of Sherwood." Edited by J.R. O'Donnell. *Mediaeval Studies*, 3 (1941) 46-93.

(William of Sherwood.) *William of Sherwoods's Introduction to Logic*. Translated by Norman Kretzmann. Minneapolis: University of Minnesota Press, 1966.

(William of Sherwood. *William of Sherwood's Treatise on Syncategorematic Words*. Translated by Norman Kretzmann. Minneapolis: University of Minnesota Press, 1968.

Wippel, John F. "The Condemnations of 1270 And 1277 at Paris." *Journal of Medieval And Renaissance Studies* 7 (1977) 169-201.

Witzel, Theophilus. "De Fr. Rogero Bacon Eiusque Sententia de Rebus Biblicis." *Archivum Franciscanum Historicum* 3 (1910) 1-22 and 185-213.

Wolter, Allan B. "Bacon, Roger." *The Encyclopedia of Philosophy*. Edited by Paul Edwards. Vol. 1. New York: Macmillan and the Free Press, London: Collier Macmillan, 1967, pp. 240-242.

Wrobel, John. See Cicero (3) and Plato.

INDICES

Since this work is divided into three major parts (Introduction, Text, and Endnotes), references in these indices will be of three kinds. References to the text will consist of a paragraph number preceded by the symbol '#'. References to the endnotes to the text will consist simply in the number of an endnote preceded by the letter 'n', as in 'n. 124'. References to the Introduction will be indicated by a page number or by page and footnote number, as in 'p. 24' or 'p. 24, n. 2'. Hence a reference to, e.g., n. 3 refers the reader to the third endnote, not to a footnote in the Introduction. More than one occurence on a page of a reference is not indicated. Names in quotation marks indicate erroneous references in the text, such as "Boethius" for Priscian.

A) Index Nominum

190   INDICES

Siger of Brabant pp. 7, 14, 18
Socrates #8. See also Sortes
Solomon #4, 5, 9
Sortes #106
Statius #4 ("Ovid") and n. 7
Steele, Robert pp. 3, 10, n. 47
Stump, Eleanore n. 98

Tempier, Stephen, Bishop p. 7
Themistius n. 98
Theyer, John p. 25
Thomas Aquinas nn. 4, 69, 145, 269

Thomas of Eccleston n. 189
Tully. See Cicero

Virgil #140; n. 233

Walter Burleigh n. 145
Weisheipl, James A. p. 3, n. 8, p. 5, n. 24;
    nn. 4, 60
William of Arnaud pp. 14, 18; n. 230
William of Auvergne n. 59
William of Ockham pp. 13, 15, 16; n. 145
William of Sherwood pp. 14, 17, 20; n. 280

B) Index Rerum

Academica (Cicero) #8 ("*Hortense*"), 13
Academics. See *Academica*
'*Ad placitum*'. See Imposition: at pleasure
Adam: and naming pp. 9, 28; nn. 246; and
    original sin n. 117
Aeneid. See *Aeneis*
Aeneis (Virgil) n. 233
Agent acting according to nature or for a
    purpose #32
Allegory. See Scripture
Ampliation p. 11; #85
Anagogy. See Scripture
Analogy p. 15; #141; that is not equi-
    vocation #142; n. 154
Analytica posteriora (Aristotle) #14, 21;
    nn. 4, 101, 167; commentaries on p. 14
Analytica priora (Aristotle) nn. 4, 96, 214,
    219
Angels, composed of matter and form
    #135
Angles, language of p. 28; n. 246
Animal talk pp. 20, 23; #36
Animals, names of p. 28; #97
Anonymi paraphrasis themistiana (Ps.-Augus-
    tine) #95
Anonymous English Commentator on the
    Logica Vetus p. 17
Anonymous G and C – 668 p. 15
Anonymous G and C 611/341 p. 15
Anonymous Laudianus n. 61
Antiquitates (Josephus) #13
Appellation pp. 3, 14, 18; equivocal p. 18
Arab commentaries p 17
Aristotelian corpus n. 20
Ars poetica (Horace) #22
'Art' #29 and n. 100
Authority #2; weak and unworthy #7, 8,
    128

Babel, Tower of p. 28

Ban, at Paris p. 2; #14
Ban on writing to Pope p. 6
Becoming #110
Being, confused and determinate pp. 4,
    14; common to present, past, and future
    #99; habitual pp. 4, 13, 17; #101;
    potential or aptitudinal #103, 109; com-
    pleted #108; proper to motion and time
    #110
Beings. See Entities

Categoriae (Aristotle) pp. 16; #21; nn. 192,
    265
Categories. See *Categoriae*
Chapters, missing, reference to p. 9, n. 39
Chicken communicating with chicks #36
"Christ was man during the three days"
    #85, 128
Chronicle of the Twenty-four Generals p. 8
Circle as sign of wine #117, 127
Coming to be #110
*Commentarium [maius] in librum Aristotelis
    Peri hermeneias* (Boethius) #61; nn. 129,
    145, 148
Commentarius in S. Mattheum evangelistam
    (Chrysostom) #10 and n. 41
Communia naturalium (Bacon) pp. 6, 7, 10;
    nn. 103, 125, 175, 255, 268, 270, 277,
    281
Compendium of the Study of Theology. See
    Compendium studii theologiae
Compendium studii theologiae: compared to *De
    signis* pp. 9, 10-11; n. 91; to *Opus maius*
    pp. 6-7, 9, 10, 12; to *Sumule dialectices* pp.
    3-4, 9; divisions of p. 9; n. 1; missing
    third Part p. 9; why written pp. 12-13;
    #2, 4, 19, 43; when written p. 9; #14,
    86
Compendium studii philosophiae pp. 8, 10, 21;
    nn. 60, 65, 69

C) Index Locorum